Pushkin and the Genres of Madness

PUBLICATIONS OF THE WISCONSIN CENTER
FOR PUSHKIN STUDIES

David Bethea, Alexander Dolinin, Thomas Shaw
Series Editors

Pushkin and the Genres of Madness

~ *The Masterpieces of 1833*

Gary Rosenshield

THE UNIVERSITY OF WISCONSIN PRESS

The University of Wisconsin Press
1930 Monroe Street, 3rd floor
Madison, Wisconsin 53711-2059
uwpress.wisc.edu

3 Henrietta Street
London WC2E 8LU, England
eurospanbookstore.com

Copyright © 2003
The Board of Regents of the University of Wisconsin System
All rights reserved
No part of this publication may be reproduced, stored in a
retrieval system, or transmitted, in any format or by any
means, digital, electronic, mechanical, photocopying,
recording, or otherwise, or conveyed via the Internet or a Web
site without written permission of the University of Wisconsin
Press, except in the case of brief quotations embedded in
critical articles and reviews.

Library of Congress Cataloging-in-Publication Data

Rosenshield, Gary.
Pushkin and the genres of madness : the masterpieces of 1833 /
   Gary Rosenshield.
p. cm.—(Publications of the Wisconsin Center for Pushkin Studies)
Includes bibliographical references.
   ISBN 0-229-18200-2 (cloth : alk. paper)—
   ISBN 0-299-18204-5 (pbk. : alk. paper)
   1. Pushkin, Aleksandr Sergeevich, 1799–1837—Criticism and interpretation.
2. Mental illness in literature. 3. Pushkin, Aleksandr Sergeevich, 1799–1837.
Pikovaia dama. 4. Pushkin, Aleksandr Sergeevich, 1799–1837. Mednyï
vsadnik. I. Title. II. Series.
   PG3358.M45 R67 2003
   891.71′3—dc21
                                                        2003005698

ISBN-13: 978-0-299-18204-5 (pbk: alk. paper)

Contents

Preface — vii

Introduction: Madness and Contexualization — 3

PART ONE: *The Queen of Spades*

1. Choosing the Right Card: Madness, Gambling, and the Imagination — 21
2. Madness and Psychoanalysis — 37

PART TWO: "God Grant That I Not Lose My Mind"

3. Freedom and the Prison House of Madness — 65

PART THREE: *The Bronze Horseman*

4. Madness and the Common Man — 89
5. Madness and the River — 131
6. Madness and the Tsar — 144
7. Madness, Narrator, and Author — 162

Conclusion: Deconstructing *The Bronze Horseman*: Dostoevsky, *The Double,* and the Pushkinian Legacy on Madness — 181

Notes — 201

Index — 247

Preface

For more than a century Pushkin has been a mythic figure on whom generations of scholars, writers, and readers have imposed their values, ideas, critical theories, and ideologies. The nineteenth-century poet Apollon Grigor'ev perhaps best expressed this phenomenon when he wrote, "Pushkin is everything to us."[1] In his *History of Russian Literature,* Prince Mirsky notes that a Pushkin cult had already taken shape soon after the poet's fiftieth anniversary in 1887: "The consciousness of Pushkin's supremacy and centralness in Russian literature and civilization grew apace, unostentatiously, but irrevocably. The twentieth century received it full grown. By the time of the Revolution, it was so ubiquitous and unconquerable that even the Bolsheviks, who are in spirit as alien to Pushkin as Dostoevsky was, excluded his name almost alone from their general condemnation of pre-Revolutionary Russia."[2]

Madness, however, has never been part of this mythology. In the Russian cultural consciousness Pushkin embodies an ego ideal of grace, harmony, light, balance, clarity—even reason. Into whatever violence or chaos Russia may descend, Pushkin is always there as a beacon of the purest light and beauty, "as a genius of pure beauty," to use the poet's own words. The narrator of Andrei Bitov's *Pushkin House* calls Pushkin "the first and only bearer of Reason in Russia [*pervyi i edinstvennyi nositel' Razuma v Rossii*]." In moments when the world seems to have lost all meaning, Russians can return to their infallible source of reason, sanity, and meaning. Even Gershenzon, one of the few to celebrate the irrational in Pushkin, marveled at the master's "chaotic perfection" [*khaoticheskoe sovershenstvo*], the paradoxical transformation of chaos into perfect order.

Often decrying chaos and praising reason, Pushkin gives additional support to the myth of balance and harmony that has arisen around him. In his unfinished folk drama, *Rusalka,* a prince, sadly observing the insanity of a man whose daughter he seduced, expresses his horror at the spectacle of madness—the loss of reason: "It is terrible to lose one's mind. It is better to die.... A human being deprived of reason is no longer a human being.... He is the brother to the beast."

The greatest tension in Pushkin's works concerning chaos and the irrational, and especially madness, occurs over the issue of truth and order. The great literary critic V. G. Belinsky refused to accept Goethe's statement that order was higher than truth, but Pushkin realized that, especially under Russian conditions, without order there could be no truth. This is why he often equates the chaos of Russian rebellion—even the challenging of authority—with madness. He is fascinated by the irrational, the violent, and the extreme, but he is also terrified by their consequences for his class, his society, and his time.

Both the Pushkin myth and the historical reality, however, are not entirely in accord with the imagination of the artist concerning the issue of madness. In fact, Pushkin himself was the first to explore the idea of madness in Russian literature—and his influence was profound. Indeed, he had a greater impact on Dostoevsky's formulations of madness, both before and after Dostoevsky's Siberian exile, than any other Russian or European writer. Of course, the majority of Pushkin's work is not devoted to madness, but, with the possible exception of Cervantes, this is true of almost every major European writer. It is difficult to write an extended piece about madness, and even harder to write several works in the same vein. Madness occupies only a small part of the opus of the Greek tragedians and Shakespeare; on the other hand, in many of their finest works it plays a crucial role. We need only think of the *Oresteia, Ajax, The Bacchants, Macbeth, Hamlet,* and *King Lear.* By comparison, the quantity and quality of Pushkin's work in which madness figures prominently is remarkable.

Most of Pushkin's works on madness were written in or around 1833. He made the last revisions of his unfinished folk drama, *The River Nymph* [*Rusalka*], in the spring of 1832; and in October 1833, in Boldino, he wrote *The Bronze Horseman* and *The Queen of Spades* and probably in that same year did his last work on the unpublished poem, "God Grant That I Not Lose My Mind." "God Grant" is one of Pushkin's peerless lyrics, *The Queen of Spades* his finest prose fiction, and *The Bronze Horseman* perhaps his supreme masterpiece. The works on madness of 1833, however, do not constitute an anomalous annus mirabilis. They represent an important artistic culmination in prose, poetry, and nonfiction, shaped by Pushkin's ruminations on the relationship between madness and rebellion. In the autumn of 1833 Pushkin effectively completed *The History of Pugachev*. Of the three prose pieces he finished after *The Queen of Spades*, the most important, *The Captain's Daughter*, is a fictional rendition of the historical work.[3] *The Bronze Horseman* was his last narrative poem, *Rusalka* his last verse drama. After 1833 he wrote only about fifteen to twenty lyrics each year. Some of them "borrow" directly from the imagery of "God Grant That I Not Lose My Mind."

In the magisterial works of 1833 the poet radically diverges from his myth, exploring areas into which Pushkin, the rational citizen, rarely ventures. Fascinated by experience lived at the edge, and receptive to ideas about the special powers of genius and prophecy, he is attracted to the idea of madness precisely because he sees there a nexus between chaos and the highest truths. An exploration into the tension between the truth of madness and the chaos of madness in Pushkin's work of 1833 is the subject of the present study.

∼

I had originally envisioned a book on the representation of madness in all nineteenth-century Russian literature. As I began to assess the significance of Pushkin's work on madness for those who came after, however, I realized that Pushkin was as much an end as a beginning, a goal as well as a means. Readers of Pushkin have engaged in a long, ongoing dialogue with one another; the present work attempts to contribute to the dialogue by examining a central, but relatively unexplored, aspect of Pushkin's oeuvre in the most important genres in which he wrote: the lyric ("God Grant That I Not Lose My Mind"), the narrative poem (*The Bronze Horseman*), and the short story and novella (*The Queen of Spades*).

The present project has other ambitions as well. First, it focuses on the more romantic Pushkin, romantic in both the period and typological sense. Pushkin is horrified by madness, but he seems compelled to explore it in all its permutations in poetry, personal experience, and history. In the works of 1833 we see the genre forms mastered by Pushkin years earlier straining to contain the disruptive energy generated by madness or its threat. Madness is not invariably valorized—

given a higher value—but it is given its due. Dostoevsky, who was attracted primarily by the romantic literature of his own time, found in Pushkin his most fruitful source of literary material, not because of the ideal forms in which Pushkin bound his subjects but because of their disruptive potential. The concluding chapter directly addresses this disruptive potential in Pushkin's legacy through a comparison of *The Bronze Horseman* with Dostoevsky's *The Double*, the most radical treatment of both madness and Petersburg in nineteenth-century Russian literature. If this monograph succeeds in bringing out more of the romantic, disruptive Pushkin, it will have accomplished a major part of its task.

All citations from Pushkin's works are from the Academy edition: A. S. Pushkin, *Polnoe sobranie sochinenii*, ed. V. D. Bonch-Bruevich, 17 vols. (Moscow: Akademiia Nauk SSSR, 1937–59); they appear in the text with volume followed by page number. All translations from the Russian are my own, unless otherwise indicated.

Pushkin and the
Genres of Madness

Introduction

Madness and Contextualization

Problems of Contextualization

It is difficult to know why Pushkin wrote so much about madness in 1833—and so little about it before or after.[1] This question highlights just one of the many problems of contextualizing madness in fiction. Unlike most traceable motifs or ideas in literary texts, madness does not lend itself to the usual literary contextualizations, a problem compounded in Pushkin by his particular locus in Russian literature. A brief examination of various contextualized themes from Pushkin's work drives this point home. Let us start with the most prosaic of motifs: card playing. A popular activity of Pushkin's time, card playing was also a common theme in Western European and Russian literature. One can compare Pushkin's use of card playing in *The Queen of Spades* with any number of other Russian and foreign works. In fact, in *The Queen of Spades* Pushkin frequently alludes to the literature of card playing, polemically engaging other texts as a means of better positioning his own work in the literary tradition. Since card playing functions not only as a motif in the text but also as an intertextual and intratextual literary subject, it becomes *hypercontextualized*. And we may never know how many intertextual references—now lost to us—indeed existed that Pushkin's audience recognized immediately. Madness cannot be subjected to this kind of intertextual analysis in a work like *The Queen of Spades*, where madness strikes the hero only in the epilogue, and by surprise.

Similar problems arise with even more broadly and easily contextualizable categories. From his early romantic verse tales to *Eugene Onegin*, Pushkin worked many variations on the Byronic hero. Although, in *The Queen of Spades*, card playing works both self-referentially and intertextually, the novella's intertextuality resides mainly in its engagement of earlier and contemporary works.[2] The Byronic hero, however, functions intertextually not only with parallel texts of other writers but with Pushkin's own work over the course of his literary career; that is, one can, with equal ease, compare Pushkin's treatment of the Byronic hero to Western models or trace the development of this type entirely within Pushkin's opus. This issue is much more complicated with respect to madness. Since almost all Pushkin's works on madness are in different genres—"God Grant That I Not Lose My Mind" is a lyric, *The Queen of Spades* a prose novella, *The Bronze Horseman* a novel in verse—and all basically derive from one year, internal contextualization is virtually impossible. One has no development to compare, and the genre boundaries one would have to cross for any synchronic comparison are formidable. Dostoevsky, by contrast, wrote about madness all his life, from his second work, *The Double*, to his last, *The Brothers Karamazov*; further, all Dostoevsky's works in which madness occurs are novels.

The intertextuality of *The Bronze Horseman*, like that of *The Queen of Spades*, has been closely studied. Wacław Lednicki and N. P. Antsiferov, among others, have shown how *The Bronze Horseman* fits into the traditional representations of Peter and Petersburg; Lednicki has further established the poem's important connections to the work of the great Polish poet Adam Mickiewicz. Again, however, the contextualization of madness in *The Bronze Horseman* presents more difficult problems. First, Pushkin did not write much about madness before 1833. Equally important, the figure of Evgenii in *The Bronze Horseman* not only is a new phenomenon in Pushkin's work, but it is difficult to find prototypes or contemporary parallels for Evgenii or his madness—the madness of the common or ordinary man—in the literature of Pushkin's time. To contextualize Evgenii's madness in Russian literature, we must resort to works written after 1833. When M. L. Gofman maintains that Pushkin is the father of madness in Russian literature, he is stating that Pushkin has inheritors (Saltykov-Shchedrin, Garshin, Chekhov) but no real forbears or contemporaries. The Russian works dealing with madness from the 1830s and 1840s are not only few—

Gogol's "Notes of a Madman" (1835) and Odoevsky's "The Sylph" (1837)—but they also differ markedly from Pushkin's in character. Dostoevsky's *The Double* (1846), the only work that directly engages *The Bronze Horseman*, treats Evgenii's madness as parody. Parallels are most productive when they either precede or are contemporary with the work under examination. Dostoevsky's *The Double*, to be sure, throws a great deal of light on madness in *The Bronze Horseman*, but it is Dostoevsky who is engaging Pushkin, not the other way around, and that inevitably shifts the focus from the earlier to the later writer.

Dostoevsky's works on madness highlight another problem in the contextualization of madness in Pushkin: the infrequency of madness as a subject in nineteenth-century literature in general.[3] It may be easy to contextualize madness in Dostoevsky within the confines of his own work, but it is far more difficult to do so intertextually with the work of other writers. Few of Dostoevsky's contemporaries, Russian or otherwise, wrote about madness. Madness does not figure in the works of Tolstoy, Turgenev, Goncharov, or Pisemsky.[4] When, in his early work, Dostoevsky, the most intertextual of writers, engages other writers on madness, he, of course, pays tribute to E. T. A. Hoffmann, but in his later work he goes back to Pushkin's *Queen of Spades* and *The Bronze Horseman*.

Because of the relative paucity of works on madness, one must contextualize madness in Pushkin by working synchronically *and* diachronically, that is, by presenting, as much as possible, Pushkin's portrayals of madness, first, in the context of the literature and culture of his own time, including his own works on madness, and, second, in the larger context of Western European literature. Certainly King Lear serves as a more productive point of comparison with Evgenii in *The Bronze Horseman* than Poprishchin in Gogol's "Notes of a Madman." Almost all monographs on madness in literature refer to Greek and Shakespearean models. It would be unfair to Pushkin not to see his contributions to the portrayal of madness, at least in part, in the context of his most illustrious predecessors. The greatest writers of the Western literary tradition all wrote brilliantly, though sporadically, about madness; we need to place Pushkin in this tradition, if we do not want to see him primarily—in terms of the representation of madness—as a writer who may have borrowed an idea or two from Hoffmann and may have influenced Odoevsky and the young Dostoevsky.[5]

Contextualization: Intertextuality and Psychoanalysis

Not surprisingly I subject madness in *The Queen of Spades* to the most extensive literary contextualization of the three works I examine in detail. I attempt to demonstrate how the novella fits in with both romantic valorizations and post-romantic devalorizations of madness characteristic of some of Hoffmann's work. One can see these alternate treatments of madness in some of Pushkin's contemporaries, or near contemporaries. Odoevsky's "Sylph" reflects the tradition of the romantic valorization of madness, in which the life of prosaic sanity is repudiated in favor of the life of mad imagination. By contrast, Gogol's "Notes of a Madman" and Dostoevsky's *The Double* constitute unmistakably deflationary and anti-romantic treatments of madness. But Pushkin also manages to capture the ambiguity characteristic of several of Hoffmann's works on madness—"The Golden Pot," in particular—in which the prosaic and the visionary aspects of madness are not mutually exclusive. As I hope to show, it was left to Dostoevsky to take Pushkin's ambiguous treatment of madness in *The Queen of Spades* to its logical conclusion in the depiction of Ivan Karamazov in *The Brothers Karamazov*.

Whereas my first chapter attempts to appreciate the madness in *The Queen of Spades* in terms of the romantic and anti-romantic traditions of Pushkin's own time, chapter 2 attempts to understand Germann's madness in terms of differing twentieth-century psychoanalytic theories. The intertextual approach of the first chapter illuminates the powers and values attributed to madness in the story, but it can go only so far in revealing the psychological complexity of Germann's madness and the existential and social issues linked to it. Much of the madness-text occurs below the surface, especially since Germann becomes clinically insane only at the very end. Freudian, Lacanian, and romantic psychoanalytical theories gain the reader entrance into the unconscious text, encoded in symbolizations of Germann's imaginings and dreams. Since each of these psychoanalytic theories places different emphases and valuations on the ego, they inevitably lead to different assessments of the causes, meaning, and consequences of Germann's madness, opening up the story to interpretations that complement and enrich one another. These theories also give us deeper insight into Germann's relation with the old countess in her various incarnations. And, finally, the psychoanalytic approach achieves two important, albeit seemingly contradictory, goals. By revealing the subterranean forces at work in Germann's psyche, psychoanalysis opens the way for a more dynamic interpretation of the social implications of Germann's madness; at the same time, by universalizing Germann as a construct of psychological forces relevant to us all, psychoanalysis takes Germann out of his specific social context and turns him into an everyman.

Unlocking the portrayal of madness in Pushkin's magnificent lyric "God Grant That I Not Lose My Mind" (chapter 3) requires a different combination of hermeneutic strategies. Since I am attempting throughout to highlight the romantic aspects of Pushkin's treatment of madness, I place the lyric not only in the context of the romantic tradition but also in the context of the romantic imagery of Pushkin's earlier work. Pushkin presses the elevation of madness much harder in the lyric than he does in *The Queen of Spades*. But just as with *The Queen of Spades*, I also employ twentieth-century psychoanalytic theories—especially those of Jung and Laing—to explore the romantic implications of the persona's imaginative journey through madness to a form of hypersanity. Here romantic psychoanalysis becomes crucial in validating the notion of madness as a conduit for attaining the highest truth. Like *The Queen of Spades*, "God Grant That I Not Lose My Mind" also devalues madness, but not in the same literary terms. To understand Pushkin's ambivalent attitude toward madness in "God Grant," we need to go outside the literary culture of Pushkin's own time to the literary tradition of the eighteenth century and to the medical culture determining the treatment of the insane in both the eighteenth and nineteenth centuries. I attempt to unravel the enigmas of the lyric by showing how the contradictory representation of madness in the poem derives from incorporating images and ideas from radically different literary and medical traditions. Pushkin actually knew a mad poet, Konstantin Batiuskhov, who received the most advanced and humane medical treatment. I try to grapple with the startling inconsistencies between the imagery of insanity in the lyric and Pushkin's knowledge of the actual treatment of the mentally deranged in his own milieu.

I employ similar inter- and extratextual approaches to explore the unusual treatment of madness in *The Bronze Horseman* (chapters 4 through 8). In the famous introduction, Pushkin presents Peter and Petersburg in conformity with the Russian literary tradition, which imagines the tsar and his city as the personification of order, harmony, and reason. But I show, in the story proper—the *povest'* of parts 1 and 2—how he challenges the tradition by tying Peter imagistically and thematically to the forces of disorder, chaos, and madness. This dramatic transformation can be seen within Pushkin's works by comparing the representation of Peter in his earlier verse tale, *Poltava* (1828), where Peter is terrible but beautiful, to the *povest'* sections of *The Bronze Horseman*, where he emerges as horrible and mad. To gain a better appreciation of the madness of the hero (Evgenii), I set his madness in and against the tradition of the mad holy fool in Russian history and culture, showing how Pushkin borrowed from and transformed the tradition to create a believable mad seer in nineteenth-century Petersburg. Since, in terms of the imagery of madness and the representation of the mad, Pushkin is far closer to the Greek imagination than to either Cervantes or Shakespeare, it is helpful to employ the various paradigms of madness found in Greek tragedy and culture, especially to further our understanding of the relationship between the angry God (Peter) of the poem and his mad subject (Evgenii), and between the new, victorious god (Peter) and the mad, vanquished god (the river). To put the romantic madness of Pushkin's Evgenii in still greater perspective, I conclude by comparing Evgenii to Dostoevsky's deflated mad hero, Goliadkin, in *The Double*, which contains the most important polemic with Pushkin's view of madness in Russian literature (chapter 8).

In *The Bronze Horseman* I have reserved the psychoanalytic approach to illuminate one of the most difficult problems of the text, the point of view of the narrator and his role in representing madness. It is impossible to fully understand *The Bronze Horseman* without appreciating how the narrator uses the madness of the participants paradoxically both to hide and reveal the truth about Peter and his mission. Although chapter 7 is specifically devoted to the narrator (chapters 4, 5, and 6 are devoted, respectively to Evgenii, the Neva, and Peter), I deal with the narrator's relation to the protagonists in all *The Bronze Horseman* chapters. At times the narrator seems well aware how close he is to rebellion against Peter, especially when presenting Evgenii's mad insights, but at other times, when portraying the mad fury of the river, he overreacts, suggesting—in a classic example of reaction-formation—a desperate need to repress the Neva's siren-like calls. The river thus necessitates still another strategy, a psychoanalytic deconstruction, first to recover the repressed counterplot concerning the Neva and then to explore the reasons for the narrator's animus. By lashing out at the river, is the narrator not attempting to compensate for his overly sympathetic portrayal of his hero's rebellion? Most important, when the narrator vents his wrath at the river, he moves from being an observer to a participant in the mad plot himself. A psychoanalytic approach to the narration allows for a more insightful interpretation of the narrator, whose role outside the introduction has been sorely neglected in previous scholarship.

Contextualization: Madness and Pushkin's Time

Although the representation of madness in Pushkin's works manifests things peculiarly his own, especially regarding the relationship between violence, madness, insight, and truth, it also reflects the psychological, social, and cultural notions of madness and its treatment in Pushkin's time. Reared on French culture of the eighteenth century, Pushkin was much better acquainted with French than with German literature, and thus with French rather than German romanticism. In many ways he was, literarily speaking, a child of the Enlightenment, a period that had no place for madness, the antithesis of Reason. Foucault has been justly criticized for his unfair treatment of the mental health reformers of the last half of the eighteenth century and early part of the nineteenth, but he has aptly characterized the depreciation and devaluation of madness—unreason—in the literature and culture of the French Enlightenment. For Foucault, the Age of Reason does not combat madness, it dismisses it, viewing it not so much as a negative presence or force but as an absence, specifically the absence of reason.[6]

However one wishes to assess the important developments in the understanding and treatment of madness at the end of the eighteenth and beginning of the nineteenth century—negatively as Foucault does or more positively as most commentators do—psychologists, physicians, and scientists attempted to eliminate the stigma of madness by changing the public's perception of insanity as a curse from God or a form of alien possession. Madness was a mental "illness" that could be treated and perhaps even cured. Foucault sees the new paradigm as a covert attempt by the scientific community to neutralize or even appropriate the power of madness for its own ends, but most still see the new attitude toward the mentally ill as motivated by genuine compassion and a desire to improve treatment.[7]

An inevitable consequence of this new attitude was a desacralization (both negative and positive) and demystification of madness, a transference of the locus of madness from the supernatural to the scientific—or, from Foucault's point of view, from the world of unreason to the world of reason—and a consequent dissociation of madness from insight, truth, and prophecy. Since Pushkin was conversant with many of the more progressive nineteenth-century ideas about the treatment of the insane, his decision to employ the images of the eighteenth century in his portrayal of madness in "God Grant That I Not Lose My Mind" suggests an informed choice rather than a cultural reflex.

At the same time that nineteenth-century psychologists were attempting to neutralize madness, or "undemonize" it, the Romantic movement was, in part, resacralizing the image of madness desacralized by the Age of Reason.[8] Pushkin, who was influenced by various currents in European romanticism, was aware of E. T. A. Hoffmann's stories—much in vogue in Russia from the 1820s through the 1840s—in which madness is sometimes presented as a conduit to a vision of a higher reality ("The Golden Pot"). One can see the direct influence of a more romantic view of madness on Russian literature as late as the 1840s, particularly in the stories of Prince Vladimir Odoevsky, a student of German romanticism and Pushkin's friend and collaborator. But even earlier Gogol's story, "Notes of a Madman" (1835), shows that literary representations of madness in popular literature were common enough that parodies on them were already being written. Hoffmann himself set the standard for undercutting romantic stereotypes, and he could treat madness with unmistakable ambiguity.

Thus Pushkin is probably subject to the influence of four distinct, though related, cultural attitudes toward madness: (1) the desacralized view of madness of eighteenth-century French culture, in which madness is seen as the antithesis of the ideal, Reason; (2) the psychological science of the late eighteenth and early nineteenth century, which attempts to counteract the predominant stereotypes of madness as a curse and redefine it as a treatable mental illness; (3) a romantic view, which, in reaction to the Age of Reason, looks again to madness, the most irrational or nonrational of mental states, as a source of the highest insight, if not prophecy; and (4) an anti-romantic reaction, which casts a skeptical, and sometimes even mocking, eye on the special powers ascribed to the mad imagination. Pushkin's works of 1833 reflect these views in different combinations and degrees. In "God Grant That I Not Lose My Mind," all four come into play.

Madness and Truth: Pushkin and the Western Tradition

Almost all books on madness in literature define their subject in terms of the Western literary tradition. I do so in this study as well—though briefly—not for historical reasons but as a way of placing the most important issues relating to the depiction of madness in Pushkin in a larger context. We have few literary coordinates for the portrayal of madness in Pushkin. Most of the works in which madness figures prominently in Russian literature are distant from Pushkin in either time (Chekhov, Kuprin, Garshin, Bely) or spirit (Odoevsky, Gogol, Dostoevsky). Madness, of course, always plays a small part in realist fiction.

Madness and Violence

In Greek literature, myth, and culture, madness is associated either with violence or truth, rarely with both. In Greek tragedy, madness, as a passion representing the antithesis of reason, order, and control, is usually linked with violence. It is thus tantamount to derangement or what we now would call mental illness. It makes no difference whether the madness is temporary or permanent or whether it manifests itself in groups or individuals. In Euripides' masterpiece, *The Bacchants,* Dionysus stirs up a group of his devotees to punish Pentheus, the King of Thebes, who has actively worked against the god's cult in his city. Pentheus is torn to pieces by a group of mad Bacchants led by his own mother, Agave, who banishes herself when she comes to her senses and realizes what she has done to her own son. In Euripides' *Madness of Heracles,* Heracles slaughters his own children. By making Ajax mad, in Sophocles' eponymous play, Hera prevents him from carrying out his plan to murder Agamemnon, Menelaus, and other Greek leaders; he mistakes a herd of cattle for his human enemies and slaughters them instead. When Ajax regains his sanity, he is so humiliated by what he has done that he commits suicide. God first makes mad those whom he wishes to destroy: *Quem deus vult perdere, dementat prius.*

The violence arising out of madness always elicits condign punishment. In Greek tragedy and myth, the greatest punishment for those who commit violent acts when temporarily insane is subsequent sanity—when the mad recover their wits and face the humiliation and horror of what they have done: usually to their own children. But madness is tied to violence in still another way—as punishment for violent or blasphemous actions. Thus, in Aeschylus's *Oresteia*, Orestes is driven to madness by the Erinyes for avenging the murder of his mother, the slayer of his father. But sleeping with Zeus, as Io learned, could result in no less of a punishment (Aeschylus, *Prometheus*) from Hera than her descendent Heracles would receive. If one were to apply this view of madness to *The Bronze Horseman*, for example, one might interpret Evgenii's madness as *engendering* his rebellion against Peter and his final derangement, after he threatens the statue, as *punishment* for his blasphemous curse, the rebellion itself.

Madness and Truth: Prophecy

In almost all cultures, alongside the connection of madness with violence exists a more beneficent link: madness and truth, usually in the form of prophecy, the mysterious ability to predict events or understand profound truths inaccessible to the rational mind. As Ruth Benedict notes: "Even a very mild mystic is aberrant in our culture. But most peoples have regarded extreme psychic manifestations not only as normal and desirable, but even as characteristic of highly valued and gifted individuals."[9] But prophecy is generally less represented in literature than it is in myth and religion. And it is rarely, if ever, associated with violence. It is Plato, the rationalist philosopher, to whom we owe perhaps the most prestigious statement about the benefits of madness. In the *Phaedrus*, he emphasizes that there is a kind of madness that almost all agree is a great evil or misfortune, but there are other kinds—prophetic, artistic, and erotic—that can be great gifts, especially the madness of prophecy.

> For that might have been truly said if madness were simply an evil; but there is also a madness which is the special gift of heaven, and the source of the chiefest blessings among men. For prophecy is a madness,[10] and the prophetess at Delphi and the priestesses of Dodona, when out of

their senses have conferred great benefits on Hellas, both in public and private life, but when in their senses few or none.... There will be more reason in appealing to the ancient inventors of names, who, if they thought madness a disgrace or dishonor, would never have called prophecy, which is the noblest of arts, by the very same name as madness, thus inseparably connecting them; but they must have thought that there was an inspired madness which was not disgrace.... In the same proportion, as the ancients testify, is madness superior to a sane mind, for the one is only of human, but the other of divine origin.[11]

Plato implicitly distinguishes between madness the playwrights portray, often associated with the most egregious forms of violence, and the madness associated with prophecy and higher truth. Prophetic madness has nothing to do with violence or with its concomitant punishments: alienation, humiliation, and wandering.[12] Plato also links the greatest poetry with mad prophecy, for the preeminent expression of the Muses is also, he says, a form of madness. Though it possesses a different realm of truth than prophecy, it, too, has nothing in common with the deleterious forms of madness. "There is a third kind of madness, which is a possession of the Muses; this enters into a delicate and virgin soul, and there inspiring frenzy, awakens lyric and all other numbers; with these adorning the myriad actions of ancient heroes for the instruction of posterity. But he who, not being inspired and having no touch of madness in his soul, comes to the door and thinks that he will get into the temple by the help of art—he, I say, and his poetry are not admitted; the sane man is nowhere at all when he enters in rivalry with the madman."[13]

The deleterious and beneficial kinds of madness, the first associated with violence and clinical insanity, the other with truth and prophecy, obviously represent polar oppositions in what, in reality, is more of a continuum. Though these two sides of madness rarely come together, prophecy as truth, precisely because it is associated with madness and implies abnormal physical and mental states, rarely comes in an unadulterated form. Even Greek culture does not see prophecy as clearly defined and beneficial as Plato does. For Plato, prophecy that is never believed can hardly qualify as good prophecy, the kind of prophecy that will confer "great benefits on Hellas, both in public and private life." Hera makes Ajax mad to save her wards, Agamemnon and Menelaus; but the prophecy of the frenzied, mad prophetess Cassandra regarding Agamemnon turns out to be useless, for her prophecy is divinely cursed. Her punishment, imposed by Apollo, is that her prophecy will never be believed. And because her prophecies are not heeded, she herself is destroyed. Though her prophecy may be true and concern the most important matters of state, it benefits no one.[14]

A curse is not required, however, for a prophet to be doubted in his or her own time. The divinely inspired prophets of the Old Testament often experience a similar fate. But whence comes the disbelief in the divine word? In ancient times prophecy, like madness, was seen as possession by an outside force. But since one could be possessed by devils as much as by God, prophecy could just as often be false as true. The Old Testament speaks of many false prophets, the New Testament of an Antichrist. Possession, madness, and inspiration can be from God, but they can also be from the devil. The mad trance of the true prophet cannot always be distinguished from the mad trance of the false prophet. Madness may make the perception and dissemination of higher truths possible, but madness alone does not validate the source; in fact, it may call into question the authority of the source, invariably the most important criterion for the assessment of truth. When prophecy is considered true, madness is seen as a gift from God, an incarnation; when it is false, it is viewed as a curse and a disease. But, as Cassandra shows, prophecy may be a curse even when it is true.

Truth and Derangement

If distinguishing between divinely or satanically inspired prophecy and visions were not a difficult enough problem, the relationship between insanity (mental derangement) and truth further complicates matters.

> Cultural values serve not only to encourage or check the experiences and acts of these individuals; they also provide the criteria by which deviant behavior of this type is judged and differentiated from other forms. Thus many societies distinguish between the insane, that is, mentally deranged individuals whose condition is chronic, and those whose behavior appears similar in some respects, but who exhibit it only in socially sanctioned situations such as religious rites, or in roles upon which the society places great value such as that of the prophet.[15]

Plato carefully distinguishes between mental derangement, violent and nonviolent, and a higher mental state, madness, associated with decodable truth. But, in many cultures, nonviolent mental derangement is often associated with prophecy. In ancient Israel Saul, the first major figure afflicted with mental illness, was said to have been possessed by demons; however, his possession seems also to have been the source of his ability to prophesy. In contrast to the class of prophesying temple priests and priestesses in Greece, the major Hebrew prophets were generally outside the class of officially sanctioned prophets associated with the Temple. Moreover, rulers, upset with untoward prophecies, often found it in their interest to discredit prophets by declaring them mentally deranged and then mistreating them. Prophets frequently exhibited behavior similar to the insane. Often they were alienated from their own people ("a prophet is not without honor, save in his own country," Matthew 13:57), left to wander the country in rags, resembling the uninspired mad (the mentally deranged). Elisha, the disciple of Elijah, must certainly have resembled a deranged man, given that he was pursued and ridiculed by young children.[16] Jeremiah, though from a prominent priestly family, was also a wanderer, lived alone his entire adult life, and was rejected by his own people. Some obviously considered him mad. Indeed, in his writings he shows signs of terrible depression, if not paranoia.[17]

Probably the closest amalgam of truth and derangement occurs in the Christian tradition of the holy fool, which achieved its greatest prominence in medieval Russia. This tradition may ultimately derive from a peculiar interpretation of Paul's first epistle to the Corinthians: "We are fools for Christ's sake, but ye are wise in Christ; we are weak, but ye are strong; ye are honorable, but we are despised" (Cor: 4:10).[18] True fools in Christ, who consciously humiliate themselves to live a life in imitation of Christ, often went about in rags, begged, and behaved as though demented. Their prophecy was highly regarded by many tsars; they could express themselves in ways that few Hebrew prophets could without risking their lives.[19] It is important to point out, however, that, although many Russians would come to regard even the truly demented as fools in Christ, the early holy fools were not insane at all but consciously took on the image of insanity in kenotic imitation of Christ.

In literature, clinical madness and prophetic madness rarely come together. As I have indicated, the Greek tragedians, with the possible exception of Aeschylus's portrayal of Cassandra in *The Oresteia*, present madness primarily as a curse and divine punishment, and rarely associate it with prophetic gifts or higher truths. Before the nineteenth century, works in the Western literary tradition in which the prophetic (or visionary) and the clinical come closest are Cervantes' *Don Quixote* and Shakespeare's *King Lear*. It is this link that is so important for Pushkin's major works of 1833, which specifically address the relationship between truth—even prophecy in the case of *The Bronze Horseman*—and mental illness. But in Pushkin we are dealing not with the inspired prophecy of temple priests, nor even the visions of kings (King Lear) and knights (Don Quixote), but with the visions of ordinary and, in some cases, even vulgar (Germann in *The Queen of Spades*) human beings.

Don Quixote and *King Lear* present somewhat different approaches to the connection between madness as mental derangement and insight. Since Pushkin combines these approaches or vacillates between them, it is important to outline them as a way to more accurately define the parameters in which madness operates in his work. The simpler case is *King Lear*, the most celebrated work before the nineteenth century in which madness plays an essential role. In *King Lear*, madness as derangement is fully compatible with the idea of insight or higher truth. Before he goes mad, Lear is presented as the epitome of unwisdom. He becomes wise only after he goes mad. "In madness, Lear finds the wisdom he never knew as king."[20] Most of Lear's statements after he goes mad express his rage at his terrible fate and at his daughters who have turned him out. But in scene 6 of act 4, he rises above his preoccupation with the wrongs done against him and sees with new and more penetrating eyes. As his position changes, he begins both to go mad *and* see the world differently, from the perspective of a vagabond rather than a king. He begins to understand the arbitrary relationship of power to justice. In response to the monologue in which Lear expresses these views, Edgar utters: "Oh matter and impertinency mixed! Reason in madness" (4.6.176). Edgar does not mean reason and madness side by side, but "mixed"; they have come together, fused to become "reason in madness."[21] It is rare in ancient Greek literature and culture to find a fusion of inspired prophecy and derangement, not to speak of reason and derangement.

Don Quixote presents a more complex case because it presents the relationship between truth and madness much more ambiguously.[22]

Since Quixote's madness is at times presented as a disease, and the vision is dependent on the disease, the truth of his vision is always subject to doubt. More important, Cervantes turns the relationship of madness and truth into an openly discussed issue within the text itself, such that the reader willy-nilly is also brought into the discussion. The novel participates in the dialogue on the relationship with its readers. In *King Lear*, this issue is not raised; it is a surprise that Lear grows wiser as he becomes madder.[23]

The problematic relationship between madness and truth that Cervantes presents—the concomitance of illness and truth—was one that Dostoevsky struggled with in the creation of Prince Myshkin in *The Idiot*. When Dostoevsky first conceived his Christ-like Prince Myshkin, he hoped to overcome some of the problems he saw in Cervantes' comic presentation of his hero. "I will mention only that of the beautiful figures in Christian literature the most finished is Don Quixote; but he is beautiful solely because at the same time he is ridiculous [*smeshon*]."[24] To Dostoevsky, Quixote is comic or ridiculous because he is mad, and his madness compromises his truth.[25] Dostoevsky attempts to overcome this problem by turning the plot structure of *Don Quixote* inside out. Whereas Don Quixote is sane at the very beginning and end of the novel, and mad in the middle, Myshkin is mentally ill at the very beginning and end, and essentially sane in the middle. Dostoevsky reduces Myshkin's period of madness in the novel proper so that it will not undermine his hero's iconic status as an incarnation of divine light. But Dostoevsky, unable to resist the temptation of heteroglossia, deconstructs his own reconstruction of Cervantes not only by bringing madness as illness back into the plot but by including it, like Cervantes, as a subject of discussion within the novel itself. Myshkin has visions of absolute beauty and truth, but he experiences them only during the aura before an epileptic attack. He wonders whether the vision is compromised by his mental instability—by his disease—especially since these visions are closely associated with the time he spent in Switzerland when he was still being treated for "idiocy." He also fears that these visions are the harbingers of a terrible relapse into mental illness. At the same time Myshkin proposes the opposite, the more romantic, interpretation: that the vision is not compromised by his mental condition at all; in fact, the ability to see the higher truths is directly attributable to the disease, to madness itself. "'What if it is a disease?' he decided at last. 'What does it matter that it is an abnormal intensity, if the result, if the moment of sensation, recalled and analyzed afterwards in health, turns out to be the acme of harmony and beauty, and gives a feeling, unknown and undivined till then, of completeness, of proportion, of reconciliation, and of ecstatic devotional fusion with the highest synthesis of life?'"[26] The implication is that Myshkin's epileptic madness, like Mohammed's, may be holy, that madness itself as illness may be the vehicle of the highest truth. But Dostoevsky, who himself suffered from epilepsy and experienced the same aura as his hero, like Cervantes, leaves the issue unresolved.[27]

An understanding of the portrayal of madness in *King Lear, Don Quixote,* and *The Idiot* illuminates for us Pushkin's portrayal of madness in the works of 1833. If we take Evgenii, the hero of *The Bronze Horseman,* as an example, we can see that, like Lear, Evgenii goes mad, clinically insane, and not only temporarily mad like Don Quixote. Like Lear's, Evgenii's mental illness becomes increasingly severe. And also like Lear, Evgenii displays the traditional characteristics of the homeless mad: destitution, wandering, begging, and alienation. *The Bronze Horseman* establishes the relationship between madness and truth in Evgenii, but, like Cervantes and Dostoevsky, Pushkin makes the relationship problematic by implying that the vision itself may be compromised, at least to some degree, by mental illness. In "God Grant That I Not Lose My Mind" and *The Bronze Horseman,* he adds a further problem to the connection between madness and truth by tying truth not only to mental derangement but also to violence.[28] He implies paradoxically that violence stemming from madness may lead to truth but that any truth arising from violence is thereby compromised. In his depiction of madness, then, Pushkin subsumes the representations of the most important writers of the Western tradition and brings together manifestations of madness—violence and truth—usually unassociated (Greek tragedy) or consciously disassociated from each other (Plato).

The devil, however, is in the details. So let us now turn to Pushkin's greatest work in prose, *The Queen of Spades,* in which the hero goes mad in the end and is confined to a mental institution, an image that evokes the poet's greatest horror in his lyric, "God Grant That I Not Lose My Mind."

PART ONE

∾ *The Queen of Spades*

CHAPTER 1

Choosing the Right Card

Madness, Gambling, and the Imagination

Introduction

Scholars have never argued that madness was central to a proper understanding of *The Queen of Spades* [*Pikovaia dama*], though the story culminates in the hero's insanity.[1] Perhaps this critical lapse stems precisely from the fact that Germann's madness strikes at the end, and only by surprise. But not to make use of the terrible conclusion of the story, namely, madness, as an essential tool for reevaluating all that has come before is tantamount, for example, to dismissing the centrality of Rogozhin's murder of Nastast´ia Filippovna and Myshkin's lapse into idiocy at the end of Dostoevksy's *The Idiot*. Whether true or not, supposedly Dostoevsky wrote the novel backward, as many novelists do. He envisioned first the conclusion and then faced the task of working out the plot and characterization leading to his preordained finale. Germann's madness at the end of *The Queen of Spades* compels the reader not only to come to grips with the idea of madness in the story but also radically to reinterpret the hero and his actions. Once the calculating Germann is associated with madness, especially in a literary and historical context in which madness can be as much exalted as maligned, the doors to interpretation swing open.

In each of the works that we will examine, Pushkin presents madness from several different perspectives, always exploring and balancing the negative and positive, sometimes explicitly, as in "God Grant That I Not Lose My Mind," and sometimes implicitly, as in *The Bronze Horseman* and *The Queen of Spades*. There is a great temptation to impose a monolithic interpretation on the problem of madness in *The*

Queen of Spades, as on other aspects of the work; but one should be guided by Dostoevsky's observation that the perfection of the story derives directly from Pushkin's ability to present mutually exclusive ideas convincingly.

> The fantastic should come so close to the real that you must *almost* believe it. Pushkin, who has given us all our artistic models, achieved in *The Queen of Spades* the acme of the art of the fantastic. For you really believe that Germann actually saw a ghost and you believe precisely that view of reality commensurate with such a vision; yet at the end of the story, that is after having read it, you do not know how to interpret it: did Germann's vision arise from Germann's nature or was he actually one of those who came in contact with another world, a world of evil and hostile spirits (i.e., Spiritism and its teachings). Now that is art![2]

Caryl Emerson has taken this idea even further, suggesting that in *The Queen of Spades*, one of the earliest and most brilliant examples of deception in narrative prose, Pushkin not only encourages different interpretations but also purposely withholds sufficient proof for any one interpretation by including only fragmentary codes. "I would suggest that the codes we get in this story, wonderfully crafted as they are, were designed by Pushkin *not* to build any single unified structure, not to solve any single puzzle ... Pushkin provides us not with a code, and not with chaos, but precisely with the *fragments* of codes, codes that tantalize but do not quite add up. He teases the reader with partial keys."[3]

Since Pushkin's ambiguous presentation of the supernatural—the use of fragmentary codes—provides a good analogy for the interpretive strategy I shall apply to the representation of madness, I would like briefly to summarize the diametrically opposed psychological and supernatural interpretations of the plot.

Germann, the hero of *The Queen of Spades*, overhears a tale about an eighty-seven-year-old countess who possesses a secret formula for winning vast sums at faro. His attempt to wangle the secret from the countess by threatening her with a gun fails when she dies of fright. The next day the countess's ghost visits Germann and reveals to him the secret, involving three cards. When he tries the secret formula, it works for the first two cards, and, though it enables him to determine that he should take the ace as the third card, he inexplicably chooses the queen, the wrong card. Believing that the countess (in the form of the queen) has wreaked her revenge on him, Germann goes completely insane. He sits in a mental hospital continually muttering: "Three, seven, ace! Three, seven, queen!" [*"Troika, semerka, tuz! Troika, semerka, dama!"*] (8:252).[4] It is easy enough to interpret everything in this story psychologically, including the countess's ghost—as has often been done.[5] But Germann seems awake and lucid when the countess visits him. Moreover, the secret he receives works, despite the choice of the wrong card. The psychological code turns out to be fragmentary; it can never prove that Germann did not see a ghost who gave him the winning three cards. Once the door is open to the fantastic, it becomes possible to reinterpret all the data from a supernatural point of view, with the understanding that the supernatural is an even more fragmentary code than the psychological.

Likewise, *The Queen of Spades* gives contradictory presentations of madness. There seems to be no compensatory wisdom or vision in Germann's clinical insanity; his final condition appears to be a fate worse than death. However, Germann's mistake, the choice of the queen over the ace, challenges this deromanticized, devalorized picture of madness (revealing it to be only a fragmentary code) and contains a key to a more romantic notion of madness as an imaginative achievement—even a breakthrough. Nevertheless, there is more evidence for the devalorized interpretation than for the romantic one because the revelation of the true value of madness can come only at the end; the epiphany must be a shock not only to Germann but to the reader as well.

Since little has been written on madness in Pushkin in general, not to speak of madness in *The Queen of Spades*, I shall first present the contextual and textual arguments for a devalorized, unromantic interpretation of madness. In the next section, "The Context of Devalorization," I outline Pushkin's gradual turn away from a romantic view of madness, a turn reflected in this period in both German literature (Hoffmann) and Russian (Gogol and Dostoevsky). In the section that follows, "The Devalorization of Madness," I detail how Germann's materialistic ideal and the various failures of his imagination deflate madness. In the last section, "The Elevation of Madness," I show, in contrast to all previous interpretations, that Germann chooses the right card, not the wrong one, and that this choice constitutes for the hero not only a validation of madness but a victory of the imagination, and thus a victory of life over death. My aim is not to refute one interpretation by the other but to bring out what Dostoevsky considered the supreme artistic quality of the story, the simultaneous validity of mutually exclusive interpretations: that is, to place the devalorized interpretation of madness in perspective and provide the case for the romantic alternative. Finally, I discuss a legacy of Pushkin's presentation of madness, showing its influence on Dostoevsky's conception of Ivan Karamazov, in *The Brothers Karamazov*, often considered the seminal work of modern Russian literature.

The Context of Devalorization

It has been generally held that Pushkin's work from 1833 and later contains few, if any, traces of a romantic view of madness. Some Soviet critics (Levkovich, for example)[6] have conceded that Pushkin may have regarded the subject—especially the relationship between poetry and madness—romantically in the 1820s but maintain that he overcame this poetic phase by the early 1830s, when realism triumphed over romanticism, reason over madness, and clarity over confusion. Indeed, his early poetry closely ties madness—as well as other extreme states—to the poetic process. Pushkin describes poetry as a "passionate illness," "fiery ecstasy," "the violence of the whirlwind," "confusion," "fever," even "sacred delirium."[7] "God Grant That I Not Lose My Mind" (1833) seems to confirm a turn toward a more anti-romantic position. In the beginning of the lyric, the persona finds his situation so desperate that he entertains the idea of parting with his reason to secure his peace and freedom; however, when he visualizes the social and personal consequences of madness, he rejects it as a solution to his problems. In the end, madness is likened not only to a fatal illness afflicting an individual but also to a plague [*chuma*] threatening a population; society perceives the madman as a threat to the well-being of the state.[8]

Pushkin was also personally acquainted with a "mad" poet, Konstantin Batiushkov, whose sad fate may not only have intensified Pushkin's fear of madness but even further separated in his mind the ideas of madness and poetry.[9] Batiushkov completely stopped writing poetry after he went insane at thirty-three—Pushkin's age when he wrote *The Queen of Spades*, *The Bronze Horseman*, and perhaps "God Grant." Pushkin had visited the mad Batiushkov when everyone thought that Batiushkov was dying (he actually recovered) and was reported to have come away from this visit quite shaken.

Pushkin's devalorization of madness runs counter, in part, to the romanticism of this period in Russian literature, typified by the works of the arch-romantic Prince Vladimir Odoevsky (1803–1869), a writer influenced by German literature and philosophy and close in spirit to E. T. A. Hoffmann. An opponent of rationalism and utilitarianism, Odoevsky wrote repeatedly about the superiority of humankind's mystical and irrational inner world and about the inextricable relationship between madness and genius, particularly madness and poetry.[10] The hero of "The Sylph" ["Sil'fida," 1837], a story reminiscent of Hoffmann's "The Golden Pot" ["Der goldne Topf," 1814], settles on his estate in the provinces and, about to reconcile himself to the philistinism of everyday life—including marriage to his neighbor's daughter—starts reading cabalistic and esoteric treatises. They lead him, through insanity, into a higher, spiritual world that reveals to him the true meaning of existence and releases him from all mundane concerns and ties. The hero is eventually "saved" by his friends, who cure his madness, but at the expense of his spiritual life. His greatest regret in life remains his cure, a view with which the author sympathizes.

The most important writers of the time, however, including Gogol, the young Dostoevsky, and Pushkin, often treat German romantic and Hoffmannian prose forms and thematics ironically and even parodically.[11] German literature made this ironic turn earlier, perhaps taking its cue from Hoffmann himself, who often wrote in an ironic vein, sometimes parodying his own writings devoted to the marvelous and the fantastic (in the late "The King's Betrothed" ["Die Königsbraut"], for example).[12] To be sure, Gogol and Dostoevsky could not have influenced Pushkin's representation of madness in *The Queen of Spades*, but their early works show that Pushkin's parodic, anti-romantic treatment of madness, though atypical for Russian literature, was not idiosyncratic; in fact, it reflected Western literary trends.

Gogol presents madness ironically in two of his most famous stories, "The Nose" ["Nos," 1836][13] and "Notes of a Madman" ["Zapiski sumasshedshego," 1835].[14] The hero of "The Nose," Kovalev, wakes one morning to find that his nose is gone and leading an independent existence, disguised as an official whose rank is much higher than Kovalev's. The story parodies the theme of the doppelgänger, which Hoffmann frequently used to represent spiritual and mental disturbance, for Gogol's characters are too superficial to have minds or spirits in which a true double could manifest itself. The hero is a typical

Gogolian *poshliak*, the epitome of self-satisfied vulgarity and mediocrity, and his double is literally a nose. The hero of "Notes of a Madman," a petty clerk with neither intellect nor spirit (and perhaps even without a soul), goes mad not because of a desire for a higher spiritual realm but because he is not taken seriously by his superior's daughter. Though the reader sympathizes with the hero's sufferings after he goes mad, the madness itself is presented as ridiculous and petty. The tragic side of the story is actually more social than personal, issuing from the brutal treatment of the hero in an insane asylum. Similarly, in *The Double* (1846),[15] Dostoevsky devalues madness in his hero, Goliadkin, and in his hero's double. The opposite of a higher self, this double does not provide Goliadkin with any vision of a higher— or a lower—realm. Emptied of all that is vital and elevating, the double is as prosaic as Goliadkin himself.

Roberta Reeder, who has made an excellent case for *The Queen of Spades* as a parody of a Hoffmannian *Kunstmärchen*, argues that Pushkin empties Germann of all that is romantically elevating: "Like many of Hoffmann's heroes, Germann is provided with choice, but prefers to blame his interest in the demonic on outside forces. His goal is not to be a great poet like Anselmus, but to gain great wealth out of sheer greed.... Like the Philistines in Hoffmann's tales, when Germann turns to the spiritual, he achieves only the demonic and never attains the heights of the realm of the good and the beautiful."[16] Pushkin thus seems not only to portray Germann's madness at the end as a spiritual death but also, through parody, to undercut all suggestions that it could have led to greater insight or a higher world or truth. In contrast to Anselmus, the hero of "The Golden Pot," who must lose his sanity so as not to become a prisoner of the world of avarice, and to Odoevsky's hero, who is cured of madness against his will, Germann appears to go mad only because his performance is inadequate to his greed; that is, he goes mad unromantically.

The Devalorization of Madness

Madness in *The Queen of Spades* seems precipitated and aggravated not by the absence of imagination but by imaginative failure. Almost every time Germann meets story and art, he attempts to appropriate them as a means of achieving great wealth. The work opens with a tale told by the countess's grandson, Tomsky, about his grandmother's secret of three cards. At first Germann disbelieves the story, but it soon begins to work on his imagination and, as he appropriates it, to take on more grotesque forms than in all its previous history.[17] The first night after hearing the story—despite the prompting of his prudent other self, which tells him that the story could not be true—Germann is already dreaming of riches. He wakes up the next morning sighing over the loss of what now seems to him not imaginary but real wealth. Rather than leading him to a higher truth, Germann's imagination panders to his material desires. Outside the old countess's house, after hearing the story:

> Germann began to tremble. The amazing story of the three cards again appeared before his imagination. He began to walk up and down near the house thinking of its owner and her marvelous gift. He returned late to his humble lodging, but he could not sleep for a long time; and when at last sleep overcame him, he dreamed of cards, a green table, piles of banknotes and heaps of gold coins. He played card after card, decisively turning down the corners of his cards, and he won continually, raking in the gold and putting the notes into his pocket. After waking up quite late, he sighed over the loss of his fantastic wealth; then he again set out to wander around the city, and he again found himself in front of the countess's house. (8:236)

Soon Germann absorbs everything and everyone into a monomaniacal plot. For example, Pushkin sets Liza, the countess's ward, as a romantic object for his hero. On the first fateful night of decision, Germann can either choose a door on his left to Liza's room (where she has arranged a tryst with him) or a door on the right, to the countess's. But Germann does not intend to sacrifice fortune for love. Rather, he must give up the heroine to forward his ambition. In a tale like "The Golden Pot," the bourgeois heroine is presented as an ideological reason for the hero to escape into the world of his imagination, but, for Germann, Liza is little more than a part of his plan to wrench the secret from the aged countess.[18]

Earlier, to win Liza's heart, Germann composes letters by copying passages out of German novels. Later he does without this aid; his letters are written "under the inspiration of passion, spoken in his own language, and they bore full testimony to the inflexibility of his desire and the disordered condition of his uncontrollable imagination" (8:233). The passion that inspires Germann is nothing but the desire for wealth, security, and independence. His language in the letters is a hodgepodge of clichés from second-rate sentimental and romantic literature. The narrator notes that these clichés were perfectly expressive of Germann's desire and imagination; his inflexible desire is made even triter by his disordered and uncontrolled fancy.

Numerous studies attempt to discover the meaning of Germann's transformations of the three cards,[19] but what may be most important about these transformations for a devalorized view of madness in *The Queen of Spades* is that they are prosaic. Germann sees all stout men, often associated in Russian literature with status and success, as aces, and he regards flowers as threes. His response to people on the street who ask him for the time indicates how close he is to the madness of the epilogue. Regardless of the time of day, he answers, in a way worthy of Gogol's comic genius, "Five minutes to the seven" [*"bez piati minut semerka"*] (8:249). The narrator concludes the above passage with another deflationary stroke. The hero should, after all, go back to Paris—the origin of the fairy tale—and take on fortune in the great gambling houses of the city. But just as the countess comes back after her death to reveal her secret to Germann when he had lost all hope, Germann spares himself a heroic challenge or quest. He is hardly inconvenienced.

His confrontation with the old countess is the scene that most deflates Germann's imagination, and thus his madness. He steals into her chambers and waits for her to return from a ball. Although he takes an unloaded pistol with him to threaten her if she proves unaccommodating, he plans to win her over the same way he won Liza, despite the seventy-year difference in the women's ages. Germann's speech to the countess provides the first and most detailed access to the linguistic contents of his imagination. It also suggests the contents of his letters to Liza and anticipates the countess's speech to him from beyond the grave. When Germann confronts the countess in her boudoir, she responds by saying that the story was a joke. In no joking mood, he falls on his knees before the decrepit eighty-seven-year-old woman and reveals why he must have her secret.

"If your heart ever knew the feeling of love," he said, "if you remember its rapture, if you have even once smiled at the cry of a new-born son, if anything human ever beat in your breast, then I implore by the feelings of a wife, a lover, a mother, by all that is sacred in life, not to reject my plea. Reveal to me your secret. Of what use is it to you?... Maybe it is connected with a horrible sin, with the loss of eternal bliss, with a pact with the devil.... Consider: you are old; you do not have long to live—I am ready to take your sins upon my soul. Only reveal to me your secret. Remember that the happiness of a man rests in your hands, that not only I, but my children, grandchildren, and great grandchildren will bless your memory and honor it as sacred." (8:241–42)

This product of Germann's disordered and uncontrolled imagination will hardly persuade the countess to reveal her secret—assuming that she has one. Aside from triteness, this speech is characterized by ridiculous non sequiturs regarding the satanic, the sacred, sin, and happiness. Germann entreats the countess by all that is sacred not to reject his plea, but he immediately remarks that the secret may be related to some horrible sin, to the loss of eternal bliss, or to a pact with the devil. He is even willing to make his own pact with the devil, taking all her sins on himself. But how can his happiness—and especially his children's—be assured if it is based on a satanic pact?

In a more traditionally romantic work, Gogol's "Portrait" (1842),[20] the imagination can be corrupted, serving the devil (comfort) as well as true art or religion. But Germann is not an artist, and though he has a most lively imagination, every manifestation of it appears as the epitome of *poshlost'*: the second-rate, the vulgar, the unimaginative, and even the ridiculous. From this point of view, any connection between Germann and the demonic—such as the countess's spirit—is as doubtful as one between Germann and the higher spiritual world.

Though Germann may be "punished" in the end for using others to achieve crass, materialistic goals, Nabokov, for one, might have argued that Germann's crimes are also against the imagination. Art, Nabokov writes, "is a game, because it remains art only as long as we are allowed to remember that, after all, it is all make-believe, that the people on the stage, for instance, are not actually murdered, in other words, only as long as our feelings of horror or of disgust do not obscure our realization that we are, as readers or spectators, participating in an elaborate and enchanting game: the moment this balance is upset we get, on the stage, ridiculous melodrama, and in a book just a lurid description of, say, a murder which should belong in a newspaper instead."[21]

Germann, both a Nabokovian melodramatic "reader" and "spectator," upsets the balance between art and life by reducing one to the other. By doing so, he kills the story and destroys himself. It is perhaps poetic justice that, in contrast to Anselmus, who is redeemed by a creative madness, Germann goes vulgarly mad. For Anselmus, madness is a means to a higher end; for Germann, it is the result of imaginative failure.

Yet it might be argued that what leads Germann to madness is not so much the coarseness of his imagination as the reductiveness. He tries, in effect, to reduce life to a simple formula. At the beginning Germann needs imagination to acquire the secret of the three cards. He is preoccupied with choosing between alternatives. He has to gain entry into the countess's house, and, once there, he needs a strategy to make the countess reveal her secret. When she dies, he cannot stop thinking creatively, for he still lacks the secret. Once the three cards are revealed to him, however, he becomes more obsessive and his world more constricted. No ingenious plans are now necessary. Three, seven, and ace made up Germann's entire existence: everything in the outside world is transformed into the new code.

> Two fixed ideas cannot exist together in the moral world just as two bodies cannot occupy one and the same place in the physical world. Three, seven, ace began to eclipse in Germann's imagination the image of the dead old woman. Three, seven, ace didn't leave him for a moment and played continually on his lips. If he saw a young girl, he would say: "How slender she is! A real three of hearts." If anyone asked him the time, he would answer: "Five minutes to the seven." Every pot-bellied man he saw reminded him of the ace. Three, seven, ace haunted him in his sleep, assuming all possible forms: The three blossomed before him in a form of a magnificent flower, the seven appeared as a Gothic portal, and the ace an enormous spider. All his thoughts fused into one: to make use of the secret that had cost him so dearly. He thought of retirement and of traveling. He wanted to compel fortune to yield up her treasure to him in the public gambling houses of Paris. Chance saved him all these troubles. (8:249)

The third and last stage of this imaginative reduction is perfectly represented in the insane asylum. All thought has vanished. All connection to the outside world has been severed. Two phrases, four words ("Three, seven, ace," "Three, seven, queen") constitute the only sign that a human being once lived in that body. Germann has, in effect, become reduced to the name of the cards, signifiers now of absolutely nothing. His imagination has revealed nothing to him; instead, it has reduced the tale that was told at the beginning (which had permuted through hundreds of variations) to a simple formula for the elimination of risk, chance, and change. (It should be noted that Germann, at least consciously, never conceives of his card playing as real gambling.) Further, it has stopped the process of interpretation and reinterpretation, reducing the life of the story to a magic formula, to a final interpretation. Germann again becomes an exemplum of madness as imaginative failure.

The Elevation of Madness

Although *The Queen of Spades* underscores the vulgarity of Germann's imagination, the story is not a monolithic devalorization of madness. Like the psychological interpretations of the story, the devalorization of madness constitutes only a partial code. In fact, Germann ultimately does the opposite of his prudent, fortune-amassing father and even does what probably no one associated with the tale of the three cards has done, especially if most of the absurdities that Germann hears at the beginning are discounted. Germann starts out with a small capital, risks everything, and loses everything. To assume that he believes in the secret and thus thinks he is not taking a risk, not really gambling, is to make him into a one-dimensional character—a figure completely coinciding with his conscious self—in a story that is above all ambiguous and complex.[22]

Given a Nabokovian view of *poshlost'*, it may seem better to have no imagination at all than the one Pushkin deals Germann, but the story, I hope to show, reveals otherwise. The narrator says not only that Germann has a lively imagination but also that he is a gambler at heart. Critics have paid much more attention to the first quality than to the second, but each is prophetic, realizing itself and combining with the other to seal Germann's fate. In the end Germann gambles; he plays not so much to win as he does to risk, to dare, to stake his life, that is, to live.[23]

That Germann is a gambler at heart is indicated in the very first passages of the text as well as in the last. At the beginning he sits on the sidelines, a passionate and imaginative observer—Pushkin stresses his strong passions [*sil'nye strasti*]—but he is able to restrain his desire.[24] "And yet he would sit night after night at the card tables, following with feverish excitement the various turns of the game" (8:235). Both his restraint and passion are present even before he hears the tale [*skazka*] of the three cards. The tale does not transform Germann; it pushes him over the edge.

The narrator abandons Germann on the very first page and does not take him up again until the middle of the next chapter, providing a span of reading time that suggests the psychological time Germann requires for the *skazka* to invade his imagination. Despite the depreciative account I give of Germann's imagination in the previous section, the narrator still describes it as active and fiery [*ognennoe*] (8:235). Germann does not passively accept the *skazka* but transforms it into his own creation, and so it reflects, as any creation must, the mind and passions of its creator. Germann knows that the story of the secret is only a fairy tale, but only this story, which represents the imaginative transformation of many generations, can affect him. A creature of the imagination, he finds the gambling less tempting than the story into which the gambling is metamorphosed.

Soon after the idea of the three cards implants itself in Germann's mind, he attempts to exert active control over the *skazka*. A plot begins to emerge in his imagination that charges all the events and characters of the tale. First Liza is plotted, then the countess, both before and after her death. Of course Germann places himself at the center of events, the quester after the great secret. However, his madness, while exacerbated by his desire to reduce the story to the names of the secret cards, can be just as easily seen as a concentration of his imaginative powers to some higher end, of which he is barely conscious.

The most important of Germann's imaginative acts involving the dead countess are the first, by which he thinks his fortune is made, and the two last, by which his doom is sealed. The first act, his imagining the ghost of the countess (for argument's sake, I do not treat the apparitions as supernatural), is not so much a self-serving device as a creative interpretation. "'I have come to you against my will,' she said in a firm voice: 'But I have been ordered to fulfill your request. Three, seven, ace in succession will win for you, but only on the conditions that you do not play more than one card a day, and that you never play again for the rest of your life. I forgive you my death, on the condition that you marry my ward, Lizaveta Ivanovna'" (8:247). This utterance is in some ways as trite as Germann's other speeches. His conception that the countess comes against her will to grant his request and forgive him seems psychologically obvious, if not commonplace. Further, he has been thinking about threes, sevens, and aces ever since he encountered the anecdote. The night after hearing it, Germann names the cards and affirms their power even as he seems to reject them. "No! Prudence, moderation, and hard work: those are my three sure cards, that is what will increase my capital threefold, sevenfold, and provide me with peace and independence."[25] And yet he curiously varies the story from the way it has been repeated in the past (perhaps to make it more convincing to himself), introducing the requirement that the cards be played on successive days. For perhaps the first time, instead of reducing the tale, Germann begins to draw it out. This expansion may reflect his desire not to win at once but to prolong the game, to continue to play for the sake of playing.

Pushkin makes Germann's role as interpreter explicit: "For a long time Germann could not come to his senses. He went into the other room. His orderly was asleep on the floor; Germann was hardly able to wake him. The orderly was drunk as usual, and it was impossible to get any sense from him. The street door was locked. Germann returned to his room, lit a candle, and wrote down his vision" (8:248).

Whatever Germann writes is an interpretation, in no way less fanciful than those of numerous critics who, after reading *The Queen of Spades*, and especially the vision episode, sat down, like Germann, to write. In this episode others as well—scholars, and artists like Dostoevsky—have thought that there was more to Germann's imagination than the clichés that riddled his speeches.

On the night of the countess's death, Germann faces a choice—on the left, Liza's apartment, and on the right, the countess's study: he chooses the door on the right, seemingly the wrong door—ambition wins out over love. On the night of the last card game, it is the card on the left—the ace—that will bring him fame and fortune, the card on the right that leads to madness. He chooses the card on the right. But this final mad act, the playing of the last card, must be viewed not as the most reductive deed of a vulgar madman but as Germann's most inspired and imaginative act in his own creation. For when he chooses the wrong card (and who but a madman would choose the wrong card when he knows the right one?) it is a choice that runs counter to his ideals of peace and comfort [*pokoi*], and of independence [*nezavisimost'*], a rebellious blow against a final resolution. The "mad" act that drives Germann permanently insane thus may be his highest act of sanity: a choice against reduction, a choice for the first time for chance, play, and life. Given Germann's extreme personality, only an act of madness can free him from his vain ideal of undisturbed self-sufficiency and permit him, for one moment, to experience, in the most intense form imaginable, the feeling of being a true, though reckless, gambler, one who can stake his life on a card. Had Germann won, of course, it would have been the greatest loss; it would have been never to have gambled—to have lived—at all.[26]

The conclusion is as unexpected for the reader as the queen of spades is for the conscious Germann. Almost all critics hold that Germann chooses the wrong card and that Pushkin punishes him by making him do so; but, in fact, the calculating Germann dies for chance and is thereby elevated. At the last possible moment, a romantic notion of madness flashes into the reader's view and sheds a different light on all that has happened previously. Before actually going insane, the hero experiences a momentary vision of the truth of his life, much as Dostoevsky's Myshkin does in his epileptic aura. At last Germann understands the emptiness of his ideal of peace and independence, and sees clearly—and recognizes the price of—the only possibility that remains for redeeming his past. For this romantic moment, as in Pushkin's *Egyptian Nights*, one must be willing to sacrifice one's life. Madness sends Germann to the asylum, but it also gives him the only moment when he must have felt really alive, living not for his father but for himself. He pays dearly for this moment. But the tragedy of Germann, a sharply polarized personality, is that, for him, there can be no compromise, no healthy gambling. It is all or nothing.[27] His choice in the end is the one he created for himself. It was he who brought the countess back from the dead. It was he who invented the cards, the secret. It was also he who plotted his final moments, giving himself no "middle" ground. It was either the ace or the queen. By choosing the queen, Germann makes a leap of the imagination that elevates him above his fellows and transforms him into a figure that has exerted a tremendous power on the Russian literary imagination to this day. But just as important, by choosing the queen, Germann also chooses to keep the story alive—open to interpretation—and to make himself part, perhaps the most intriguing part, of the next redaction of the tale, a warning to all proponents of closure.

Pushkin's ambiguous and ambivalent representation of madness in *The Queen of Spades*—as simultaneously the epitome of *poshlost'* and romantic epiphany—is probably not what Gofman had in mind when he speculated about Pushkin's legacy for Russian literature in terms of madness. But this strange idea of madness perhaps constituted Pushkin's principal legacy for the mature Dostoevsky. In "The Gambler" (1867), Dostoevsky wrote his own version of *The Queen of Spades*, and in Raskolnikov in *Crime and Punishment* (1866) he created an updated Germann. But it is in the representation of Ivan Karamazov's madness that the implications of Pushkin's treatment of madness seem to be taken to their logical conclusions.

Toward the end of *The Brothers Karamazov* (1880),[28] in a passage that echoes Germann's encounter with the countess's ghost, Ivan Karamazov confronts a ghost, the creature of his imagination. A doctor from Moscow has just diagnosed Ivan as "having something perhaps even like a brain disorder" [*"vrode dazhe kak by rasstroistva v mozgu"*] in which "hallucinations ... are quite possible" [*"galliutsiatsii ... ochen' vozmozhny"*] (15:70). "And so he was sitting there now, almost conscious himself of being delirious, and, as I have said already, staring persistently at some object on the sofa against the opposite wall. Someone suddenly appeared sitting there, though God knows how he walked in, because he had not been in the room when Ivan Fyodorovich entered the room on his way back from his visit to Smerdyakov" (15:70). Ivan senses something mean and seedy in his devil. Ivan may curse him and call him a lie, an illness, a ghost, an embodiment of only one side of himself, a reflection of Ivan's most loathsome and stupid thoughts and feelings, but what most disturbs Ivan is the visitor's banality, his *poshlost'*. The devil says archly that his dream is "to become incarnate ... in some fat, two-hundred-and-fifty-pound merchant's wife and believe everything she believes in" [*"voplotit'sia ... v kakuiu-nibud' tolstuiu semipudovuiu kupchikhu i vsemu poverit', vo chto ona verit"*] (15:73–74), and he claims that not only artists have extraordinary hallucinations but "the most ordinary people, officials, journalists, priests" [*"sovsem samye zauriadnye liudi, chinovniki, fel'tonisty, popy"*] (15:73–74). The devil, however, deftly counters Ivan's characterization of him as banal: "How could such a banal devil come to such a great man?" [*"Kak, deskat', k takomu velikomu cheloveku mog voiti takoi poshlyi chert?"*] (15:81). Banality, brilliance, and hallucination are inseparably bound in Ivan's madness.

This unusual sort of madness brings Ivan, as it does Germann, face to face with the choice that will determine his fate, a choice between opposite worlds. Though Ivan's choice differs from Germann's, Dostoevsky, like Pushkin, focuses simultaneously on the banal and the romantic aspects of his hero's madness. More important, however, Dostoevsky intimates something larger than a dual, or ambiguous, interpretation of madness—*poshlost'* or revelation. He posits a different kind of madness, perhaps a particularly Russian form, not a madness that leads now to false salvation (the ace) and now to transfiguration (the queen) but one that both threatens damnation and promises transfiguration at the same time—or perhaps even a madness without closure. Through Dostoevsky's transformation, Pushkin's concept of madness may have become, to Nabokov's consternation, one of the most dynamic of Pushkin's legacies to nineteenth- and twentieth-century Russian literature and culture. Nabokov seemingly attempts to have the final word in *Despair* in which the main character, Hermann (*Germann*), a mad writer prone to hallucinations and obsessed with a double, is punished for imaginative failure: "Hell shall never parole Hermann."[29] But it is not in Nabokov's power to end the story by dealing Hermann/Germann the wrong cards; whatever end he chooses for his hero, Nabokov is fated, somewhat like Pushkin's Germann, to become still another intriguing link in the self-renewing legacy of *The Queen of Spades*.

CHAPTER 2

Madness and Psychoanalysis

Introduction

In the previous chapter I attempted to show how Pushkin simultaneously makes powerful cases for both the devalorized (anti-romantic) and valorized (romantic) notions of madness in *The Queen of Spades*. These opposing positions manifest themselves in the cultural and literary context of Pushkin's own time where madness itself appears primarily as a literary category. Germann, seemingly the epitome of practicality, turns out also to be a creature of the imagination. Though initially driven by the desire for wealth, he increasingly gets caught up in the story he hears and the plot he creates. In literary terms, what seems to be devalorization of madness can also be seen as its elevation, not an elevation in general but one for Germann, or Germann's type, in a specific literary and psychological context.

The present chapter turns the focus from the literary to the psychological, more specifically, the psychoanalytical. Again it takes its lead from Dostoevsky, who maintained the equal validity of two mutually exclusive interpretations of *The Queen of Spades*, the psychological and the fantastic. The last chapter showed that two seemingly mutually exclusive literary notions of madness were equally sound artistically; the present chapter shows how the story can similarly embrace two apparently exclusive psychoanalytic theories of personality, one based on the ego psychology of Freud and the other on the anti-ego psychologies of Lacan and other "romantic" psychoanalysts.

There are obviously significant differences between these sets of polarities. A comparison of the romantic with the anti-romantic aspects of *The Queen of Spades* is grounded in the literary culture in which Pushkin himself was immersed; that is, he was acquainted with both romantic and anti-romantic portrayals of madness in European literature. When applied to nineteenth-century literature, psychoanalytic interpretations represent twentieth-century adaptations of psychological concepts and constructs unknown to the authors being analyzed. There is nothing intrinsically problematic about this since all interpretation of past literature, to some extent, represents an attempt to understand it in terms of contemporary sensibilities and practices, to understand its relevance and significance for us. This is one of the functions of the never-ending process of reinterpretation. Psychoanalysis does not illuminate all literary works, and even those that it does enlighten, it does not do so equally; but it works well with *The Queen of Spades*. It sheds light on Germann's madness, and it also opens up avenues for exploring the larger significance of madness in general.[1]

Since psychoanalytic models of personality diverge dramatically in their understanding of the role of the ego in mental health, they lead, in literature as in life, to different assessments of madness. Contradictory psychoanalytic interpretations do not cancel one another out; they shed equal, but different, light on the same phenomena. In this chapter I first analyze Germann's madness using a traditional Freudian personality model based on American ego psychology. This model, which privileges the ego, accounts, more satisfactorily than previous interpretations, for Germann's rapid transition from remarkable self-control (superego) to ultimate risk (id) and finally insanity. I then turn to a contrasting model of personality based on Lacan's mirror stage, a model which suggests that not the contest between the id and the superego, but the identificatory strategies of the ego (the preoccupation with the ace of spades, the *tuz*) are responsible for Germann's madness and demise. I apply the romantic psychoanalysis of Deleuze, Guattari, Laing, and others to take this devalorization of the ego one step further—the ego is not only demoted but madness itself is elevated as a conduit of ultimate truth: Germann chose the right card, the queen. Lastly I come back to Lacan, for Lacan's devaluation of the ego, in contrast to romantic psychoanalysis, does not celebrate untrammeled desire or madness. For Lacan, Germann's choices—either ace or queen—are both rejections of the symbolic order and thus as antithetical to the Lacanian "ideal" as ego psychology. In Lacan, madness can break through the constraints of the ego and glimpse important truths; but not all madness is creative. In the last section I employ Lacan again to explore the relation between Germann and his creator (the implied and historical author) and to assess more fully Germann's place in the symbolic order. Is Germann—whom Dostoevsky, without irony, called a colossal figure—condemned irrevocably to a devalorized Lacanian madness: linguistic idiocy? Or does he "escape" his creator's prison and come to play, as a type, a larger social (symbolic) role than his confinement in an asylum implies?[2]

I intend the following psychoanalytic interpretations not to be *strictly* Freudian or Lacanian but rather theories of personality suggested by Freudian, romantic, and Lacanian models of the ego and the unconscious, in their widest senses, adapted as interpretative strategies for understanding literary texts. These models, being both prescriptive and descriptive, not only describe the role the ego and unconscious play in the life of civilized men and women, but they also suggest the role they should play.[3] Further, I am not presenting Freud and Lacan as psychoanalytic antitheses. Lacan understood his own work not as a replacement but as a recovery or rediscovery of Freud, a means of exposing the distortions of the ego psychologists: Freud's, mostly American, followers and "heirs." Lacan capsulizes his own approach in his interpretation of Freud's famous statement on the ego and the id in his *New Introductory Lectures* (Where id was, there ego shall be [*Wo es war, soll Ich werden*]) not as an authoritative pronouncement but as a metaphor inviting multiple interpretations, one of which informs the interpretations offered here. But at times I take the same liberty with Lacan as Lacan takes with Freud, stretching his model to accommodate Pushkin's text.[4] On the other hand, I have tried not to take liberties with Pushkin's texts. In the psychoanalytic interpretations I propose here, every effort has been made not to violate the spirit of Pushkin's story; nor do these interpretations exceed in extravagance or fancy the numerous numerological, masonic, and cabalistic interpretations that the story has inspired over the last two centuries.[5]

Freud

In the last decades of his life Freud worked continually on a tripartite model of personality centered around the ego and its attempt to mediate between the instinctual drives emanating from the id and the internalized constraints on those drives imposed by the superego. Freud never meant these concepts to be understood as static, reified entities but rather as dynamic functions and relationships; he himself continued to rework and refine them to his death. (I use these concepts, in my discussion of Freud, Lacan, and others, as a form of metaphoric shorthand, not reifications of psychological processes.) The followers of Lacan refer to Freud's later psychological theories, somewhat disparagingly, as ego psychology, because these theories emphasize the positive role of the ego. For Freud, the ego should be the hero of the narrative of personality since the mental health of the individual depends directly on the ego's ability to mediate the opposing demands of its two merciless masters, the superego and the id. The more successfully the ego keeps the unrealistic strictures of the superego and the libidinous demands of the id in check or satisfied, the more energy and psychic space it can appropriate from the id for its own realistic and rational purposes. Progress for the personality occurs when the domain of the ego expands at the expense of the id and superego. At the end of the third lecture in his *New Introductory Lectures on Psychoanalysis*, Freud writes: "Nevertheless it may be admitted that the therapeutic efforts of psycho-analysis have chosen a similar line of approach. Its intention is, indeed, to strengthen the ego, to make it more independent of the super-ego, to widen its field of perception and enlarge its organization, so that it can appropriate fresh portions of the id. Where id was, there ego shall be [*Wo es war, soll Ich werden*]. It is a work of culture—not unlike the draining of the Zuider Zee."[6]

For ego psychology, madness represents the direst of all imaginable fates for Germann; it signifies death-in-life. Germann embodies the antithesis of Freud's wish for a stronger, more independent, and enlarged ego. Throughout the story Germann's ego undergoes a progressive deterioration, ending in complete failure. At the beginning his concern for his patrimony (his inheritance, in all its senses, from his father) and his desire for gambling (even for its own sake) coexist in a state of tense and fragile equilibrium. He greatly values his ego ideal (that is, the ideal of the superego) of position, wealth, and progeny, but he takes little joy in it, for it demands prudence, moderation, and hard work [*raschet, umerennost', and trudoliubie*], the three *reliable* cards of the superego that represent values Freud describes as essential to civilization but also responsible for its discontents.[7] As E. M. Forster says in *Howard's End*: "Those who prepare for all the emergencies of life beforehand may equip themselves at the expense of joy."[8]

The demands of the id, however, rival those of the superego. Germann is not, as many have argued, interested in cards solely as a way of increasing his fortune without risk.[9] As the narrator says, Germann is "a gambler at heart" [*"v dushe igrok"*] (8:235); gambling constitutes the very core of his desire, of his irrational self. To follow in one's father's footsteps, must one increase one's patrimony three and seven times? When Germann says that he is not in a position to sacrifice what is necessary to obtain the superfluous, he means that his father's idea (perhaps the German idea in contrast to the Russian one) requires only preservation of, and addition to, the family fortune, not its geometric increase.[10] His dream of sudden immense fortune, then, represents less a desire to preserve and add to his father's patrimony than a desire to gamble. It is often argued that the three magic cards derive from Germann's wish to increase his capital, as he says, threefold, sevenfold,[11] and become independent and wealthy, a *tuz* (an ace).[12] But, in fact, it is the desire to gamble that transforms the various combinations in faro into a plan for self-aggrandizement; the cards become the signifiers of Germann's libidinous desire, not a means to fortune.[13]

Since Germann is really more passionate than cool and calculating, he seems bound to take matters to their extreme conclusions.[14] On the one hand, his passion for gambling clashes with the superego's demand for *raschet, umerennost'*, and *trudoliubie*. On the other hand, the superego—always ready to exact punishment, in guilt, for the ego's concessions to libidinal satisfaction, for even courting desire—will not easily countenance giving in to passion. For the superego, according to Freud, does not distinguish between desire and satisfaction, that is, thoughts and deeds: "The distinction ... between doing something bad and wishing to do it disappears entirely, since nothing can be hidden from the superego, not even thoughts."[15]

Germann has long haunted the gaming tables; he would sit whole nights, following with feverish excitement the various changes in the course of play. He openly admits that gambling fascinates him [*igra zanimaet menia sil'no*] (8:227). Soon after hearing Tomsky's tale about his grandmother's success at cards, all the libidinal forces that have been held in check by the ego seek expression in the desire to gamble, not so much for the sake of fortune but for the sake of gambling itself, that is, for the sake of risk, chance, and danger. Germann wishes to exchange the three sure cards of the superego—no matter what the sacrifice—for the magic cards that will attain for him "the superfluous": the desire of the id. Horrified at the possible abandonment of the ego ideal, the superego marshals its forces, pressing for prudence, moderation, and hard work. But neither "side" can gain complete ascendancy: gambling is unacceptable to the superego; a life of continued moderation is no longer acceptable to the id.

Previously the ego had been able to hold these contending passions in check through compromise. Before hearing the story [*skazka*] at the Narumovs, Germann has done well for himself, working his way through the military ranks. After he hears the story, the old compromises and restraints no longer work. Germann disguises his passion for gambling as a higher form of prudence, as a means of fulfilling his obligation to add to his patrimony and establish his own line, "the paternal order of genealogy," as Kristeva describes it.[16] It seems like an ideal compromise—although a paradox—a scheme of gambling without risk. The imaginative shape of the compromise is revealed in the account of the countess's visit. Ostensibly the countess comes to Germann to give him the secret cards, assuring him of victory (the desire of the id); but it is a victory with strictures: he is not to forget his goal of settling down and starting a family; he must marry the countess's ward, Liza; he must not forget the legacy of his father; and he must never gamble again—all demands of the superego. But this attempt simultaneously to placate the id and superego, to realize the paradox, is doomed to failure. Germann's ego is not weak; it is simply unable, after his imagination has been inflamed, to contend with the increasingly powerful and uncompromising demands of both id and superego. Since there can be no rational—ego-engendered—solution to Germann's situation, no resolution of the conflict between the superego and the id, the ego increasingly leaves the field to its irreconcilable and more powerful masters.

This struggle within Germann reaches its terrible conclusion at the gambling tables, where only play can decide the issue. On the last day, the day of the third card, Germann, though teetering on the edge of madness, is still sane.[17] He is still sane for he has not yet really gambled. Since his first two cards have won as predicted and have thus proved reliable, he cannot know that he has really risked anything. But the makeshift compromise of the ego is now rejected in favor of libidinal desire. Germann now must really play, gamble, risk; he must show himself that he has not been given three sure cards, for those three cards are nothing but the formula of calculation, the absence of risk, the ego ideal. He must now lose in order to win; he must lose to prove that he has really played. He must choose the wrong card; he must choose the queen (desire) and not the ace (the ideal of the father).[18] But the loss of everything, of his entire patrimony, brings upon Germann the punishment of the father—the embodiment of the superego—whose prescriptions he flagrantly violated in pursuit of forbidden libidinal desires, symbolized by the queen of spades, the queen mother, the ultimate object of forbidden desire, who is transformed in the story by the superego into a temptress, witch, biblical snake, and destroyer. The symbolically realized desire for the mother must always entail the loss of patrimony, for patrimony is the prime compensation of the child for renouncing the rights to the mother.[19] Germann, in a sense, never really had a choice at all; the ace and the queen, each in its own way, is the wrong card; each leads to a life completely unacceptable to the other. The final scene merely works out the fate, the madness, latent in Germann's character from the very beginning, from the moment he first heard the tale of the three cards.

The ego's compromise of gambling without gambling is destroyed on contact with the real world. In contrast to the draining of Zuider Zee—Freud's vision of the aggrandizement of the ego at the expense of the superego and the id—in *The Queen of Spades* we have a bursting of the dikes: the power of the ego is nullified. In the end, neither desire nor civilization survives. The personality suffers a complete collapse and then disintegration; Germann goes hopelessly insane. Madness becomes a metaphor of nonbeing.

Lacan: The Mirror Stage

Whereas the Freudian model suggests an unfortunate, perhaps even tragic Germann, the "victim" of powerful forces he cannot control, it does not cast the desires of the id or the constraints of the superego as villains. Had the ego proven stronger or the demands of the id and superego weaker, a viable, though not necessarily happy, compromise could have emerged. By contrast, the Lacanian model adopts a pejorative attitude toward the idea of mediation, the hallmark of ego psychology. From a Lacanian perspective, the problem lies not in the failure of the ego but in its near "success": the choice of the ace.

For Lacan, the ego does not represent the ideal, the real self, that is, the part of the personality whose control over, and growth at the expense of, the unconscious constitutes the sine qua non of healthy adult psychological development.[20] Rather, it is one of the earliest aspects of the personality to be formed—occurring in the pre-linguistic, pre-Oedipal stage of human development (the imaginary stage)—and remains for a person's entire life an obstacle to overcome, almost a prison from which to be liberated. Lacan describes the ego as an alienating identity, and he repeatedly ascribes to it, in varying degrees, paranoia, narcissism, aggression, and *méconnaissance* [false knowledge]. The ego evolves in what Lacan calls the mirror (or imaginary) stage, when the child first sees himself in the mirror—his mirror image—and gains a false, idealized image of himself as a whole, unified integral self. The ego's quest of wholeness, autonomy, and mastery of its environment involves a futile exercise reflecting the most superficial ends of the personality. Worse still, it stands in the way of the truth of the unconscious.

For Lacan, the ego always misreads the truth that comes from the unconscious, for the truth of the unconscious can be glimpsed only through its metaphoric condensations and metonymic displacements, when the individual emerges from the mirror stage and enters the symbolic order, which is based on, and mediated by, language. Only by entering the symbolic order can the individual overcome the demands of the ego for unity, wholeness, and fixity and open himself up to the linguistically mediated manifestations of the unconscious. The mature subject has access to the repressed because the mature subject lives in the world of language (the symbolic); whereas the ego—which derives from a pre-symbolic, pre-Oedipal phase of development, in which identity (the mirror), not difference (the symbolic), is dominant—struggles against the very notion of a shifting, indeterminate, and linguistically mediated truth.

Ego psychology equates the collapse of Germann's ego—madness—with spiritual and mental death. For Lacanian psychology, by contrast, Germann's main problem rests in the ego itself. Before the *skazka* Germann seems arrested in the mirror stage of development. He has devoted his whole life to a rational, closed, infallible plan of existence. Unwilling to sacrifice the necessary for the superfluous, he seems to desire most of all "peace and independence" [*pokoi i nezavisimost'*] (8:235), the false ego ideal of stasis, wholeness, autonomy, and mastery of the future. At the beginning of the story he resists all temptation to diverge from his plan; in fact, he must steel himself against the promptings of the unconscious precisely because he senses that he is a gambler at heart.

Germann's rational side, however, is not merely a manifestation of a strong paternal superego, for his "patrimony" is not the father (the law of the father of the symbolic order) but a mirror image of his materialistic ego ideal. Germann does not pass precipitately from a small fortune and sanity to ruin and madness, for, from a Lacanian point of view, he has reached the nadir of his psychological "fortune" at the very beginning, as he controls the forces raging within, as he continues to stand by, refusing to take part in the life that seethes around him. As we have seen, Germann is already on the make; he has a position in the Engineers, and, given the experience of those of German origin in the tsarist state and military bureaucracies, he seems destined to eventual prestige and even a larger fortune. His patrimony has been preserved intact, and he will soon be adding to it, just, as we must presume, his father did before him.

But once Germann hears about the countess's secret of the three cards, he becomes overwhelmed by his ego ideal. His dreams—in which the unconscious in its various disguises should most reveal itself—do not seem to reflect unconscious content at all; they contain no ingenious displacements and compensations that point to the truth of the unconscious. Immediately after hearing the countess's story, Germann spends a restless night thinking of nothing but the three cards. "The anecdote about the three cards had a powerful effect on his imagination; all night he could not stop thinking about it" (8:235). But the content of his dreams is almost identical to his conscious thoughts and therefore requires little interpretation. "He returned late to his humble lodging, but he could not sleep for a long time; and when at last sleep overcame him, he dreamed of cards, a green table, piles of banknotes and heaps of gold coins. He played card after card, decisively turning down the corners of his cards, and he won continually, raking in the gold and putting the notes into his pocket. After waking up quite late, he sighed over the loss of his fantastic wealth" (8:236).

The same transparent wish fulfillment reveals itself in many of Germann's other daydreams, hallucinations, and nightmares. For example, the above dream is repeated in a more dramatic form in the fifth chapter. Here Germann again returns from the countess, this time from the dead countess who has, he imagines, just winked at him from her coffin. He throws himself on his bed fully clothed and falls into a deep sleep. The countess visits him from beyond the grave, revealing her secret to him and stipulating perfectly acceptable conditions. He must play on three successive days—the bank probably does not have enough money to cover three successive wins in one day. He must never play again—why should he play again, once he has attained his fortune? He must marry Liza—if he is going to be a wealthy man he will need a wife, and Liza is pretty, charming, and undemanding.

When Germann wakes up the following day to play his first card, he is obsessed with the names of the cards he has learned from the countess. The narrator's description of Germann's thoughts and dreams show clearly Germann's incipient schizophrenia and again the lack of a significant distinction between Germann's conscious thoughts and his dreams. "Three, seven, ace began to eclipse in Germann's imagination the image of the dead old woman. Three, seven, ace didn't leave him for a moment and played continually on his lips. If he saw a young girl, he would say: 'How slender she is! A real three of hearts.' If anyone asked him the time, he would answer: 'Five minutes to the seven.' Every pot-bellied man he saw reminded him of the ace. Three, seven, ace haunted him in his sleep, assuming all possible forms" (8:249). The merging of Germann's waking life and dream life, indicating the erasure in Germann's mind of himself from the real world, prefigures, of course, final schizophrenic breakdown. As the narrator says: "All his thoughts fused into one: to make use of the secret which had cost him so dearly" (8:249). But the three cards of Germann's obsession do not seem to harbor any special unconscious code: they are merely the cards Germann must choose to attain his ego ideal of peace and independence—that is, identification—characteristic of the mirror stage. "He thought of retirement and of traveling. He wanted to compel fortune to yield up her treasure to him in the public gambling houses of Paris" (8:249).

Pushkin sets up the card game to give Germann the possibility of achieving his ego ideal: an achievement of absolute mirror identity. Germann will become exactly what he dreamed of becoming. Further, on three successive days, he will exactly match his three winning cards. On the last day he will achieve the ultimate identity and union with, of course, the ace. But when the opportunity arrives, when the ego ideal is virtually in his grasp, Germann makes a mistake: he chooses the wrong card. More important, he chooses the wrong card *unconsciously*. For the first time, the conscious and unconscious content of Germann's mind fail to coincide; in fact, they radically diverge. At long last, the unconscious reveals itself in all its power and truth—in *difference*; it reveals to him, and to us, the illusory nature of the dream of independence, peace, and unity—the insufficiency of the ego ideal. When it appears that ultimate unity may be achieved, the story seems to declare itself for ultimate separation, disunity, and disruption; the unconscious has spoken. In the end, *The Queen of Spades* speaks the truth of the unconscious.

For Freud, the draining of Zuider Zee is at best a hope, for he is essentially pessimistic about human happiness. The cultural institutions essential for preserving the human race also prevent the satisfaction of elemental sexual and aggressive desires. Germann's madness suggests the fate potentially lurking for us all just beyond the juggling act of the ego. For Lacan, whose psychology seems at times a never-ending attempt to deconstruct the metaphor of Freud's Zuider Zee, the ego, rather than being man's greatest hope, is at best an obstacle to truth. Lacan interprets Freud's *"Wo es war, soll Ich werden"* not as "the ego must dislodge the id"[21] but, rather, that the ego must be at home where the id—or rather the true subject, "the unconscious . . . *itself*"—was:[22] that is, "in the field of the dream" where the voice of the gods is heard, where the subject "must come into existence."[23] I must be somewhere other than where I am now.[24] From a Lacanian point of view, madness in *The Queen of Spades* seems not so much the paradigmatic failure of a Freudian compromise but the price we sometimes must pay for the existential experience of truth.

But does this Lacanian interpretation of Germann's "fortunate" mistake really elevate Germann's madness? Does it even mean that he has chosen the right card? To answer this question we need to see Lacan's view of desire against the background of romantic psychoanalysis, which takes the valorization of madness to its extreme conclusion.

Romantic Psychoanalysis/Anti-Psychiatry

In the previous chapter I argued that, though Germann's choice of the queen was disastrous both morally and spiritually, it could nevertheless be seen as the right choice. The queen was an unconscious decision taken against the shallow ideal of bourgeois comfort and security—or, in Lacanian terms, against the mirror stage ideal of autonomy, stasis, and identity. Yet a Lacanian interpretation, however much it privileges the unconscious over the ego, cannot take the romantic leap from ace to queen that some of the more romantic or revolutionary psychoanalytic writers—like Laing, Deleuze, and Guattari—might suggest or even advocate.

From a more romantic psychoanalytic point of view, the real Germann seeks not security and autonomy, the most superficial side of his self, but adventure and risk. The real Germann, unknowingly, has taken a journey to the other side in exploration of his true being, namely, the being associated with unconscious desire.[25] Whereas, at the beginning of the story, Germann's passionate nature and the desire of the unconscious are effectively repressed—Germann having not once deviated from his ideal of prudence, moderation, and hard work—at the end, the irrational and the unconscious take over completely. There are traces of the old ego ideal; stout men remind him naturally of aces. But he also sees them transformed into spiders, a displacement that reveals his unconscious revulsion toward his ego ideal, an ideal that has caught him in its fatal grasp. As previously noted by Rosen,[26] sexual imagery abounds. Young girls turn into threes, and threes into flowers; sevens become Gothic portals. Germann seems less a man who holds the secret of the three cards than a gambler possessed by one enormous desire: to play, nothing more. Whether he wins or not must now be irrelevant. Dostoevsky sees the very same desire in Raskolnikov, who really plans a robbery to commit a murder, not a murder to commit a robbery. Germann must test whether he can dare to place everything on a card, to find out *not* whether he is man or a mouse, as Raskolnikov conceives of his deed, but whether he is a creature of imitation and identification, an automaton in the mold of his father, or whether he is a man, a creature of passion and desire, who can stake his whole existence on a game of pure chance.

Pushkin presents the last three days of Germann's sanity with the utmost conciseness. We learn little about Germann's state of mind on the first two days. We know that after the first day of play Germann drinks a glass of lemonade and goes home. There is nothing more to tell, for everything rests on the third day. *The Queen of Spades* begins with Germann silently watching others play; now he silently plays himself. The *skazka* has become a reality—for him. The irrational has taken up residence in the light of day.

The playing of the three cards on successive days seems at first curious.[27] But perhaps Pushkin is giving Germann time to experience, for a few short days, the life of desire: on the second day to experience the repetition, which in psychoanalytic theory is essential for the validation of experience, and to peak, of his own volition, only on the last day. Life happens in the gaps, the breaks, and the ruptures, not in the everyday. "Life can happen to us only in an instant, like a flash of lightning, and only on condition that we be open to it and move toward it."[28] Ordinary life has been sacrificed for life lived on an entirely different plane, in which the self is in direct contact with its essence, its unconscious desire. To be sure, the rebellion against the father (Germann's father) and the mother (the countess) cannot long go unpunished. Germann, as we have seen, inflicts the punishment on himself. But it is a triumphant destruction that he unconsciously brings down upon himself, for, in the end, only by losing could he have really played, risked the necessary in order to obtain the superfluous. For, as Cixous says, "risk is the other word for life.... We can say that being is without shelter [*sans abri*], without protection, but salvation is precisely in risk."[29]

For romantic psychoanalysis, the story presents Germann's madness, his pathetic reduction to a body without a mind, not as an incontestable mark of perdition but as a sort of triumph in disaster. Given his ego ideal at the beginning of the story, Germann progresses from a blind, illusory sanity to a few moments, if not a few days, of truth in madness—of mad risk, in the sacrifice of "the necessary" for the "superfluous." In fact, Germann "sacrifices" the superfluous for the necessary. Germann's madness is the price he must pay to find himself. It is, at least, a human being who goes mad. Madness, for Germann, a man imprisoned by a repressive ego ideal, marks the end of the path to liberation and a higher form of sanity. Germann's madness not only culminates the process that began after he heard Tomsky's *skazka*, it also validates that process.

Germann's madness lacks the traditional heroic stature. He fails to achieve that insight, compassion, and wisdom sometimes vouchsafed to the mad tragic hero, like Lear, or to the mad artist, genius, or religious seer, like Dostoevsky's Prince Myshkin. He treats Liza unconscionably. But for romantic psychoanalysis *The Queen of Spades* is less a tale about man in his relation to the social world than a tale about the perdition and salvation of the individual soul in terms of the individual's relation to himself.

The price of the truth, for Germann, is and perhaps could not have been anything other than insanity. R. D. Laing, who sees the journey to the other side as essential to all spiritual rebirth, concedes that "not everyone comes back to us again."[30] Yet "we have to blast our way through the solid wall, even if at the risk of chaos, madness, and death. For from this side of the wall, this is the risk. There are no assurances, no guarantees."[31] Certainly Germann would have seemed more spiritually and morally diminished had he achieved his ideal of security and autonomy, the "negative" ideal of Kalinovich and Chichikov, an estate of a thousand souls.[32] Is not his embracing—at last—of the irrational a victory of the individual, of the personality in its attempt to overcome the stultifying imprisonment of the ego ideal?

Achilles is given the choice of an undistinguished long life or a short illustrious one. He chooses glory over long life.[33] Perhaps what he really chooses is life lived at a fever pitch over one of uneventful security. Soon after Germann hears the story of the three cards he chooses the madness of the irrational over the sanity of the ego ideal. For a few weeks he lives at an intensity he never dreamed of—such is the force of his repressive ego ideal. He burns out quickly, but for the first time in his life he does not calculate; he lives. On the third day it is no longer possible for Germann to win at cards, that is, to attain his father's desire, to gain "a thousand souls," and not at the same time to lose his own soul, to cut himself off even more completely from himself and the truth of desire, life—from his sense of being alive. "Far from having lost who knows what contact with life, the schizophrenic is closest to the beating heart of reality, to an intense point identical with the production of the real."[34] Seen from this point of view, Germann's fate in *The Queen of Spades* embodies the essence of psychoanalytic romanticism.[35]

Lacan: The Desire of the Other

But no Lacanian interpretation can view Germann's madness as a victory if the hero retreats into an autistic shell, incessantly muttering nothing but "Three, seven, ace. Three seven, queen": the ultimate linguistic reduction, the nullification of semantic difference. Might not the choice of the queen be almost as flawed a choice as selecting the ace? In fact, from a Lacanian perspective, until the unconscious breakthrough at the very end, the queen, just like the ace, may correspond not to the highest truth, the truth of unconscious desire, but to a form of imaginary desire, a "lower" form of desire associated, like Germann's desire for fortune and stasis, primarily with the ego.[36]

The traces of imaginary desire associated with the queen can be inferred, however, not from Germann's dreams—which, as we have seen, offer little material for deciphering—but from Tomsky's *skazka*. All readers, like Germann, have assumed that when Germann hears Tomsky's tale he becomes obsessed with the desire to make his fortune without risk, simply by learning the countess's secret. It seems perfectly consistent—albeit irrational—that a superstitious man, obsessed with fortune, would pursue a secret bound to make him fabulously rich without risk. But this is only one of the vectors (plots) of imaginary desire, that is, the achievement of Germann's ego ideal, the replication of his father's identity. There is, however, another very different plot of imaginary desire associated with Saint-Germain, the hero of the countess's tale about pleasure, not fortune.

The secret of this other desire resides not in the cards themselves—they are, despite Germann's wishes, signifiers not signifieds—but in the relationships they call into play in Tomsky's tale. Germann secretly yearns not for a specific person but for an entire age called up by the tale. In the present age the ego ideal has displaced pleasure; everyone is seeking, in one way or another, his fortune.[37] Tomsky's tale takes Germann back to what seems to him (we are obviously not speaking of facts) an age when desire reigns supreme; a completely frivolous time preoccupied with gambling, magic, and love; an age whose dominant figures know nothing of prudence, moderation, and hard work. The countess, *la Vénus moscovite*, gambles without any regard for her losses, and her secret friend, Saint-Germain, can solve her monetary problems without recourse to anything so prosaic as a loan. With no money at all, she presents herself at the gambling salon to bet on three cards in succession and "wins back everything" (8:229). She does not win a fortune—for what purpose? She wins only enough to repay her debt and return unimpeded to her frivolous life, in the French capital, that is, to a life of pleasure.

For Germann, the young countess is not so much a particular beauty but the Other, the object of desire itself. "You should know that about sixty years ago my grandmother used to travel to Paris, where she created a sensation. People would run after her, just to catch a glimpse of *la Vénus moscovite*. Richelieu paid court to her, and grandmother insists that he almost shot himself from her cruelty" (8:228). Not even Richelieu was able to attain her! Pushkin describes in copious detail, though through Germann's eyes, the countess's bedroom/boudoir. It is certainly faded, just as the countess, but it also has definite reminders of the age that catered to the frivolous desires of fashionable women. "In all the corners, he could see porcelain shepherdesses, table clocks made by the famed Leroy, little boxes, *roulettes*, fans and playthings for ladies, invented at the end of the last century together with Mongolfier's balloon and Mesmer's magnetism" (8:240). Just as Germann stands transfixed before the countess's house, he now seems "mesmerized" by the playthings associated with the countess's youth—an attachment to objects characteristic of all fetishists.

But Germann is equally, if not more attracted to his namesake but antithesis, the "remarkable" Saint-Germain—the Lacanian object of the (m)other's desire. The identity of the real Saint-Germain is irrelevant; the only important Saint-Germain is the one who speaks to Germann. Tomsky says, "You've heard of Count Saint-Germain, about whom they tell so many marvelous stories. You know he passed himself off as the Wandering Jew, the inventor of the elixir of life and of the philosopher's stone, and so forth. He was laughed at as a charlatan, and Casanova in his memoirs says that he was a spy; however, Saint-Germain, despite his mysteriousness, was a man of very respectable appearance, who knew how to behave in society" (8:228).

Tomsky's tale is hardly credible, even downright ridiculous in parts; he even seems purposely to tell the tale in a way that undermines it.[38] But, for Germann, the figures of the tale are as real as the secret the countess supposedly possesses. Saint-Germain belongs to that society of desire; he has a respectable appearance and knows how to behave in society; on the other hand, he is not bound by it or to it; he is not identical with it. Affable, presentable, carefree, eccentric, generous, accommodating, he is a man who can easily say that for the resolution of life's problems "money is not necessary" (8:229). To Germann, Saint-Germain stands on the outside, as spy, necromancer, Wandering Jew, and alchemist, a seeker after life's greatest secrets; he is someone who has had access to the countess, the epitome of desire for an age obsessed with desire; he is the father who has enjoyed the desire [*jouissance*] forbidden to the child. As Lacan says: "Nowhere does it appear more clearly that man's desire finds its meaning in the desire of the other, not so much because the other holds the key to the object desired, as because the first object [goal—G.R.] of desire is to be recognized by the other."[39] In other words, Germann seeks the countess because he wishes to be recognized, acknowledged by Saint-Germain—as his son?—who as *Other* defines his being, his position as a subject.

If Germann seeks only the secret of the cards, the countess must be seen, like Liza, as a means to an end. But if the *skazka* opens up the more passionate, imaginative, irrational sides of Germann, it must open him up far more to the pursuit of desire—however imaginary—than to the pursuit of the prosaic ideal of comfort and independence.[40] Germann thus seeks out the countess less to learn the secret of the three cards than to confront the countess—not the countess herself but the countess that has come in his mind to represent an age of desire, a world that exists locked up within his own psyche.[41] From this point of view, Germann needs the cards to get to the countess, not the countess to get to the cards. The need to learn the secret is a pretext for other ends.

When we first meet Germann after Tomsky tells the tale, he is already obsessed by the tale and the possibility of fabulous fortune. He is already thinking of persuading the countess to reveal her secret to him. Dismissing the absurdity of the tale and idea, Germann says to himself: "Can one really believe it? No! Prudence, moderation, and hard work; these are my three reliable cards. They are what will increase my capital threefold and sevenfold, and bring me peace and independence." Since, as Shaw has pointed out, one of the meanings of ace (*tuz*) in Russian is a wealthy man of comfort and independence, the three cards three/seven/ace are given to Germann from the very beginning; or, rather, while dismissing the tale as unsubstantiated nonsense, Germann invents (imagines) the three cards for himself. No sooner does he invent the cards—that is, in the very next sentence—than he finds himself [*ochutilsia*] in front of the countess's house. Again the cards lead to the countess, not the other way around.

> Pondering these matters, he suddenly found himself on one of the main streets of Petersburg, in front of a house of old-fashioned architecture....
> "Whose house is this?" he asked a policeman.
> "The Countess N.'s," answered the policeman.

> Germann began to tremble. The amazing story of the three cards again appeared before his imagination. (8:236)

The magic of the three cards works; it has led him, without his consciously knowing it, to his real destination. The narrator writes that Germann began to tremble [*zatrepetal*]. The Russian verb *trepetat'* also means to experience a thrill, a palpitation of the heart. Germann experiences a thrill of horror but, even more tellingly, perhaps even a secret thrill of delight [*jouissance*]. His imagination is immediately set aflame again and he begins to circle the countess's house. On returning home, he cannot fall asleep; when he does, he dreams of nothing but gambling. He wakes up, and the process begins again—the psychoanalytic repetition compulsion. Again he wanders aimlessly about the city, winding up once more (the same Russian verb, *ochutilsia*, is repeated) in front of the countess's house. The first time was obviously no accident.[42] Germann interprets the coincidence as an unknown force drawing him to the house.

This is an unknown force, but it is an internal not an external one. Germann returns to the house—home—precisely to find out what this force is, this force that has existed in him all the time but only now is claiming its due. Freud describes uncanny experiences like Germann's, including his own, in terms of repetition compulsion.[43] He defines the uncanny [*unheimlich*] as that which is most intimate [*heimisch*]—because it is associated with home—but which is repressed. "In this case, too, the *unheimlich* is what was once *heimisch*, home-like, familiar; the prefix 'un' is a token of repression."[44] The repetition compulsion is a sign of an almost demonic unconscious desire, that is, the unconscious repressed striving for expression or, in Lacanian terms, insisting to be heard.

When Germann finally enters the countess's boudoir, he discovers, of course, in addition to the accoutrements of the eighteenth century—the century of desire—a decrepit old woman, hardly *la Vénus moscovite*. But there is also something of a demonic, witchlike quality about the old woman; she cannot satisfy Germann's desire, but she can assist him in discovering the hidden: the repressed within himself.

After frightening the countess to death, Germann comes to her funeral. He must somehow revive her, so he wishes her back. He steps up to the coffin, and, as he bends over, he thinks that the countess winks at him. He steps backward, misses his step, and falls flat on his back. He is mistaken for the countess's "natural son" [*"pobochnyi syn"*]; that is, the countess is mistaken for his mother, the ultimate object of desire.⁴⁵ The countess beckons him; that is, he beckons her. In the evening Germann prepares for the return visit about which she has given a sign. It cannot be to give him the secret of the cards; he already has that. The cards are again a pretext, a rationale for the countess's visit. She tells him what he wants to hear. He must play; he must come to terms with his desire. She says this under the cover, the manifest content, of the secret that will gain him a fortune. But we must remember, from the point of view of pleasure/desire associated with the countess, fortune is nothing but death, his ego ideal. But the truth of desire, of the unconscious, can be listened to only under the guise of the acceptable. Now Germann is ready for the final confrontation, the agon, between his ego ideal, symbolized by the ace, and his desire, symbolized by the countess, the old lady, the witch. Germann makes a terrible "mistake" at the end but only in terms of the manifest content of the story, for when Germann unconsciously chooses the queen, he is only following his desire to the very end. When he chooses the queen, he calls the countess back, just as he did in his dream. In the end, therefore, he seems to renounce his dream of fortune, his ego ideal, and gives himself up to desire—at last. Now he is wedded to the countess forever.

But can the unconscious choice of the queen really be equated with the truth of the unconscious that Lacan describes in terms of discovery and surprise? Does Germann's choice take to its conclusion what Lacan has said about the truth of the unconscious? "What occurs, what is *produced*, in this gap, is presented as *the discovery*.... The discovery is, at the same time, a solution—not necessarily a complete one, but, however incomplete it may be, it has that indefinable something that touches us ... namely *surprise*, that by which the subject is overcome, by which he finds both more and less than he expected—but, in any case, it is, in relation to what he expected, of exceptional value."⁴⁶

It is not too difficult to understand why Germann goes insane after sacrificing fortune for desire. He realizes that his mistake has cost him everything: what he once possessed and what he had dreamed of possessing (his ego ideal). In terms of the superego, he is punished both for abandoning his ego ideal and for desiring what is prohibited. But why must he go insane so autistically? Why must he be condemned to repeat "Three, seven, ace. Three, seven, queen" over and over again, as though he had not already made the ultimate choice and paid the highest price. Why is he reduced to signifiers now bereft of all reference? How can a man, who has ventured so close to the truth of the unconscious, which is structured like a language, be condemned to repeat the same signifiers, now completely bereft of meaning? What happened to the cards or to the cards in relation to Germann?[47]

Lacan, to be sure, writes disparagingly of the ego ideal and presents the idea of madness as essential to human freedom and our definition as subjects. "Not only can man's being not be understood without madness, it would not be man's being if it did not bear madness within itself as the limit of his freedom."[48] He does not, however, promote the madman or the schizophrenic as an ideal, as do anti-psychiatrists such as R. D. Laing and material psychiatrists (or schizoanalists) such as Deleuze and Guattari. For Lacan, Germann is neither a schizophrenic of genius nor a traveler to the other side who has a hope of coming back with a new truth. In the epilogue his absence of true speech underlines Germann's complete destruction; he has retreated into another world, the Real Order, cutting the ties of language to which the individual owes his existence as a human subject.[49] For Lacan, there can be no true existence without the language of the Other, especially not true unconscious life, since the unconscious is related to the desire of the Other, and thus the *language* of the Other. From a Lacanian perspective, we cannot view Germann's choice of the queen, though far superior to that of the ace (the ego ideal, the wish for autonomy and security), as ultimate truth—even for Germann. Either card represents a serious mistake, although of a different degree and order.

Lacan ascribes the difference between the psychotic and neurotic personality to what he calls the foreclosure of the paternal metaphor and its substitution—in the imaginary sphere—by a delusional metaphor in which the signifier and signified are stabilized.[50] "It is an accident in this register and in what takes place in it, namely, the foreclosure of the Name-of-the-Father in the place of the Other, and in the failure of the paternal metaphor, that I designate the defect that gives psychosis its essential condition, and the structure that separates it from neurosis."[51] The human being becomes a subject by taking his/her place in the symbolic order, by accepting the symbolic father as author-of-the-law[52]—Freud's totem that binds the brothers of the clan—and living by its attendant socio-linguistic proscriptions and empowerments. The choice of either card, then, constitutes a refusal to enter fully into the symbolic order, to accept the law based on difference and lack.

To understand Germann's refusal to enter into the symbolic by choosing the queen, we need to examine more closely how Germann incorporates the *skazka* into his life and how he pursues the countess and Saint-Germain, the symbols of pleasure/desire. Germann's obsession with the ace symbolizes his desire for identity and stasis. The ace signifies the elimination of all difference between demand and need, that is, desire. Germann is closer to the truth of the unconscious and his personality when he pursues the countess and his alter-ego/antithesis, Saint-Germain, but his obsession with the countess and Saint-Germain also reveals his desire to retreat to, or bring back, an already dead past. The ego (the ace) wishes to freeze the present, not to enter the next stage, the precarious realm of the symbolic, the domain of the infinitely postponing and deferring signifying chain of the symbolic order. The story shows the futility not only of attaining the ego ideal but of pursuing desire without the mediation of language—that is, through magic—outside the symbolic.

Germann should have seen through the *skazka*, but fairy tales, like dreams and daydreams, do not have to be artistically convincing to be psychologically meaningful; they need only strike the appropriate chord. He can no more become the son of Saint-Germain and the illegitimate son of the countess than he can bring back the age of desire they represent. Nor can he displace Saint-Germain and gain possession of the countess for himself. The countess makes fun of Germann's attempts to become Saint-Germain—the desire for the mother—winking at him both at her funeral and at the final game of faro. Thus, while Germann's efforts to transcend his ego ideal is presented positively in the story, the form that it takes—his desire to possess the mother, to become Saint-Germain—represents an attempt to foreclose the paternal metaphor. Germann, however, finds it no easier to take the place of the father when he is no longer there or possess the mother when she is eighty-seven years old. For the father is most there, symbolically, as the name-of-the-father, as law, when he is no longer physically present. To enter in the symbolic order, Germann must repress the desire to replace the father and possess the mother; he must forego the desire of the primary process and live in the mediated world of language and difference, in which the signifier continually slides over the signified. Germann uses language, the names of the cards, to achieve identification and unity, whether it is to achieve his ego ideal (the ace) or to become undifferentiated from his desire (the queen). To choose either the ace or the queen must mean to lose, for the cards—the queen and the ace—represent not the symbolic order, the goal as well as the process of adult life, but the dead end of a reactive and reactionary agenda: wealth and the satisfaction of desire. Germann reveals his priorities when he passes Liza by. To love Liza is to accept the law of the father, to renounce the mother, and to enter the symbolic order. Germann's punishment is "symbolically" appropriate. Since the symbolic order is characterized by the dominance of language—of desire mediated by language—when Germann goes mad he loses language. He is reduced to mumbling the two phrases that brought about his ruin, phrases that no longer can signify anything, for the signifying chain has been broken. Germann becomes a true infant—he who does not speak—and a true idiot, a completely private person.

This transformation of Germann into a private, nonspeaking person starts well before the finale. Germann withdraws more and more into himself as the story progresses. At the beginning, even when he is among company, he stands aside from the play. He is the only one who does not gamble. All the countess's sons were gamblers; only the "natural" son never gambles. When he does finally play, it is one against all. If he wins, he has promised never to play again, which implies that he may completely withdraw from society. Since the story presents playing/gambling as a symbol of life, of the chance and risk that are necessary for human freedom, Germann's promise never to play again constitutes a foreclosure of the paternal metaphor. To play is continually to live in the world of difference, to keep possibilities open, to refuse reduction, to accept that there never can be a perfect coincidence between demand and need, and that there is no coincidence between the ace and fortune, on the one hand, and between the queen and desire, on the other.

Lacan: The Symbolic Order

Is there something even more latent in the Lacanian paradigm, relating to Germann's inability to enter the symbolic order, that demands further explication, or must we content ourselves with still another explanation, however different, of Germann's insanity? What does Germann's madness say about his relation to the putative author? Clearly the narrator shows contempt for Germann's materialistic ideal and scorn of feminine charms: Germann uses Liza and then passes her by for the countess. Germann's imagination seems limited to clichés: the rumor that Germann has three crimes on his conscience and that he has the soul of a Mephistopheles seems ridiculous. Germann seems to have the profile of Napoleon—even Liza thinks so—but this could easily be a studied pose, as clichéd as the letters he writes to Liza.[53] But Pushkin not only creates a disparaging portrait of his hero; he also "punishes" him severely. Worse than killing him off, he strips him forever of his sexual and linguistic powers, the powers that meant most to Pushkin himself. It is a fate worse than death—a death-in-life that Pushkin had imagined or would soon imagine in "God Grant That I Not Lose My Mind."

But something other than a reduced Germann also comes across in Pushkin's portrait, something that impressed Dostoevsky enough to call him a "colossal type." Pushkin deromanticizes his hero, but something of the romantic escapes in Germann's choice of the queen. He shows him to be a philistine but also a gambler willing to stake everything on a card. He reduces him to a driveling idiot with no issue, incapable of ever taking his place in society (the symbolic order); but again something of the symbolic, and the threat of the symbolic, remains—even prevails.

What is this threat? Why does Pushkin prevent Germann from entering the symbolic? Scholars have closely examined and analyzed Pushkin's apprehensions regarding the social transformations threatening Russian society and its class structure.[54] Pushkin must have seen if not Germann, then the forces he represents, as a direct threat to everything he valued. Like many of his contemporaries, he abhorred and feared the materialistic culture he saw arising in Europe and Russia, a culture whose idea he distilled in Germann's monomaniacal pursuit of gain. He attempts to take away Germann's power, but he cannot; he is too consummate an artist to do so. Passionate, rash, and determined, Germann is potentially a dangerous rebel against the established order.[55] Dostoevsky sees him as the epitome of Petersburg, because he recognizes in him a prophetic type—the potential revolutionary—a *raznochinets*, who would soon enough abandon his desire for gold (the ace) and the lost other/mother (the queen) and invest elsewhere his passion, determination, monomania, and—yes—his willingness to gamble for the ultimate stakes. He would eventually take his place in the symbolic order and radically transform it in his own image.

Lacanian psychoanalysis effectively erases the traditional Cartesian separation of the external social world and the autonomous self, of the political and the private spheres, since the subject comes into being by virtue of adopting the social rules and strictures of the symbolic world of language. Though Lacan represents the truth of the unconscious—which is available, and only available, through language—as socially derived, as formed in interaction with the Other, he also views this truth as inherently subversive, as something that continually challenges institutions, order, and convention. After all, that is why it is repressed. For Lacan, the captive "self" lives entirely in the imaginary, imprisoned by a false image of identity and autonomy, whereas the true subject—though he may not be completely autonomous, though he may even be "decentered"—by virtue of living in the symbolic order gains access to the creative power and freedom of "the words that will make him faithful or a renegade."[56] The subversiveness, the challenge, of Germann, is that his desire is not entirely personal, it is also social and political, and it is precisely the social and political ramifications of Germann that Pushkin attempts to repress.[57]

Pushkin, like Dostoevsky, wishes Germann would go away, but such a wish—wishful thinking—represents only the manifest content of *The Queen of Spades*. The realization and fear that Germann is really Russia's future, not her past, constitutes a deeper, more latent level of the text, a level that reveals the author's *unconscious* desire to keep Germann down, to deal him all the wrong cards, to drive him insane. The excellence of the story is that it resists, as it were, the attempts of its author. The story, not the author, speaks the truth of the Lacanian unconscious. For better or worse, Germann represents the true legacy of Peter the Great; he can be denied only temporarily. Eventually the Germanns will enter the symbolic order, and, when they do, they will hold all the cards, reshuffle them, and give all the signifiers new meaning. The secret, of course, is that the cards as signifiers can have no meaning in themselves. It may be small consolation, but we also know that the Germanns, too, will hold these cards only temporarily, for they will inevitably be passed on to and redefined by others who have also waited their time before the house of the ancient countess.

Though the various psychoanalytical approaches to Germann's madness take the reader different places, they each reveal something important about the role madness plays in the tale. If *The Queen of Spades* is large enough to accommodate the simultaneous validity of the fantastic and the realistic, it can likewise accommodate radically disparate interpretations of madness, which in itself is not the most easily definable of mental categories. A Freudian interpretation sees Germann's madness as a metaphor—taken to its logical conclusion—for the tragic situation of man in civilization. Romantic psychoanalysis, in valorizing Germann's mad choice of the queen, emphasizes the risks the individual may need to take to escape from an alienating environment given over to conformity and material aggrandizement. Finally, Lacanian psychology is perhaps, *horribile dictu*, more in the spirit of Pushkin; while leaving room for the participation of unconscious desire in Germann's choice of the queen, it exposes at the same time the failings of two different kinds of imaginary desire associated, respectively, with the queen and the ace. Each obsessive and exclusionary choice leads, though by different paths, to an unredeemed solipsistic madness, to the foreclosure of the symbolic. But this ultimate foreclosure (clinical madness) appears in a very different light when seen against the relationship between the hero and narrator/author. Germann's madness—the deprivation of language and sexual life, the foreclosure of the symbolic—may reflect the author's desire to prevent Germann's entry into the symbolic order, to counter, at least imaginatively, his fears regarding the role of the Germanns in Russia's future.

Germann's full-blown madness strikes only at the end. Before the choice of the queen, Germann is obsessive but not clinically mad. Yet Germann's final madness informs the entire story. Because of their brevity and compactness, lyric poems are read forward, backward, and all at once, almost as though they were spatial entities. Although *The Queen of Spades* is a speedily moving, temporal narrative it demands the same kind of reading, especially backward reading: the incorporation of the ending in the interpretation of all that precedes it. And nothing in the story demands this kind of reading more than the hero's sudden final madness.

In these last two chapters, I have explored various literary and psychoanalytic approaches to the valorization and devalorization of madness. I shall similarly pursue these approaches in the next chapter devoted to Pushkin's famous lyric, "God Grant That I Not Lose My Mind." Whereas in *The Queen of Spades* madness comes only at the very end, in "God Grant That I Not Lose My Mind," madness explicitly informs every line.

PART TWO

~ "God Grant That I Not Lose My Mind"

CHAPTER 3

Freedom and the Prison House of Madness

Since in *The Queen of Spades* full-blown madness strikes only at the end, it does not appear as an explicit subject. Even at the conclusion, it is handled as concisely as possible—just two sentences in the brief epilogue. Furthermore, the rather impersonal third-person narrator keeps his distance from his hero, whom he treats ironically throughout. By contrast, "God Grant That I Not Lose My Mind" [*Ne dai mne Bog soiti s uma*] (1833)[1] is perhaps the most personal of all Pushkin's lyrics, and it addresses the issue of madness from the very first line.[2]

Whereas *The Queen of Spades* focuses on the past, "God Grant That I Not Lose My Mind" looks to the future. It posits a persona who is *not* mad but one who *imagines* madness and carefully weighs the advantages and disadvantages of madness for his specific situation. Thus, from beginning to end, it presents an explicit and detailed argument both for and against madness as a solution to the persona's problems. It makes explicit the horror of the epilogue in *The Queen of Spades*, but it also makes explicit the other side of madness, a side we get only a glimpse of in *The Queen of Spades*—that is, the madness associated with imagination, insight, breakthrough, even poetry. "God Grant That I Not Lose My Mind" provides a bridge, in terms of exegesis if not in a chronological or genetic sense, to the issue of madness in *The Bronze Horseman*.

> God grant that I not lose my mind.
> No, easier were the staff and bag;
> No, easier toil and want.

It is not that my reason
I treasure; not that with it
   I would not part:

Were they to leave me
At liberty, how eagerly would I
   Make for the darkling wood!
In flaming frenzy would I sing,
Forget myself within a haze
   Of shapeless, wondrous dreams.

And I would hark my fill of waves,
And I would gaze, with gladness filled,
   Into the empty skies;
And strong were I, and free were I
Like to the whirlwind gashing fields,
   And breaking forests down.

But here's the rub: go off your mind
And men will dread you like the plague,
   And straightway lock you up,
Will put the madman on a chain
And, through the screen like some small beast,
   Will come to harass you.

And in the night I shall not hear
The nightingale's clear voice,
   Nor the rustling murmur of oak groves—
But my companions' cries,
And the night warders' curses
   And shrieks, and clanging chains.[3]

Не дай мне бог сойти с ума.
Нет, легче посох и сума
   Нет, легче труд и глад.
Не то, чтоб разумом моим
Я дорожил; не то, чтоб с ним
   Расстаться был не рад:

Когда б оставили меня
На воле, как бы резво я
    Пустился в темный лес!
Я пел бы в пламенном бреду   10
Я забывался бы в чаду
    Нестройных, чудных грез.

И я б заслушивался волн,
И я глядел бы, счастья полн,
    В пустые небеса;   15
И силен, волен был бы я,
Как вихорь, роющий поля,
    Ломающий леса.

Да вот беда: сойди с ума
И страшен будешь как чума,   20
    Как раз тебя запрут,
Посадят на цепь дурака
И сквозь решетку как зверка
    Дразнить тебя придут.

И ночью слышать буду я   25
Не голос яркий соловья,
    Не шум глухой дубров —
А крик товарищей моих,
Да брань смотрителей ночных
    Да визг; да звон оков.   30

    Although "God Grant That I Not Lose My Mind" does not explicitly identify the persona as a poet, it addresses the relationship between imagination and madness, specifically poetry and madness. The madman of the poem sings, in a passionate delirium, about forests, skies, fields, and forests, and he identifies himself with nightingales. For Pushkin, there is no way of testing madness other than measuring it against poetry, a practice with important contemporary literary precedents, especially in the work of E. T. A. Hoffmann, the German romantic with whom Pushkin was most familiar.
    At the heart of the poem stands a contradiction or inconsistency between two of its sections: section 2 consisting of stanzas 2 and 3, and

section 3 consisting of stanzas 4 and 5.[4] In section 2 the persona argues that if going mad implied only losing one's reason, then he would gladly do so, for madness then would open up for him the limitless resources of the creative imagination.[5] The imagery in which this opening up is conveyed is as romantic as anything to be found in Pushkin. By contrast, in section 3, in which the poet finally rejects madness as a solution, the anti-romantic, devalorizing images of madness characteristic of the eighteenth century predominate. The tension between these two radically different points of view is never completely resolved. On the one hand, we may simply be dealing with an unfinished poem. On the other, either section 2 (the valorization of madness) or section 3 (the devalorization of madness) may be read otherwise—making the poem either a coherent devalorization or elevation of madness throughout. To appreciate the full range of Pushkin's representations of madness in "God Grant"—and its potential connections with *The Queen of Spades* and *The Bronze Horseman*—I shall explore each of these possible interpretations, first examining the poem as a work in which the tensions are left unresolved and then as a work in which the tensions are artistically resolved in radically different syntheses.

Madness: Freedom and Imprisonment

Although "God Grant" begins with the persona's plea to not go insane, the persona soon makes a case for madness. In the second half of the first stanza, he states that he does not fear madness because he values reason or because he would not part with it; in fact, he fantasizes about the poetic freedom resulting from the loss of intellect [*razum*]. The second and third stanzas present the persona's fantasies of being released from his confinement and of experiencing new creative powers. Whereas the poem begins with a negative wish—"God grant that I not lose my mind"—the second and third stanzas move to the positive hypothetical mood.[6] And, in contrast to later stanzas, almost all the verbs are in active voice.[7] The nominative "I" [*ia*] is the explicit subject of every statement; it is also the rhyme word in lines 7 and 16. The rhyme "me/I" [*menia/ia*] in lines 6 and 7 further highlights the change from passive to active voice. The persona welcomes the enhancement of his creative powers and his new sense of agency: he would set off for the dark wood [*temnyi les*]—the world of poetry—where, singing in passionate delirium [*plamennyi bred*], he would forget himself in the haze [*chad*] of shapeless [unharmonious; *nestroinykh*] dreams.[8] In the third stanza the persona further gives in to his fantasies of power, freedom [*volia*], flight, and even destructiveness. He would not only retain his poetic gifts with the loss of intellect, but, freed of reason's impediments and encumbrances, he would achieve an enormous gain in creative breadth and power. And when he descends to earth, it would be like a whirlwind leveling fields and destroying forests.

The style and imagery of this section is romantic throughout. The language is elevated, the rhythm free flowing. The third and sixth lines of stanza 3, in contrast to all other lines in the poem in this position, convey ease and expanse. The passionate or fiery [*plamennyi*] delirium of line 10 recalls the importance of the element of fire in German romanticism, often associated with poetry and madness, as in Hoffmann's "The Golden Pot," in which the hero chooses poetic madness (symbolized by the fiery salamander) over a life of bourgeois confinement. Empty skies [*pustye nebesa*], rather than implying "skies without God"[9] or "freedom from ... even God,"[10] suggest unlimited physical, spiritual, and creative space, in which the persona-poet can soar freely; it is not so much a freedom from but a freedom to and for.[11] This sense of soaring is built up in the cascading succession of hard and soft "l's," especially in the anaphoral lines of stanza 3: *I ia b zaslushivalsia voln / I ia gliadel by, schast'ia poln / I silen, volen byl by ia* [And I would hark my fill of waves / And I would gaze, with gladness filled / And strong were I, and free were I]. The violence of the last lines of stanza 3, which speaks of a whirlwind leveling fields and destroying forests, even suggests a challenge to the Pushkinian ideal of harmony, a kind of poetics of discord composed of "wondrous and unharmonious dreams" [*chudnye nestroinye grezy*].

For Russians who see Pushkin as the poet of supreme balance, light, and harmony, it is difficult to accept that "God Grant That I Not Lose My Mind" makes any favorable associations between madness or disharmony and poetry. But the second and third stanzas of the lyric seem to suggest otherwise. The persona is immediately attracted to the dark wood, not to the bright light of truth. His singing will be unrestrained by the fetters of reason; rather, it will resemble mad delirium. He wishes to lose himself in a world of "discordant dreams," where his only interlocutors will be the waves and empty skies.¹² Pushkin's lines recall Shelley's in "To a Skylark," where the persona speaks of the "shrill delight" of the skylark and the "harmonious madness" it inspires in the poet. Nor is this a constructive, socially oriented poetics: the persona revels in his destructive license and power; he would be like a wanton whirlwind leveling fields and forests in its path.¹³

In the fourth stanza, however, the persona is violently brought back down to earth, where he is forced to contemplate the terrible social and imaginative consequences of actually going mad. In the last two stanzas (section 3) he seems to see himself as mad but not insane, that is, deprived of reason but still possessing, in some form, the gift of poesy. The mad poet finds himself—perhaps with Coleridgian "flashing eyes" and "floating hair"—among the clinically (unpoetically) mad.¹⁴

The abrupt transition from elation to despair in stanza 4 is reinforced by dramatic changes in style and imagery. The persona as subject suddenly becomes the persona as object. Whereas he had envisioned himself uprooting trees and leveling forests, he now sees himself the object of the violence of others. The freedom [*volia*]—or license—is now on the other side, as are the strength and the power, embodied in the implied but unnamed "they." The first-person, both as subject and object, is absent. Instead, the demeaning second-person singular pronoun object "you" [*tebia*], reserved here for fools and animals and perhaps even for those of the lower class, dominates. Pushkin further highlights this contrast by placing the two pronominal "you's" [*ty*] in a rhyme pair, lines 21 and 24, and by giving the ends of each of these lines a similar rhythmic pattern: *tebia zaprut/tebia pridut*, a pattern which starkly contrasts with the mellifluous style of the third and sixth lines in the previous stanza (lines 15 and 18). In addition, the style of this last stanza is startlingly prosaic, descending, according to Étkind, to the outright "common" [*do vul′garnoi rechi*].¹⁵

The "misfortune" [*beda*] of line 19 refers back to the poverty [*bednost′*] of lines 2 and 3, where the persona first confronts the frightening prospect of "staff," "labor," and "hunger" [*posokh, trud*, and *glad*],¹⁶ as do the consonantal pair of "if you go mad" [*soidi s uma*] at the end of line 19 and "to go mad" [*soiti s uma*] at the end of the first line. The rhymed pair "mind/plague" [*uma/chuma*] in lines 19 and 20 underlines the persona's fears even more strongly than in lines 1 and 2, where "out of one's mind" (*s uma*) rhymes with the relatively less terrible "staff" (*suma*).

But the persona's public humiliation may, in fact, be less horrible than the destruction of his poetic world. In the mental ward he realizes that he will be even less free than in the "outside" prison of his social milieu. Further, the sounds of poetry will be completely stifled by the cacophonous non-discourse of his fellow inmates. He will no longer be able to hear at night the clear and bright [*iarkii*] voice of the nightingale, with which the persona associates himself in the rhymed pair in the first lines of the fifth stanza (lines 25–26): "I/nightingale" [*ia/solov'ia*]. Nor will he be able to hear the rustling murmur [*shum*] of the oak groves. He will hear only the cries [*krik*] of his comrades [*tovarishchi*], the curses [*bran'*] of the warders watching him at night, and the rhythmic but monotonous clanking and clanging of chains [*Da vizg; da zvon okov*]. The sounds of the madhouse and the prison replace the sounds of nightingales and oak groves. Nature and poetry are lost more irrevocably than before, replaced by even more oppressive social institutions for dealing with society's outcasts. One can hardly imagine the persona echoing Byron's "Prisoner of Chillon": "My very chains and I grew friends." The sounds in the persona's prison are chained as much to the prison wall as to his body. There can be nothing more painful than the contrast the persona draws in the last stanza between the mellifluous *absence* of nightingales and oaks and the discordant *presence* of shrieks and chains. This seems an even far worse fate than that of Keats's persona in "Ode to a Nightingale," who, in imagining his death, focuses also on the nightingale pouring forth its soul in vain.

> To cease upon the midnight with no pain,
> While thou art pouring forth thy soul abroad
> In such ecstasy!
> Still wouldst thou sing, and I have ears in vain—
> To thy high requiem become a sod. (55–60)

The idea of absence also informs the depressing conclusion of the last stanza. The mellifluous first three lines of this stanza obviously recall the lyric longings of stanzas 2 and 3, but now in negation. The important pair "I/nightingale" [*ia/solov'ia*] conveys a cruel irony. Neither the "I" nor the "nightingale" indicate a turn to the active lyric mode of stanzas 2 and 3 but rather a continuation of the dire implications of stanza 4. The persona seems to make the consequences of madness even more painful to himself by emphasizing not only the horrors he will experience (the presence) but also what he will no longer experience (the absence): "the bright voice of the nightingale." The rhyme "I/nightingale" in the first two lines emphasizes now not identity (though it is the only exact rhyme with "I" (*ia*) in the poem) but difference and distance. The last three lines of the stanza directly recall the terror of stanza 4; the style changes abruptly and accordingly with a heavy, jerky drumbeat of realized ictuses and monosyllables. The mellifluous "golos iarkii solov′ia" [the nightingale's clear voice] and "shum glukhoi dubrov" [the rustling murmur of oak groves] are replaced by the "krik" [cries], "bran′" [curses]," and "zvon" [noise] of his fellow inmates, his warders, and his fetters. The rhyme pair "oak groves/fetters" (*dubrov/okov*), indicating nature, poetry, and the persona in chains, contrasts dramatically with the images of infinite space, power, and license in stanzas 2 and 3.

Madness without Poetry

But there is something troubling about this interpretation. Though the argument is consistent, the imagery of section 2 (stanzas 2 and 3) and section 3 (stanzas 4 and 5) is at odds. The persona seems to argue that it is possible to lose one's reason [*razum*] and retain one's creative powers, even expand them. What the persona, therefore, fears most is not madness but society's treatment of the mad, which will result in an imprisonment even more destructive to his imagination than his former condition. But while Pushkin's portrayal of madness as freedom derives from nineteenth-century romantic sources, his description of the treatment of the insane clearly derives from the eighteenth century. Pushkin knew that the insane of his class, especially mad poets, were no longer treated the way he imagines it in the poem. Why, then, does he revert in "God Grant" to the notions and imagery of the eighteenth century for representing the treatment of the mad? Further, the inclusion of eighteenth-century depreciative images of madness in section 3 seriously undercuts the nineteenth-century romantic imagery established in section 2. Why revert to eighteenth-century images of madness when they at least implicitly undercut nineteenth-century romantic notions of the imagination?

When the persona imagines that he himself is in the insane asylum chained to the walls of his cell, the object of malicious amusement for visitor-spectators, he is calling up the visitation of insane asylums, one of the most popular forms of public entertainment in the eighteenth century.

> As late as 1815, if a report presented in the House of Commons is to be believed, the hospital of Bethlehem exhibited lunatics for a penny, every Sunday. Now the annual revenue from these exhibitions amounted to almost four hundred pounds, which suggests the astonishingly high number of 96,000 visits within a year. In France, the excursion to Bicêtre and the display of the insane remained until the Revolution one of the Sunday distractions for the Left Bank bourgeoisie. Mirabeau reports in his *Observations d'un voyageur anglais* that the madmen at Bicêtre were shown "like curious animals, to the first simpleton willing to pay a coin." One went to see the keeper display the madmen the way a trainer at the Fair of Saint-Germain put the monkeys through their tricks. Certain attendants were well known for their ability to make the mad perform dances and acrobatics, with a few flicks of the whip.... It was madness itself, madness in flesh and blood, which put on the show.[17]

Pushkin's rhymed association of "madness" (*s uma*) with its rhymed partner "the plague" (*chuma*) reflects the eighteenth century's view of the insane as a dangerously contaminated population that had to be separated from society. Foucault argues that the quarantine of lepers during the Middle Ages provided the paradigm, in succeeding periods, for separating and imprisoning other undesirables, particularly the mentally ill. In the next-to-last stanza, the "grating" [*reshetka*] and "the locking up" [*zaprut i posadiat*] conjure up these older images of imprisonment. The lines in which the speaker sees himself treated as a mad fool [*durak*] whom people come to tease like some little animal [*zverok*] echoes the perception of the mad in the Age of Reason as not only bereft of reason but equal to animals, that is, subhuman.

But this treatment of the insane has virtually nothing in common with the treatment of a mad poet whom Pushkin knew quite well, Konstantin Batiushkov. It has been said that "God Grant That I Not Lose My Mind" reflects the influence of Pushkin's last visit, on 22 March 1830, to what most assumed to be a dying Batiushkov.[18] Batiushkov is usually considered to have gone mad in 1821, when he was thirty-four, Pushkin's age in 1833, and the probable date for "God

Grant That I Not Lose My Mind." Since his illness had come on gradually, Batiushkov knew that he was ill and sought help. But by 1827 he was declared incurably insane by German doctors, after which no attempts were made to treat him. Batiushkov suffered from persecution mania [*sumasshestvie na pochve manii presledovaniia*] as well as severe bouts of depression, hypochondria, and melancholy. In the early years of his illness, he made several attempts on his life, believing that only death would relieve his suffering.

Batiushkov's unhappiness was unmistakable, but his fate differed considerably from the one the persona/poet envisions for himself in the last stanzas of Pushkin's poem. Batiushkov received the best medical care of the day in Germany and then later in Russia. He stayed in a sanitarium and was looked after by a good-hearted doctor, Anton Dietrich, a great devotee and translator of Russian poetry, who took a special interest in the recovery of his patient. After having cared for Batiushkov for four years in Germany and then two years in Russia, Dietrich finally returned home. In Russia "the mad poet" received excellent care on his estate, especially from his sister, who devoted the rest of her life to his well-being; earlier, when he was still in the sanitarium, she had even moved to Germany to be near him. Further, sympathetic friends and fellow poets frequently visited Batiushkov in Vologda. Most important, he was not at all a "madman." Though he suffered from paranoia and acute depression, he had relatively normal periods during which he could carry on intelligent conversations on almost any topic.[19]

Pushkin clearly knew many of the details of Batiushkov's illness, and he was aware of the excellent and loving care he received. As Alekseev argues, in 1830, the then severely ailing Batiushkov surely made a strong impression on Pushkin[20]—there were times when Batiushkov did not recognize old acquaintances—but Batiushkov hardly fits the image of an incarcerated madman: chained, closely guarded, feared like the plague, and teased by curious spectators. The last stanzas of "God Grant That I Not Lose My Mind," then, derive less from Pushkin's personal experiences or probable readings about contemporary developments in the treatment of the insane than from the literary and cultural images and concepts of the mad, and their treatment, of a previous age. The poet seems to need the most horrible image of madness that he can conjure up, and he finds it in the cultural storehouse of the eighteenth century.[21] This, however, leads to significant inconsistencies. The last two stanzas, from the more romantic perspective, seem like an eighteenth-century intrusion into a nineteenth-century romantic poem about the relationship between madness and poetry. But these two stanzas are not only anachronistic in terms of the treatment of the insane (and insane poets), they introduce eighteenth-century associations of madness—madness as incompatible with poetry. For the eighteenth century, madness is a misfortune [*beda*][22] whose place is outside both society and poetic discourse.[23] It is the primary negation and absence, specifically the absence of reason and thus truth.

From the classical point of view, then, the confined persona may seem at best a *former* poet, a madman who has lost the creative imagination (poetry) because he has lost his intellect. The persona will not hear the voice of the nightingale and the dull rustle of the oak groves not so much because they will be drowned out by the cries of the insane but because madness will prove ruinous to the creative imagination. Ia. L. Levkovich argues for this deromanticized view of madness in her attempt to refute the position (held, among others, by Lednicki, V. Nepomniashchii, Catharine Theimer Nepomnyashchy, Glebov, and Bocharov) that the poem associates poetry with madness.[24] She argues that the poem's "disharmonious" or "shapeless, wondrous dreams" [*nestroinye, chudyne grezy*], "haze" [*chad*], "fiery frenzy" [*plamennyi bred*], and the destructive nature of "license" [*volia*] constitute the antithesis of true poetry for Pushkin. Rather than advancing any romantic notion about the positive relationship between madness and poetry, "God Grant" affirms the "realist" connection between reason and inspiration. Levkovich concedes that Pushkin may earlier have had a more romantic view of poetry and madness. In fact, she cites similar phrases from previous poems, where poetry is not associated with health and clarity but with illness and confusion: "fiery infirmity" [*plamennyi nedug*] and "wondrous dreams" [*grezy chudnye*] from "Conversation of a Bookseller and a Poet" [*Razgovor knigoprodavtsa s poetom*]; "confusion" [*smiaten'*] from "The Poet" [*Poet*]; and "lyric excitement" [*liricheskie volneniia*] from "Autumn" [*Osen'*].[25] But to Levkovich this was Pushkin in his earlier, romantic stage, a stage he had overcome in his late thirties, when realism triumphed over romanticism, reason over madness, and clarity over confusion.[26]

Furthermore, with regard to both the mistreatment of the insane and the devaluation of the mad imagination, "God Grant" bears a striking resemblance to Gogol's grisly description of Poprishchin's torments in the insane asylum in "Notes of a Madman," a description that was probably also influenced by eighteenth-century images of the mad.[27] Poprishchin thinks he is the king of Spain. His last diary entry echoes not only the last two stanzas of "God Grant That I Not Lose My Mind" but the lyric's second and third stanzas as well.

> Today, they shaved my head, though I shouted with all my might that I did not want to be a monk. But I can no longer recall what happened to me when they began to pour cold water on my head. I never in my life experienced such hell. I was about to fly into a fury, so that they were barely able to restrain me.[28]
>
> No, I don't have the strength to endure it any longer! God, what are they doing to me? They're pouring cold water over my head! They are not attending to me, they don't see or hear me. What have I done to them? What are they torturing me for? What do they want from a poor, unfortunate man like me? What can I give them. I have nothing. It is beyond me, I can't bear all these torments. My head is burning and everything is spinning round before me. Save me! Take me away! Give me a troika with horses swift as a whirlwind [*vikhor'*]! Climb aboard, driver, and let the bells ring! Soar away horses, and carry me from this world! Farther, and farther, so that nothing, nothing is visible any longer. Over there the sky [*nebo*] whirls before me. A little star shines in the distance; the moon and the forest with its dark [*temnye*] trees rush by; a gray-blue mist spreads over under foot; a string twangs in the mist. On one side is the sea [*more*], on the other, Italy.[29]

Poprishchin, like the persona in "God Grant That I Not Lose My Mind," has visions of whirlwinds, skies, seas, and dark forests. But here the strains of lyric flight and the terrible sights and sounds of the insane asylum do not appear in separate visions, as in "God Grant," but are conflated by the confused mind of the madman. If the last stanzas of Pushkin's lyric are viewed in terms of the eighteenth-century tradition, or in Gogolian terms, then the persona visualizes himself in the insane asylum bereft of his imagination not because of his confinement but because of a mental illness incompatible with the creative imagination.

The poem thus seems to contain two essentially antithetical and irreconcilable views of madness and the imagination. Stanzas 2 and 3 present an essentially romantic view of the possibilities of creative imagination wondrously enhanced by madness, whereas stanzas 4 and 5 portray a basically classical view of madness which implies that any romanticized view of madness in terms of the unfettered imagination is itself a mad fancy.

I doubt whether one can completely resolve the problems raised by the poem's stylistic, cultural, social, and imagistic discordances. But to do proper justice to Pushkin's magnificent lyric, first I would like to discuss the possible reasons for the poem's seeming inconsistencies—some inconsistency in a poem about madness might not, after all, be entirely inappropriate—and, second, to offer antithetical new readings of section 2 (less romantic) and then section 3 (less "eighteenth-century"), which point to more unified interpretations.

An Unfinished Poem?

I mentioned earlier that the glaring differences between sections 2 and 3 of "God Grant That I Not Lose My Mind" might be ascribed to the poem's incompletion.[30] To be sure, the extant draft may be a complete poem, but the extremely personal nature of the poem may have made Pushkin reluctant to publish it; of course, the personal nature of the poem may also explain why Pushkin may have abandoned a poem that he knew he would never publish.[31] Perhaps the lyric was an experiment in which the poet explored the consequences of madness for his poetry and his spiritual well-being. When the poem failed—or succeeded—to deliver the desired therapeutic effect, the purpose of its composition, it was abandoned.

Internal artistic problems may also provide insight into why the poem may not have been completed. One reason that "God Grant That I Not Lose My Mind" seems incomplete is that it ends so abruptly; it is as though the poem lacks the final stanza or stanzas that would have resolved the thesis and antithesis of sections 2 and 3 into a higher synthesis. Section 2 revels in images of freedom, power, open space, and expanded states of consciousness; the last section emphasizes imprisonment, powerlessness, and mental confinement. Each of these alternatives may have represented unacceptable possibilities for the author: on the one hand, the abandonment of the self to unconstrained desire [*volia*], the id of section 2; on the other, its subordination to insufferable societal constraints, the punishing superego (perhaps tsar the father) of section 3. The unfinished poem may reflect the persona's inability to reconcile madness with poetry, a sort of lyric distillation of Freud's *Civilization and Its Discontents*. Any synthesis would have involved bad faith. Madness cannot lead both metaphorically and realistically to the heightening of the persona's imaginative powers and their complete negation; that is, to freedom and empowerment at the same time as confinement and debilitation. But in the poet's vision, the mad poet and the madman without poetry coexist within the same persona in *poetically* unresolved tension.

Nor does incompletion necessarily imply imperfection. "God Grant That I Not Lose My Mind" is one of the most formally perfect of Pushkin's lyrics. The expression of poetic madness is conveyed in Pushkin's most perfect mellifluous romantic style. It is almost as though Pushkin refuses to resolve the tensions in the poem by formal means, to resort to the canonic means by which paradoxes in lyric poetry are usually held in aesthetically *satisfying* tension. Does "God Grant" constitute a case of "harmonious discord" [*stroinaia nestroinost'*]?[32] Does it represent a darker, centripetal, Dionysian side of Pushkin's genius, not only in addition to, as Gershenzon has argued,[33] but also perhaps even at the expense of his Apollonian light, balance, and clarity, his "almost un-Russian sunniness" [*pochti nerusskaia solnechnost'*)?[34] If the poem's power derives from the tension borne of discord, then it may not be so much unfinished as intentionally unresolved. "God Grant" is complete in its incompletion, in its resistance to completion, a completion that would have been a betrayal of its poetically irresolvable tension.[35]

Testing of Extremes

Like *The Queen of Spades*, "God Grant That I Not Lose My Mind" presents both romanticized and deromanticized notions of madness, but it takes each of those positions to greater extremes. These completely valorized or devalorized representations of madness in "God Grant" become clear only in more internally consistent interpretations in which the contradiction between the romantic flights of section 2 and the devalorized associations attached to the classical view of madness in section 3 are resolved. Practically, this involves either deromanticizing section 2 so that it harmonizes more with the desacralized view of madness in the last section or by treating the last section more romantically so that it supports, not undercuts, the romantic interpretation of madness and poetry in section 2. I shall begin with the case for deromanticization.

Section 2 of "God Grant That I Not Lose My Mind" suggests almost a poetics of madness, a poetics of excess and a freedom from all restraints, not only from reason. Whether the forests, waves, skies, and fields are real or metaphoric is unclear. The persona is taking leave not only of society and reason but also the forms and intellect that characterized his previous poetry. He is testing the limits of Pegasus without rider, exploring the new limits of woods, sea, and sky. These flights of imagery reach an enigmatic conclusion in the last lines of stanza 3 in which the persona is transformed into a whirlwind [*vikhor'*], rooting up fields and leveling forests.

But the destructive imagery of the last two lines of the third stanza may undermine the romantic poetics of madness presented in the preceding lines. It may reflect the persona's apprehensions regarding the consequences of madness for poetry, specifically of a poetics that begins in freedom but ends in destruction. The persona starts out retreating playfully into the dark wood [*temnyi les*] but concludes wantonly devastating fields (the work, the plantings of others), and, even more important, the very woods [*lesa*] that served before as his refuge and inspiration in line 9. The rhyme pair "I/fields [*ia/polia*], which metonymically juxtaposes the fields and the persona, suggests destruction is reflexive: the whirlwind within ravages the poet-persona's own creations as well as those of others. In the end, poetic madness leads to the destruction of poetry itself. Section 2, then, may be interpreted as testing the possibilities of the statement in the last lines of the first stanza in which the persona expresses his willingness to part with reason in exchange for complete poetic freedom. Exhilarated, emboldened, and strengthened by the prospects of his new imagined freedom—all reflected in the form—the persona concludes with the destructive consequences of that freedom for his imagination: the devastation of the very forest to which he repaired.

Thus interpreted, section 2 provides the evidence for the wish/prayer of line 1: "God grant that I not lose my mind."[36] It is as though the persona writes so as to frighten himself from taking leave of his senses, to prove to himself that for poetry madness is not a solution but a form of self-destruction even more unacceptable than the prison he seeks to escape from. The last lines of section 2, therefore, lead directly into section 3, which underscores the social consequences of madness devoid of imagination. The destruction of the imagination is not presented as sufficiently terrible to compel the persona to choose sanity; he must imagine the social consequences of going mad as well. Here the mad poet Batiushkov is no longer the issue, because the poem is now driven by irrational fear, by a need to conjure up the terrifying images of madness—akin to the imagery of Gogol's "Notes of a Madman"—and not by Pushkin's knowledge of the actual treatment of mad poets. The persona chooses eighteenth-century images of madness precisely because, emptied of all traces of sacralization and romanticization, they represent madness for him in its most horrible form: that is, not only social humiliation, imprisonment, and dehumanization—where the loss of reason is likened to the plague (madness/plague [*s uma/chuma*]) but also to the loss of poetry. Explored imaginatively, "the undiscover'd country" gives the poet pause. The second section of the poem becomes one with the third, leading back to the prayer of the first line. Madness is no solution to the persona's dilemma; it turns out to be the worst alternative that he can *creatively* imagine.

Madness as Return

Although, just as in *The Queen of Spades*, a good case can be made for the devalorization of madness in "God Grant That I Not Lose My Mind," the case for a valorization, I hope to show, is just as strong. The reason why it has not been made as often as its opposite is the same as in *The Queen of Spades*: it is based in the deepest levels of the poem and requires an imaginative, romantic interpretation. It also requires a romantic Pushkin that goes against the image of the myth: the icon of classical perfection.

In the previous section I presented a deromanticized interpretation of section 2 of the poem so that it would lend support and lead into the devalorization of madness in section 3. I would now like to present a consistent and coherent romantic interpretation of madness in the poem by demonstrating that section 3 strongly supports the romantic view of madness, and that madness is not only a valid metaphor for the enhancement of poetry but also for the persona's spiritual death and resurrection. I have just argued that one way of interpreting the "logic" of "God Grant" is to imagine the persona conducting a journey into the world of insanity, which reveals to him the destructive aspects of madness for the imagination and conjures up its greatest horrors (section 3). It is thus a journey designed to maintain the poet-persona's sanity, for it compels him to see it either as an imaginative world that turns against itself or as social humiliation and degradation. If, however, we look at the persona's journey into madness in sections 2 and 3 more romantically—for example, in terms of the psychology of Karl Jung and R. D. Laing—the journey becomes transformed from an experience that devalorizes madness to one in which madness becomes either the means to Jungian psychic integration and greater creativity or a conduit toward what Laing calls "hypersanity," a higher truth of the unconscious[37]—madness not as breakdown but as breakthrough.[38]

To Jung, the journey into the darkness of the unconscious is essential to all psychic health and spiritual regeneration. For the visionary artist, especially, it is the path to enhanced creativity. The terror of the dark side is understandable, but it is impossible to see the light before "we have ventured into and emerged again from the darkness."[39] "Light is born of darkness.... It is from the depths of our own psychic life that the new spiritual forms will arise."[40] Moreover, there is no possibility of spiritual or artistic growth without coming to terms with the destructive as well as the creative parts of our psyche, without coming to know our shadow, our madness. For Jung, neurosis and the threat of madness are more than just dangers, they can also constitute creative attempts to confront the demons within and overcome them. Jung quotes Hölderlin: "*Wo Gefahr ist, Wächst das Rettende auch* [Where there is danger, there too is salvation]."[41] In fact, frequently "it is as though, at the culmination of the illness, the destructive powers are converted to healing forces."[42] For Jung, the dark forest [*temnyi les*]—Dante's *selva oscura*—is the symbol of the unconscious and also of all those forces, potentially both creative and destructive, that tend to obscure or devour reason.[43]

Jung's views thus offer an alternative reading of the persona's vision of his destructive powers in the third stanza. In realizing the destructive sides of his powers, the persona is not experiencing disillusionment but rather undergoing a descent, exploration, and return, whereby, out of despair and destruction, he is able to achieve a poetic sublimation commensurate with the depths into which he has plunged. The poem therefore not only represents the journey, it becomes the journey by "imitatively" reenacting it at every level. Jung writes of the famous fifteenth-century German alchemist Theophrastus Paracelsus that "he was a veritable whirlwind, tearing up everything by the roots and leaving behind a pile of wreckage. Like an erupting volcano he laid waste and destroyed, but he also fertilized and brought to life."[44] In Portuguese legend, Jung notes, the wind is a symbol of fertilization and creation.[45] Jung's interest in Paracelsus lies not in his scientific achievement but in the nature of his spiritual journey, particularly the delicate balance and interaction in his soul between the forces of destruction and creation. The destructive whirlwind in "God Grant That I Not Lose My Mind" does not discredit the potential of madness; rather, it offers a vision of the poet's creative powers that can be released—or perhaps regained if one sees the poem as a confession of the poet's declining creativity—only through a journey within, a journey the persona not only contemplates but completes in and through the poem itself.

To the even more romantic and maximalist R. D. Laing, the soul's journey into madness is a necessary withdrawal from the world both in time and place into the unexplored and unknown (the darkling wood [*temnyi les*]; the empty skies [*pustye nebesa*]), a death-in-life essential for the rebirth of the personality. Perhaps this is what even the anti-romantically inclined Gofman implies when he writes that "Pushkin is bright [*svetel*] not because he does not notice the darkness and the gloom, or forgets about them, but because he overcomes and conquers them."[46] According to Laing, the journey within—madness—"is potentially liberation and renewal as well as enslavement and existential death."[47] It is a transcendental process by which we escape the time and space of our present world and experience both new heights (section 2) and also new depths of being, Coleridge's "through caverns measureless to man" (section 3). There is nothing the poet does not experience: air [*pustye nebesa*], fire [*plamennyi, chad*]; water [*volny*]; earth [*temnyi les, lesa, polia*]). Thus stanzas 4 and 5 do not conflict with the poetic flights of stanzas 2 and 3 but reinforce them, for the "enslavement and existential death" they describe is necessary for the "hypersanity" which is poetic madness. There is no flight without a descent. From a Laingian point of view, "God Grant That I Not Lose My Mind" need not be about poetry at all. Rather, it reenacts the journey that, potentially, we *all* must take. The "I" [*ia*] of the poem becomes the universal "thou" [*ty*]: the reader. It is *not*, however, a journey back to normality but a regeneration of the personality.

As we have seen, the last stanzas, which visualize the social humiliation that the persona will experience, are not to be taken literally in any interpretation. They are no less hypothetical than the persona's flights of imaginative fancy in stanzas 2 and 3. Pushkin could not have realistically feared being locked up in an insane asylum and taunted by curious spectators. Read biographically, the last stanzas seem more to describe the prison of Petersburg high society (implied in the first three lines of stanza 2 beginning with the phrase: "If they left me in peace" [*Kodga b ostavili menia / na vole*], from which the poet is attempting to escape. He is terrified that he will eventually find himself essentially in the same place from which he had hoped to escape. Sanity and madness make no difference; each leads to a similar prison.

The last two stanzas closely correspond to Laing's "enslavement and existential death"; they constitute an objective correlative of the persona's greatest fears: personal abuse and debasement; social humiliation and disgrace; and the complete loss of the creative imagination. But this seeming death-in-life is precisely what the persona must experience before he can be spiritually reborn and, similarly, what the poet must experience before he can return to poetry. Like Dante, he must descend to the very lowest point before he can experience a personal rebirth or a poetic resurrection. At the end of the poem the doors of the prison slam shut, but he who writes the poem is not the one imagined in the insane asylum, but one who has imaginatively transcended this madness, partly through the writing of the poem itself. The last stanzas, which at first may seem to undercut a romantic interpretation of madness for poetry, when conceived as a metaphor of "enslavement and existential death," paradoxically support the most romantic of all interpretations.

Furthermore, although the contrast between sections 2 and 3 is dramatic, there is a strong formal, non-thematic link between these seeming discordances. The last four lines of stanza 3 all have the terminally stressed open vowel *a* in rhymed (masculine) position, and all the rhymed words are quite close euphonically: *nebesa* [skies], *by ia* [I], *polia* [fields], *lesa* [forests]. These unusual rhymes enhance the romantic effect of the third stanza.[48] But this pattern is carried over, uncharacteristically, into the following stanza (stanza 4) where the first two lines have similar rhymes—*s uma* [madness], *chuma* [plague]—resulting in the consecutive *nebesa, by ia, polia, lesa, s uma, chuma*. The euphony suggests a significant underlying connection between the contrasting forms of madness, a connection that supports a more romantic understanding of the relation between madness and the creative imagination.[49]

Moreover, the prayer in the first line, "God Grant That I Not Lose My Mind," does not undercut the need for madness at all. In Laingian terms, the prayer may reflect the resistance of the demonic ego[50] to the persona's desire and need to explore the truth of his own unconscious, a resistance that the rest of the poem negates; for it is precisely the soul's journey into the other world and its triumphant return—as reenacted in the poem—that makes possible the reconstitution of the ego and the hypersanity of true poetry.

The order of stanzas, then, should not be seen as a regression, from ascent (section 2) to a *final* descent (section 3). The persona of the poem is not the madman left in the asylum but a man who has progressed—as Shaw has suggested for the persona of an important earlier poem, "The Demon" [*Demon*] and for the author-narrator of *Evgenii Onegin*[51]—through a three-stage process of development. The first stage, in section 2, is a period of initial enchantment. "God Grant That I Not Lose My Mind" even seems to echo here the *shum dubrovy* [the rustling murmur of the oak grove] and *noch'iu pen'e solov'ia* [the nocturnal singing of the nightingale] of the first stage of "The Demon." The second stage is a period of disenchantment, which the later poem, "God Grant," takes to greater depths than "The Demon." The last stage is not so much one of "mature re-enchantment" (29) as in "The Demon," but one of reassessment, in which the persona must reenact the earlier stages, in their proper progression, in order to arrive at the hypersanity of the mature poet as well as the mature individual. The testimony of the success of the poetic enterprise in "God Grant That I Not Lose My Mind" is, just as in "The Demon," the magnificent lyric Pushkin has written about the entire process, the synthesis of the experience that has arisen out of the thesis of section 2 and the antithesis of section 3.

Although I have argued here for what I believe is the richer, romantic interpretation of "God Grant That I Not Lose My Mind," the poem, like all Pushkin's works of 1833 about madness, is open to conflicting interpretations of the role of madness in spiritual and moral development; for these masterpieces are, as Chekhov might characterize them, not satisfying answers but brilliant settings of the question. The same panoply of opposite points of view regarding madness is even more magnificently displayed in *The Bronze Horseman*. As we shall see, in no other work does Pushkin integrate madness on so many levels and present such a strong a case for the special powers of the mad imagination.

PART THREE

The Bronze Horseman

CHAPTER 4

Madness and the Common Man

In *The Bronze Horseman*, the hero, Evgenii, a minor official [*chinovnik*] in the Petersburg bureaucracy, goes mad after he loses his fiancée, Parasha, in the devastating Petersburg flood of 7 November 1824. Instead of flowing into the Gulf of Finland, the Neva reverses its course and overflows its banks, inundating the city and the islands in the river. Parasha's little house, which is on one of these islands, is completely washed away. Evgenii goes mad about two-thirds of the way through the poem, when he realizes that Parasha has perished in the storm. The narrator then recounts the actions of his mad hero till his death at least one year after the flood.[1] Evgenii dreams of living a quiet and modest life with his wife and children; of being buried by his grandchildren; of living, as it were, ahistorically. His fate and madness, however, are bound up with Peter the Great and his legacy.

Of Pushkin's three eminent works of 1833 dealing with madness, *The Bronze Horseman* stands out as the one in which madness plays the most far-ranging role. In the lyric "God Grant That I Not Lose My Mind," the parameters of madness are understandably limited. The persona is not mad; in fact, after flirting with the freedom and possibilities that madness might bring, he rejects madness as a solution to his unhappy state. Although poetry is not explicitly mentioned, one can easily imagine the persona as a poet in a situation similar to Pushkin's own circumstances during the 1830s. One may argue, perhaps, that the poem is making a statement beyond the personal and poetic,[2] but it seems located outside any specific time and place, outside history and politics. In *The Queen of Spades*, Germann's madness emerges only at the very end. Though in the previous chapters, I have tried to integrate the psychological dynamics and political implications of the story, his madness does not figure *openly* in the novella's historical and social context as does Evgenii's in *The Bronze Horseman*.[3]

Since the hero's most important act in *The Bronze Horseman*, his open threat to Peter the Great, occurs after he goes mad, but considerably before the end of the poem, Pushkin has much more time to develop Evgenii's madness. The reader can follow the stages of the hero's insanity and the author's changing attitude toward his hero's plight. The situation is similar to that of *King Lear*, in which Lear goes insane during the course of the play and essentially remains mad until the very end, though wiser than when he was sane. Pushkin needs not only to differentiate between stages and forms of madness but also to contrast the sane and mad Evgenii, for each stands in a different relationship to Peter, his city, and his mission. Since Russia's mission and Evgenii's fate are explicitly addressed through the historical Peter, madness touches on every personal, social, historical, and political issue both factually and metaphorically. The wind, the river, and the rain participate in the idea of madness no less than Peter and Evgenii. Since Peter plays so important a role in Evgenii's madness, Pushkin cannot begin his story—and his story is essentially about Evgenii—without first introducing and establishing Peter. For in the beginning there was Peter.

God and Subject: Peter

The most famous of the sayings about madness inherited from the ancient world attributes the cause or agent of madness to God, a god, or gods: *Quem deus vult perdere, dementat prius* ("Whom God wishes to destroy, He first makes mad").[4] Though the Gods, of course, can destroy mortals without first making them mad, when madness does strike in Greek myth and literature, it is of divine origin, usually punishment for an act of disrespect or dereliction of duty. Lycurgus, who persecuted Dionysius, was driven mad by the god. In his madness he killed his son with an axe, imagining that he was lopping off a vine.[5] But this is hardly a uniquely Greek concept. In Deuteronomy (28:15–68), madness figures twice among the curses that will come down on the Jewish people if they fail "to hearken unto the voice of the Lord thy God" and "to observe to do all his commandments and his statutes": "The Lord shall smite thee with madness" [*sumasshestvie*, 28:28]; "Thou shalt be mad" [*soidesh´ s suma*, 28:34]. *The Bronze Horseman* presents an unusual example of this phenomenon when the little hero, no Prometheus, openly threatens, even challenges, the god of the city and the god of the nation: Peter. The introduction [*vstuplenie*] creates the god, or demigod, that makes Evgenii's madness into something greater than a psychological aberration. To understand Evgenii's madness, which is as much a social and historical illness as it is a psychological condition, it is therefore essential to understand Evgenii's relation to Peter the Great.

To build Peter up to the proper godlike majesty, Pushkin resorts to the ode.[6] The laudatory ode was hardly a vibrant genre in Russian literature in 1833, but in *The Bronze Horseman* it provides the necessary contrast with the story proper—*povest´* in Russian—contained in parts 1 and 2. (Pushkin gives the subtitle *Petersburg Tale* [*Peterburgskaia povest´*] to the entire work.) *Povest´* in Russian is usually a prose narrative of intermediary length, longer than a short story and shorter than a novel—what we might call a novella. It features an unheroic (middling) subject and an un-heroic protagonist. Despite its title, *The Bronze Horseman* is actually the last and finest of Pushkin's verse tales, called *poemy*, the first of which, written in 1819 (*Ruslan and Liudmila*), vaulted Pushkin to fame. In contrast to the *povest´*, the *poema* recounts romantic or heroic events of national significance. By giving *The Bronze Horseman* the almost oxymoronic subtitle *Peterburgskaia povest´* [*A Petersburg Tale*], Pushkin calls attention to the fact that *The Bronze Horseman* is not a traditional *poema*, although it is in verse, but rather a verse tale that more resembles a *povest´*.[7] It is an attempt to combine the heroic and prosaic in verse suitable to both.[8] But the true measure and significance of Peter for Russia (and for Evgenii) cannot be adequately conveyed in a "story" [*povest´*] alone, especially in Evgenii's story: they must be represented, at least in part, by a genre that appropriately establishes Peter's stature, the ode: the highest of all poetic genres and, in some ways, the polar opposite of the prosaic *povest´*. Pushkin does not attempt to link the genres formally. He sets them in immediate juxtaposition. Each of the protagonists is addressed separately in his proper genre.

The glorification of Peter, his mission, and his vision for Russia was standard practice in the laudatory ode in Russian literature of the eighteenth century, even when the more immediate object of praise was later tsars or tsarinas. The ode to Peter at the beginning of *The Bronze Horseman* may be considered to be the last great ode in this tradition.⁹ The model for the glorification of Peter and his legacy was actually set not in an ode but in a panegyric funeral oration given by the most influential churchman of his time, Feofan Prokopovich, in which he likened Peter to, among others, Samson, Moses, and Solomon. Peter "has resurrected [*voskresivshii*] Russia as though from the dead, and he has elevated her to great power and glory. Rather he has begot and raised her."¹⁰ The most famous ode writers of the eighteenth century often likened Peter to God. Lomonosov writes: "He was your God, your God, O Russia." And Derzhavin, the preeminent poet of the eighteenth century, intones: "Has God descended to earth in his shape?" The memoirist Krekshin writes of Peter's creative powers: "Our Father [*Otche nash*], Peter the Great, thou hast led us from nonbeing to being [*ot nebytiia v bitie*]."¹¹ Many nineteenth-century fiction writers continued this deific tradition in portraying Peter.¹²

The Bronze Horseman's introductory ode portrays a mission realized. In one hundred years Russia has been transformed into a mighty and feared power, and this transformation is most brilliantly reflected in the city Peter founded and planned. Where there once existed an almost uninhabited swamp, impenetrable to the rays of the sun, now stands a bright, beautiful, vibrant, and proud metropolis. The narrator often and forthrightly proclaims his love for Peter's creation: its beauty and grandeur, its social and military life, its royalty and imperial mission. The statue of the Bronze Horseman represents the new god of the place, the city god, who looks out onto the river he has vanquished but not destroyed, and who protects, with his outstretched hand, the city's inhabitants from the threat the old gods continually pose. The ode is not a story [*povest'*]; it is an offering to the deity of the place. If the Neva and foreign powers must reconcile themselves with Peter, far be it for the poet to disturb the great tsar's eternal sleep.¹³

Before Peter had overcome and contained the local river gods, there was nothing but desolate waves. He looked upon the waters and ordered a new city to be built over and around it; a new world arose where only chaos had existed before. Peter is presented as possessed with an idea that, as in John, precedes or is virtually identical with creation itself, with the beginning of things. "In the beginning was the Word, and the Word was with God, and the Word was God. The same was in the beginning with God. All things were made by him; and without him was not anything made that was made" (John 1:1–3).[14] In the second line of *The Bronze Horseman*, the word *he* [*on*, intro. 2] serving as an implied reference to Peter, is expressed in italics, the only italicization in the poem.[15] It is a clear reference to the God of John. The echo reinforces Peter as a carrier of not only the idea but of the Word, and thus his association with deity. Likewise, as in John, the opening lines of *The Bronze Horseman* stress the darkness that hovers over the land and the sea. The forest is deprived of light because of the fog-enshrouded sun. Peter is the new sun, as Petersburg, his creation, especially in summer, is the quintessence of wondrous unending light, light even into night. Pushkin emphasizes the translucent twilight [*prozrachnyi sumrak*, intro. 49], the wondrous moonless light [*bezlunnyi blesk*, intro. 49], and the dawn that refuses to permit the nocturnal darkness [*nochnaia t'ma*, intro. 49] to infringe on the golden skies. Even in winter he can think only of the brilliance [*blesk*, intro. 63] of balls and of young girls' cheeks brighter [*iarche*, intro. 62] than roses.

But the first lines of *The Bronze Horseman*, like John, also echo Genesis: "In the beginning God created the heaven and the earth. And the earth was without form, and void; and darkness was upon the face of the deep. And the spirit of God moved upon the face of the waters." In the Russian translation the earth is void [*pusta*], "the face of the deep" is just "the abyss" [*bezdna*], and "the face of the waters" is just "waters" [*vody*]. Curiously, in the first lines of *The Bronze Horseman*, the waves are desolate [*pustynnye volny*, intro. 1]. Whereas in Genesis the spirit of God moved [*nosilsia*] over the waters, Peter looks over the coursing water [*reka neslas'*, intro. 4]. An interesting transformation takes place: whereas in Genesis the spirit of God is moving over the waters, in *The Bronze Horseman* it is Peter's vision that passes over the "moving" waters. All this occurs before God creates light and Peter creates his city of light. Pushkin's ode, especially when it deals with Peter himself, takes the genre as far as it can go, not mere glorification of Peter but metaphoric deification.[16] Of course, this is not the only view of Peter that emerges from *The Bronze Horseman*, nor even from the introduction, but it is the one with which the poem begins, and it is the one that sets up the parameters in which madness operates.[17]

God and Subject: Evgenii

Just as Pushkin creates a godlike Peter in the introduction, he conversely makes the hero of his *povest'* an average, modest man, in almost every way the antithesis of Peter. Lednicki argues that Pushkin progressively reduced his hero's status in successive versions of the poem.[18] Evgenii is the subject of the god. The narrator accordingly adopts a very different attitude toward his little hero. The narrator's different relation to Peter and Evgenii is directly reflected in terms of address. "He" [*on*, intro. 2] is the direct antithesis of "My poor, poor Evgenii" [*bednyi, bednyi moi Evgenii*, 2.89]. The narrator loves Peter's creation, the realized idea of the god-man. He admires and glorifies the visionary who made Russia a great and feared imperial power. But Evgenii is far more the *narrator's* creation.[19] Even those critics who have taken "Peter's side" in *The Bronze Horseman*—or the side of historical necessity—see the narrator's attitude toward Evgenii as unambiguously sympathetic.[20] The narrator often keeps an intellectual distance from Evgenii, but he also becomes affectively involved with Evgenii as he tells his hero's sad tale. Evgenii bears the name of the hero of Pushkin's novel in verse, *Eugene Onegin*. Therefore his name, not surprisingly, has a pleasant ring [*zvuchit priiatno*, 1.14] and hints at sound and healthy origins (Evgenii).[21] He calls him "our hero" [*nash geroi*, 1.12] and "my Evgenii" [*Evgenii moi*, 2.16]. As misfortune strikes him, he is "the unfortunate" [*neschastnyi*, 2.37], "the poor man" [*bedniak*, 2.127]; and, as he goes mad, "the unfortunate madman" [*bednyi bezumets*, 2.166; *bezumets bednyi*, 2.193] and "my madman" [*bezumets moi*, 2.220].

Unlike the more negatively characterized Germann of *The Queen of Spades*, Evgenii does not overly worry about fame and fortune, though his family name may be an ancient and respected one, and though he sometimes wonders why he was not fated to have an easier life.[22] Again in contrast to Germann, he is willing to secure his "independence" by means of hard work [*trudit'sia den' i noch' gotov*, 1.52]. He does not dream of a vast fortune of a thousand souls or of a brilliant future but of a humble and simple family life with his beloved Parasha, "his dream" [*ego mechta*, 1.151]. Seeing Evgenii's dream [*mechta*] in the context of Pushkin's life, we can more easily understand the sympathetic treatment of Evgenii, who desires honor, independence, simple pleasures, and freedom [*volia*], that is, to be left in peace. Whereas in *The*

Queen of Spades Pushkin places a considerable ironic distance between his narrative persona and the mad Germann, in *The Bronze Horseman* he bridges the emotional gap between narrator and character by depicting Evgenii, in some ways, as a simplified version of his own lyric persona of the 1830s. Evgenii is the epitome of the private person, with limited ambition and dreams, with life-cycle interests and concerns, a denizen of Peter's city but at the same time the antithesis of Peter, who epitomizes empire, will, and history.

Evgenii's Madness: History and Etiology

The narrative proper (part 1) begins with the river rising. Evgenii cannot fall asleep because his mind is agitated [*v volnen'e raznykh razmyshlenii*, 1.30]. But at this point he seems much more worried about his everyday affairs and his plans for the future than about the river. Only after the narrator recounts his hero's concerns about the future does he add that Evgenii also thought about the Neva. But he thinks about it not because he fears it—it has not seemed to him to pose any real threat—but because the raising of the bridges means being separated from Parasha for two or three days. And this thought again brings him back to his future plans of achieving family happiness. The passage closes with the culmination of his dream [*mechta*]: burial by his grandchildren. Evgenii grows more apprehensive about the howling of the storm and pounding of the rain but, in contrast to his thoughts about his future, it does not keep him awake: he falls asleep [*Sonny ochi on nakonets zakryl*, 1.67–68]. Whatever his ancient roots might be, he has accepted Peter's "new deal." Evgenii may not like many of the changes that have taken place in Russian society, most of which have been initiated in Petersburg, but he has, as it were, made a contract with Peter, reconciling himself to his diminished social standing for a modest place in the new order, sacrificing ambition for security. According to Lednicki, "the outstretched hand of the tsar, in the conception of the sculptor, was supposed to be 'a protective hand' [*main protectrice*]."[23] One of the most prominent writers of the time, A. N. Radishchev, wrote of the monument that "the outstretched arm shows that the great man, having eradicated the vices frustrating his efforts, now offers protection to all those worthy of being called his children."[24] In Prince Viazemsky's poem, "Petersburg" (1818), Peter still raises his "protective arm" over the city.[25] In the Old Testament the outstretched arm or hand—or mighty hand and arm—is associated with God, Moses, and Aaron. The hand has many meanings, but it was with a mighty and outstretched arm that God protected the children of Israel from the wrath of Pharaoh. In return for his protection and intercession, God demanded that the Jewish people remember their covenant with him by wearing a sign on their hand (which is reenacted ritually by Orthodox Jews six days a week) "for with a strong hand hath the Lord brought thee out of Egypt" (Ex. 13:9). But Peter, the god-protector, proves incapable of commanding the elements and protecting the city. When the embankment, which holds the Neva in check, fails, Petersburg becomes the plaything of nature.

If Peter the Great cannot protect the city, it is hardly surprising that his lesser heirs also cannot. Alexander I and his generals are helpless in the presence of the superior forces of nature. Pushkin emphasizes the difference between the promise and the reality by comparing Peter the Great with Alexander I (1801–1825). Alexander, who at the time still "ruled with fame" [*So slavoi pravil*, 1.108] laments: "Tsars cannot command the divine forces of nature" [*S bozhiei stikhiei tsariam ne sovladet'*, 110–11]. When Peter stood beside the desolate waves, he was full of great thoughts and looked into the distance [*Na beregu pustynnykh voln / Stoial on, dum velikikh poln / I vdal' gliadel*, intro. 1–3]; Alexander steps out onto his balcony and gazes at the waters in despair. Here Pushkin links the two tsars euphonically: we have *stoial on* (intro. 2) for Peter, and *vyshel on* (1.111) for Alexander. And then Alexander sits down [*on sel*, 1.111]: that is, he acknowledges the powers greater than his own. Pushkin also repeats, for each of the tsars, the key words *duma* [thought] and *gliadet'* [look]. Whereas Peter was full of great thoughts and peered into the distance, Alexander, in reflection [*v dume*, 1.112], gazed [*gliadel*, 1.113] at the terrible destruction.

It is no surprise, then, to learn that Evgenii is trapped by the river. We do not know exactly how it happened, but Evgenii has climbed one of the guardian lions in front of a new edifice in order to escape the flood. Though Evgenii has not yet gone mad, the narrator implies he is not far from it. He is sitting immobile atop the lion, hatless, arms crossed, and frightfully pale. He does not sense the waters rising, lapping at the soles of his boots. Nor does he sense driving rain whipping his face or hear the violently wailing wind rip off his hat. He is behaving exactly as he will behave later, when, after having gone completely

Madness and the Common Man

mad, he becomes a vagabond. His desperate glance is immobile, fixed on the islands where Parasha lives. He understands what has probably happened. There is little hope that Parasha and her mother, in their frail little house, could have survived the flood. Evgenii had just been contemplating his dream of long-lived happiness. He sees now that his dream [*mechta*] may have been little more than an empty dream [*pustoi son*, 1.153]; more than that, life itself may be nothing but a mockery of heaven over earth.

Evgenii sits on the lion almost bewitched, riveted to the spot. Around him there seems to be only water. But right in front of Evgenii, with his back turned to him, still unfazed, still rising high over the raging river, still *standing* with an outstretched hand [*c prostertoiu rukoi*, 1.162] is the idol (the god) on his bronze steed.[26]

At the end of part 1, then, Evgenii is close to madness. Only the need for certainty keeps him sane. When the water subsides he visits Parasha's island, and then he immediately goes mad when his worst fears are confirmed. The narrator presents his madness through his hero's chilling outburst of laughter. "He burst out laughing" [*on zakhokhotal*, 2.65]. In order to dramatize the terrible effects of the flood, Pushkin singles out an individual who is driven mad by his misfortunes. He does not need to treat the other victims of the calamity in detail. So, on the day after the flood, the Petersburg sun rises again, and, though the inhabitants have had a terrible scare and some have lost a great deal, no one seems to have suffered so great a loss as Evgenii. Now the narrator makes Evgenii's madness explicit. He also begins openly to show his profound compassion for his hero, which is elicited even more by his madness than by his loss.

> But my poor, poor Eugene ...
> Alas! his turbid mind   2.90
> Against those dreadful shocks
> Did not stand up. The noisy tumult
> Of the Neva and of the winds resounded
> In his ears, of horrid thoughts
> Speechlessly full, he roved about.
> He was tormented by a kind of dream.
> There passed a week, a month—he
> Did not return to his own place.
> His forsaken nook

> Was let upon expiry of his term 2.100
> By the landlord to a poor poet.
>
> [*No bednyi, bednyi moi Evgenii ...*
> *Uvy! ego smiatennyi um* 2.90
> *Protiv uzhasnykh potriasennii*
> *Ne ustoial. Miatezhnyi shum*
> *Nevy i vetrov razdavalsia*
> *B ego ushakh. Uzhasnykh dum*
> *Bezmolvno polon, on skitalsia.*
> *Ego terzal kakoi-to son.*
> *Proshla nedelia, mesiats—on*
> *K sebe domoi ne vozvrashchalsia.*
> *Ego pustynnyi ugolok*
> *Otdal vnaimy, kak vyshel srok,* 2.100
> *Khoziain bednomu poetu.* (2.89–101)]

We have seen how Pushkin employs similar structures, words, and phrases invidiously to establish an ironic contrast between the tsars Peter and Alexander. He uses a similar device to reinforce the distance separating his hero and the tsar, emphasizing the stability and strength of Peter's ideas and city, and the fragility and shakiness of Evgenii's mind. Even during the flood the Bronze Horseman remains with outstretched hand as impassive and imposing as ever. But Evgenii, in contrast to Peter [*stoial on,* intro. 2], could not withstand [*ne ustoial,* 1.92] the blows of the last day. Whereas Peter is a man of great ideas [*Stoial on, dum velikikh poln,* intro. 2], Evgenii is full of silent, horrible thoughts [*uzhasnykh dum / Bezmolvno polon, on,* 1.94–95]. The ode concludes with the warning that Peter's eternal sleep or dream not be disturbed [*trevozhit' vechnyi son Petra,* intro. 91]. Here Evgenii's dream or sleep or vision is tormented. In the ode the narrator notes that one hundred years have passed in order to remind his readers how much of Peter's vision has been realized. He needs just one month to show how far Evgenii's madness has progressed. Peter remains rooted to his place above the Neva; Evgenii abandons his home, which the narrator calls an empty (deserted) corner [*pustynnyi ugolok,* 2.99]—another echo of the first line of the poem—and has become a vagabond, a wanderer.

In Greek literature and culture there existed a common metaphoric and physical convergence of wandering and madness.[27] All types of wandering were viewed as dishonorable, even shameful; the proper place to be was at home. To be mad was to stray from right reasoning. Wandering is not only alienation from home, it is also alienation from self, mind, and the gods, and, as we have seen, a form of divine punishment. We might amend the saying "when god wishes to punish men he first makes them mad" by adding that after he makes them mad he makes them wander, physically expelling them from their homes or preventing them from returning home.[28] Madness drives Orestes from his home. The mad Io is driven all over the world.

According to Foucault, vagabonds and madmen were often perceived as belonging to the same category, or at least they were treated in the same way.[29] In some cultures the harmless mad are permitted to wander the streets; however, in others, and Russian culture is a good example, mad wanderers may achieve special respect as holy fools. Evgenii abandons his house and all his goods, takes leave of his senses, and becomes a stranger to the world [*On skoro svetu / Stal chuzhd*, 2.103–4]. In contrast to Evgenii, the Bronze Horseman is the epitome of permanence, stability, imperturbability, reason, and order. The statue stays put, undisturbed and commanding amid the surging waters.

In Greek tragedy madness is seen as an invasion of an alien force, something foreign and dark that separates the afflicted person from others and makes him a stranger in the world. In *The Bronze Horseman* we see this aberration in the descriptions of Evgenii's degraded condition. He becomes a beggar. His clothes are ragged and threadbare. Children throw stones at him, and coachmen often give him a taste of their whip. He becomes completely disoriented. The narrator describes him as being not beast nor man, neither dweller on earth nor specter. He has been reduced to something indeterminate. Thus, as the narrator builds Peter up, he concomitantly uses madness to take Evgenii down to the lowest level imaginable: a homeless, bedraggled, wandering madman, with no kith or kin, completely alienated and estranged. The narrator's emotional sympathies, however, move in the opposite direction. The lower Evgenii falls in fortune, the more empathy, sympathy, and compassion he elicits. It is only this, poetically speaking, that Evgenii has left at this point, the only thing that has not been stripped from him.

The sympathy the narrator expresses for Evgenii echoes the persona's representation of himself as a madman in "God Grant That I Not Lose My Mind:" he imagines himself locked up, chained to a wall, ridiculed, and essentially reduced to the status of an animal. We find the same sympathy in the unfinished poem *The Mermaid* of 1832, in which a nobleman [*kniaz´*] is overwhelmed at the pathetic spectacle of a miller who goes insane after his daughter, seduced and abandoned by the nobleman, drowns herself. The nobleman argues that death is better than insanity and that a person deprived of reason is no longer a human being; he is more related to a beast than to a man.[30]

But just as Evgenii seems to have reached the ultimate in despair, the narrator elevates him. On the anniversary of the flood, Evgenii, sleeping on the wharf, once again hears the terrible wind and the lapping of the Neva's dark waters. The poor fellow woke up [*Bedniak prosnulsia*, 2.127]. In the previous sections Pushkin emphasizes Evgenii's falling asleep. Here he not only wakes up but seems to take a far more active role, all reflected in the grammar itself. Almost all the verbs of this section are active. Evgenii jumps up, recalls something, rises to leave, and heads off to wander but stops suddenly. He begins to look around and realizes that he has come to the very same spot (where the lions guard the large house) where he first confronted Peter and the flood. The Neva, the statue of the lion, and the sculpture of Peter are now inextricably linked in his mind. But Evgenii's meeting is no accident. The narrator writes that Evgenii found himself [*ochutilsia*] under the pillars of a great house. Pushkin uses exactly the same device and word in *The Queen of Spades*, when Germann *reappears* at the countess's house.[31] Germann interprets the coincidence as an unknown force drawing him to the house. Likewise, an unknown force draws Evgenii to Peter. It is as though he now seeks the confrontation. The lion has a raised paw, like an outstretched hand. It stands, like the statue of Peter protecting the city, more precisely the building of the city. The description of the Bronze Horseman echoes almost exactly the last lines of part 1.

> The idol on the bronze steed *stands* with outstretched arm
> [*Stoit s prostertoiu rukoiu / kumir na bronzovom kone*, 1.162–63]

> The idol on the bronze steed *sat* with outstretched arm
> [*Kumir s prostertoiu rukoiu / sidel na bronzovom kone*, 2.142–43]

The only major differences in these lines is the reversal of the position of the word *idol* [*kumir*] from the second to the first line and the change of the word *stands* [*stoit*] to *sat* [*sidel*]. This signals the reversal, at least for this moment, of the respective positions of the protagonists. It is Peter who is now sitting instead of standing, and Evgenii who has woken and jumped up [*vskochil*, 2.131].[32] It is he, not Peter, who begins to gaze. As Evgenii looks at the statue of Peter this time, he shudders. But it is a shudder of sudden vision and insight as well as one of fear. He has now linked together the lions and the Bronze Horseman, and thus the relation between the flood, his unhappy fate, and Peter.

The mad Evgenii circles the monument, looks directly into the countenance of the ruler of half the world, and is overcome by anger. Clenching his teeth, tightening his fingers into a fist, Evgenii warns Peter that he will get his due: *Uzho tebe!* For the mad Evgenii, this threat requires enormous courage. He has challenged the god, not only the god of the place but of city and empire.[33] He starts to run, for it seems to him that the face of the tsar—hitherto immobile, imperturbable, and stolid—has turned to him angrily. The tsar then begins to chase him through the streets of Petersburg. This is the last and most devastating blow Evgenii suffers. If he was of weak mind before, after this episode he is completely intimidated and unhinged. When, afterward, he comes upon the statue by chance, more frightened and confused than angry and indignant, he doffs his worn cap, without even raising his eyes, and chooses another itinerary. The implication is that Evgenii continues to live the life of a half or wholly insane street person to the end of his days. He is found dead next to Parasha's little house, which has washed ashore on another island. We do not know how long Evgenii's wandering lasted. But it seems to have ended when he came upon the house of his beloved. A barge stops at the island to carry it away, burying Evgenii's cold corpse on the spot.

It is clear who has lost this skirmish. At the very beginning of the poem, we find Peter standing on the shore thinking of empire and glory: "Upon a shore of desolate waves / Stood he" [*Na beregu pustynnykh voln / Stoial on*, intro. 1–2]. The little house is described in two lines: "A dilapidated little house / Like a black bush it had remained by the water" [*Domishko vetkhii / Nad vodoiu ostalsia on, kak chernyi kust*, 1.215–16]. These parallel lines highlight Peter's victory and Evgenii's defeat. Evgenii ends his life as a mad, destitute errant, destroyed by the god's city and personally by the god he thinks he has angered. The dark (black) bush [*chernyi kust*] recalls the vegetation that lined the Neva's banks before Peter transformed them into illuminated embankments. *Vetkhii* [dilapidated, shoddy, or pitiful] recalls the tattered nets [*vetkhii nevod*, intro. 28] of the Finnish fisherman. Here Peter is set against the dilapidated and abandoned little house, and now, by association, against Evgenii's lifeless body.

In Greek tragedy and myth, madness can be either of short or long duration. Madness is short when a god wishes to punish an offender by making him aware of the terrible acts he committed while mad. The ultimate punishment is the return to sanity (Ajax, Agave, Hercules). Madness is long in duration when the madness is itself the punishment (Orestes). In *The Bronze Horseman*, Pushkin works out the "punishment" differently. Although Evgenii does not regain his sanity, we do not know how long he roamed the streets of Petersburg. The narrator talks about repeated, chance meetings with the Bronze Horseman. The confrontation with the statue occurs approximately one year after the flood, which is meant to be a historical event. Few details suggest a time when Evgenii might have died, and even these are ambiguous—perhaps purposely so.[34]

Madness: Wrath and Punishment

The saying that "Whom God wishes to destroy, He first makes mad" has in modern times been understood metaphorically, but among the ancients the phrase was taken quite literally: madness was seen as an illness and a curse, an incursion or invasion of some alien spirit into the mind and body. That is why remedies for madness often involved exorcism. Because it was a curse, it had a malign purpose; it had to be the agent of an ill-disposed or angered god.

We can see this principle operating in Sophocles' *Ajax*. After Achilles' death, the Greek leaders decide to give Achilles' armor to Odysseus. Ajax views this as an egregious slight and plans to kill both Odysseus and the leaders who have so humiliated him. To prevent this from happening to her wards, Athena makes Ajax mad. Instead of killing his rivals, Ajax mistakenly slaughters a herd of cattle. After Athena restores his sanity, Ajax considers his action an even greater humiliation than the incident involving Achilles' armor. He finds no way out of his situation, given that the gods have conspired against him, other than to commit suicide. But why did Athena have to destroy

Ajax by making him mad? If she were just protecting her wards, she could easily have destroyed Ajax in many other ways. But Ajax was prideful and refused to attribute his talents in war to anyone other than himself. Insulted by such hubris, Athena sought revenge. Death was not enough; Ajax had to be humiliated. Madness is not only punishment, but it is humiliating punishment. Whoever is at fault is of no practical significance in a conflict between a god and a mortal. In private matters, when insulted or not paid proper respect, gods may do with mortals what they will. Even Athena barely succeeds in extricating Orestes from the Furies, and that only after many years of Orestes' terrible persecution and a very close vote in a trial. In some cases it makes no difference that a mortal may have inadvertently angered a god or acted in a manner that, from a human point of view, is morally defensible, even praiseworthy. A god can usually wreak his or her revenge with impunity. Any type of disrespect or improper behavior, as perceived by the gods, is a form of human pollution (Orestes) that must be resolved by punishment.

One can easily see variations of these ideas in "God Grant That I Not Lose My Mind" and *The Queen of Spades*. In *The Queen of Spades* one might argue that Germann is not only destroyed by his madness, but that the madness is visited upon him by the god of the story, whether a mysterious agent of justice, the narrator, or Pushkin himself, the implied author. "Authors" or "texts" do not punish all crimes equally or consistently—and they do not, of course, punish all crimes—but they do punish those who have violated something that is of special significance to them. In the previous chapters we have seen that Germann constituted a threat to the author's society, class, and ethos. The author thus not only destroys Germann, he discredits his idea by showing it to be a form of madness or something that must inevitably lead to madness. For a criminal whose crime is an idea, madness is an appropriate punishment.

We know that Evgenii angers the Bronze Horseman when he threatens him and is thereby made even more insane. But what relevance does the idea "Whom God wishes to destroy, He first makes mad" have for Evgenii? What, in fact, has he done to elicit the anger of the gods in the first place? What act of pollution has he even inadvertently committed? Evgenii seems an innocent victim who happens to find himself between the overwhelming forces of nature and Russian history, to be in the wrong place at the wrong time. Since the narrator is so sympathetic to almost every aspect of Evgenii's story, both before and after his misfortune, we know that Evgenii has not in any way angered the god of the tale, as Germann most probably did in *The Queen of Spades*. Evgenii demonstrates no hubris. Though he has perhaps a better lineage than those who are now his social betters, he does not seem resentful. He has modest ambitions and aspirations.[35] Further, the narrator describes these modest aspirations as though they comprised his own ideal of private bliss: to be able to enjoy family life outside the path of history, to be part of the natural life cycle, and to be fortunate enough to be buried by one's grandchildren. Evgenii's ambition is too small to bother a god, let alone anger one. Although Peter undoubtedly plays the role of a god in the poem, before the flood Evgenii in no way incurs his wrath. He is neither a moral nor an intellectual rebel.

The most innovative alternation that Pushkin makes in the disposition of madness is to place the source of anger not in Peter, the god or demigod, but in those who turn against Peter, first the river and then Evgenii, thus essentially reversing the traditional relationship of god (Peter) to subject (Evgenii) in terms of anger. Furthermore, madness is both the cause and result of Evgenii's anger. The poem does not address Evgenii's anger until his confrontation with the monument, but the confrontation strongly implies that Evgenii's anger had been building up ever since he found himself stranded in the flood astride the lion and began to make connections between cause and event. His immediate concern for the safety of Parasha overcomes all other thoughts and emotions, including anger. However, when the inclement weather of the following autumn takes him back to the time of the flood and he comes upon the Bronze Horseman, a full year of growing anger and resentment—little of it directed against the river itself—comes to a head.

> His chest tightened. His brow
> Was pressed against the chilly railing,   2.170
> His eyes filmed over with dimness,
> Flame ran over his heart,
> His blood seethed. Scowling he stood
> Before the prideful statue
> And, teeth clenched, fingers tightened into fists,   2.175
> As though possessed by some black power,

"All right then, wonder-working builder!"
He whispered with a shudder of spite,
"I'll show you ...!" And suddenly full tilt
He set off running.

[*Stesnilas' grud' ego. Chelo*
K reshetke khladnoi prileglo,   2.170
Glaza podernulis' tumanom,
Po serdtsu plamen' probezhal,
Vskipela krov'. On mrachen stal
Pred gordelivym istukanom
I, zuby stisnuv, pal'tsy szhav,   2.175
Kak obuiannyi siloi chernoi,
"*Dobro, stroitel' chudotvornyi!*"
Shepnul on, zlobno zadrozhav,
"*Uzho tebe ...!" I vdrug stremglav.*   (2.169–79)]

Here we see the intense anger in Evgenii's mind finally boiling over. His heart is aflame; his teeth and fingers are clenched; he seems as though he is overcome by a dark power [*chernaia sila*, 2.176]. Evgenii's anger and madness are inextricably tied. As Evgenii sees Peter as the cause of his misfortune, his anger grows stronger and more focused. His madness feeds this anger. In order for him to express his anger, he needs to go beyond the point of self-control and sanity. Only in madness can Evgenii dare to express his wrath, to challenge the demigod, the ruler of half of the world.[36] Evgenii knows the tsar's reaction to his challenge because he imaginatively constructs it. It is a one-time challenge. After the November anniversary he reverts to his former resigned and nonconfrontational approach: avoidance and submission.

Madness and Insight: The Elevation of the Hero

To make the best case he can for Evgenii's point of view, Pushkin must present Evgenii and Peter, at least on some plane, as worthy rivals. Before Evgenii's confrontation, the narrator shows, if anything, that madness demeans Evgenii, reducing him to the level of an animal. Madness thus increases the distance between Evgenii and Peter. It is only the compassion the narrator expresses for Evgenii's suffering that redeems him. But after the confrontation the narrator uses madness to elevate his hero to Peter's level. Judging by the standards of Erich Auerbach, Evgenii must be one of the major literary achievements of the nineteenth century, for *The Bronze Horseman* raises its "hero," a man of ancient family but also of modest means, status, and ambition, to the level of a great emperor, ruler of half the world [*derzhavets polumira*, 2.168]. Throughout the text of the *povest'*, similar words, syntactic structures, and phrases are employed in the presentation of both Evgenii and Peter. But, until the great confrontation, these consonances appear to be more ironic contrasts than attempts to show inherent and larger similarities. The great "confrontation scene" changes all this. In order for the narrator to raise Evgenii to the level of Peter, he must lend his hero some assistance. He must, in fact, mentally fuse with him so that it will not be Evgenii's actions alone that elevate Evgenii but rather the power of his thoughts, insight, and vision. Through madness Evgenii begins to see as Peter sees, and perhaps as madly as Peter sees.

The "confrontation scene" comprises two sections: lines 2.145–64 and 2.165–96. The entire first section and the first part of the second are transcribed below. The first section presents Evgenii's insight into the relationship between his fate and Peter's (2.145–52) and then unexpectedly returns to a tone and point of view similar to the introduction (2.153–64). The second section is also in two parts: the first deals with the transformation of Evgenii's insight into threat (1.165–80), the second with Evgenii's terror and flight from the statue through the streets of the city (2.180–95).

SECTION ONE

Evgenii shuddered. Fearfully clear 2.145
Became his thoughts. He recognized
The place where the flood had sported
Where the rapacious waves had crowded,
Rioting viciously about him,
And the lions, and the square, and him, 2.150
Who motionlessly loomed,
His brazen head in the dusk,
Him by whose fateful will
The city by the sea was founded ...

Madness and the Common Man

Awesome is he in the surrounding gloom!   2.155
What thought is upon his brow!
What power within him hidden!
And in that steed, what fire!
Whither do you gallop, haughty steed,
And where will you plant your hooves?   2.160
Oh, mighty potentate of fate!
Was it not thus, aloft hard by the abyss,
That with curb of iron
You reared up Russia?

[*Evgenii vzdrognul. Proiasnilis′*   2.145
V nem strashno mysli. On uznal
I mesto, gde potop igral,
Gde volny khishchnye tolpilis′,
Buntuia zlobno vkrug nego,
I l′vov, i ploshchad′, i togo,   2.150
Kto nepodvizhno vozvyshalsia
Vo mrake mednoiu glavoi
Togo, ch′ei volei rokovoi
Pod morem gorod osnovalsia . . .
Uzhasen on v okrestnoi mgle!   2.155
Kakaia duma na chele!
Kakaia sila v nem sokryta!
A v sem kone kakoi ogon′!
I gde opustish′ ty kopyta?   2.160
O moshchnyi vlastelin sud′by!
Ne tak li ty nad samoi bezdnoi,
Na vysote, uzdoi zheleznoi
Rossiiu podnial na dyby?]

SECTION TWO

Round the idol's pedestal   2.165
The poor deranged man walked
And cast fierce glances
Upon the countenance of the ruler of half the world.
His chest tightened. His brow
was pressed against the chilly railing,   2.170

His eyes filmed over with dimness,
Flame ran over his heart,
His blood seethed. Scowling he stood
Before the prideful statue
And, teeth clenched, fingers tightened into fists,   2.175
As though possessed by some black power,
"All right then, wonder-working builder!"
He whispered with a shudder of spite,
"You'll get yours ...!"
And suddenly full tilt
He set off running. It seemed   2.180
To him that the dread tsar's face,
Instantly aflame with wrath,
Was slowly turning ...
And he runs down the empty square
And hears behind him—   2.185
As if it were the rumbling of thunder,
A heavily ringing gallop
Over the quaking pavement
And twilit by the pallid moon,
Arm reaching forth on high,   2.190
There speeds after him the Bronze Horseman
Upon the clangorously galloping steed;
And all night, wherever the wretched madman
Might turn his steps
Behind him everywhere the Bronze Horseman   2.195
Was galloping with heavy clatter.

[*Krugom podnozhiia kumira*   2.165
Bezumets bednyi oboshel
I vzory dikie navel
Na lik derzhavtsa polumira.
Stesnialas' grud' ego. Chelo
K reshetke khadnoi prileglo   2.170
Glaza podernulis' tumanom,
Po serdtsu plamen' probezhal,
Vskipela krov'. On mrachen stal
Pered gordelivom istukanom
I, zuby stesnuv, pal'tsy szhav,   2.175

> *Kak obuiannyi siloi chernoi*
> *"Dobro, stroitel' chudotvornyi!"*
> *Shepnul on, zlobno zadrozhav,*
> *"Uzho tebe ... !" I vdrug stremglav*
> *Bezhat' pustilsia. Pokazalos'*   2.180
> *Emu, chto groznogo tsaria,*
> *Mgnovenno gnevom vozgoria,*
> *Litso tikhon'ko obrashchalos' ...*
> *I on po ploshchadi pustoi*
> *Bezhit i slyshit za soboi—*   2.185
> *Kak budto groma grokhotan'e*
> *Tiazhelo-zvonkoe skakan'e*
> *Po potriasennoi mostovoi.*
> *I, ozaren lunoiu blednoi,*
> *Prostershi ruku v vyshine,*   2.190
> *Za nim nesetsia Vsadnik Mednyi*
> *Na zvonko-skachushchem kone;*
> *I vo vsiu noch' bezumets bednyi,*
> *Kuda stopy on obrashchal,*
> *Za nim povsiudu Vsadnik Mednyi*
> *S tiazhelym topotom skakal.* 2.195] (5:147–48)

When Evgenii comes upon the statue on the anniversary of the flood, through madness and shock he achieves insight into the meaning of Peter, not only in relation to himself but for all of Russia. To appreciate this, we need to unpack the enigmatic passage in which the perspectives of the hero and narrator come eerily together. Although the thoughts in the first section (lines 2.152–64) seem to belong simultaneously to both Evgenii and the narrator, they nevertheless convey antithetical ideas. These ideas are initially presented as Evgenii's vision, as the insight he gained through madness; however, the narrator's point of view has as much to do with the presentation of Peter as Evgenii's. The syntax, the vocabulary, the ideas all seem beyond Evgenii; they far more resemble the ode than anything that has been hitherto presented in Evgenii's consciousness or ken. "Him by whose fateful will the city by the sea was founded" [*ch'ei volei pod morem gorod osnovalsia*, 2.154] refers back to "here will a city be founded" and "we have been so destined by nature" [*zdes' budet gorod zalozhen* and *prirodoi nam suzhdeno*, intro. 13–15]. "What thought is upon his brow"

[*Kakaia duma na chele!s* 2.156] refers back to "stood he, full of lofty thoughts" [*stoial on, dum velikikh poln*, intro. 2]. The narrator's switch from the impersonal "he, who" [*togo, ch'ei*] to direct address in the second person singular "thou" [*ty*] echoes the conclusion of the introduction where he addresses the city as "thou" [*krasuisia, toboi*, intro. 84]. The section also echoes the end of the introduction in its declamatory tone indicated by the interjection "Oh" [*O*] and the exclamation marks (the only such punctuation in part 2 of the poem). Again, like the conclusion of the introduction, this section ties Peter to Russia and the city, the only two places in the poem where Peter, Petersburg, and Russia are mentioned together. The word *Russia* itself occurs nowhere else but in these two passages. As in the ode, the narrator expresses the same admiration of Peter's power, vision, ambition, daring, and will. It seems that it is not Evgenii—or not only Evgenii—who admires Peter's vision and will, and wonders about Russia's present and future.

Thus the narrator, through his hero, injects the point of view of the ode into the *povest'*, just at the *povest'* intrudes itself at the end of the ode. At the end of the ode the narrator expresses his sympathy for Evgenii; toward the end of the *povest'* the narrator again expresses his awe before Peter. In order for the point of view of the ode to be incorporated into the entire poem, Peter cannot be presented solely from Evgenii's viewpoint. To do so would obviously diminish Peter and the gravity of his conflict with Evgenii.[37]

But, more probably, the confrontation scene presents a fusion of perspectives, points of view, motivated in part by Evgenii's madness. The confusion Evgenii suffered since being stranded by the flood, which was exacerbated after he finally understood that Parasha had perished, is dissipated for a few moments when he confronts the statue on the anniversary of the flood. Madness raises Evgenii's mind and thoughts to the narrator's level. There is no way for the narrator to express his hero's new insight into Peter other than to use his own language, the language of the ode. It is through his madness that the common man gains a higher insight into the mission of Peter the Great. But this insight cannot be presented entirely in the hero's own words.[38]

In the second section (line 2.177), for example, when Evgenii threatens the statue, he uses an unexpected description for Peter, almost as though he has appropriated the narrator's words about Peter from the previous section. He calls Peter "wonder-working builder" [*chudotvornyi stroitel'*, 2.177]. Since this passage is clearly from Evgenii's point of view, we can see why it is also possible that the portrait of Peter in the previous section could represent Evgenii's point of view as much as the narrator's. If Evgenii can call Peter "a wonder-working builder," then he can also think of Peter as "the one who by his will founded the city by the sea."

There is even further justification for reading the whole passage from Evgenii's point of view.[39] Once Evgenii recognizes the statue, he realizes that it is Peter, the builder, who is responsible for his terrible plight. He becomes as terrified by the statue of Peter as he was by the flood. "How awful he is in the surrounding gloom!" seems much more a transcription of Evgenii's consciousness than the narrator's. If we also read the rest of this section as a transcription of Evgenii's unexpressed thoughts, then all the observations he makes about Peter can be seen as motivated by his fear, horror, and doubt. The word *terrible* [*uzhasen*] now attaches to the thought [*duma*], strength [*sila*], and fire [*ogon'*] of Peter. Likewise, the rest of the passage can be read as Evgenii's questioning of Peter's direction for Russia. The line "Oh, mighty potentate of fate" [*O moshchnyi vlastelin sud'by*, 2.161] must be read, then, just as ironically as Evgenii's invocation of Peter in the second section: "All right then, wonder-working builder" [*Dobro, stroitel' chudotvornyi*, 2.177]. Through his madness, Evgenii is able not only to understand who is responsible for his fate but also to see with greater breadth and penetration into the meaning of the historical Peter. He understands the greatness of the idea, the power, and the will at the same time that he recognizes their horrible consequences for himself and others. He is raised to the narrator/author's level of insight, although he cannot share the narrator's emotional and intellectual perspective, for he has become one of Peter's victims.

It has been the fashion ever since the romantics to privilege the idea of madness as insight, to see it almost as a blessing. In her criticism of E. R. Dodds's famous chapter, "The Blessings of Madness" Ruth Padel writes: "Our own age is peculiarly placed to value, even idealize, truths available to madness. Hence the title of E. Dodds's chapter. His organizing image reflected a groundswell, a reevaluation of madness, emerging in anthropology and psychoanalysis in the mid-twentieth century. Literature on schizophrenia brought out ways in which schizophrenics disregard the fictional communications and conventional assumptions on which ordinary life runs, and express emotional truths that sanity deliberately, conveniently, obscures."[40]

As we have seen Jung, Laing, and many romantic psychoanalysts such as Deleuze and Guattari fit squarely into this tradition. But it is a tradition that has excellent ancient roots, especially in the thought of Plato. "It might be so if madness were simply an evil; but there is also a madness which is a divine gift, and the source of the chiefest blessings granted to men. For prophecy is a madness."[41] In Shakespeare, the poet, as well as the lover, is likened to a madman. Indeed, in the confrontation scene, Pushkin transforms a mad lover into a visionary, whose eye, in a fine frenzy rolling [*vzory dikie navel,* 2.167], looks from heaven to earth and earth to heaven, giving shape and form (with the help of the poet) to things hitherto unknown, apprehending, in his seething brain, more than cool reason comprehends.

Madness and Holy Foolishness

Pushkin further validates Evgenii's mad insights by ingeniously grounding them in the Russian tradition of holy foolishness. "Holy fools for the sake of Christ" [*radi Khrista iurodivye*] were believed to possess remarkable insight; they also demonstrated the temerity, on occasion, to tell the truth to tsars. Those who take on the ideal of voluntary foolishness in Orthodoxy renounce reason, as well as the comforts of this world, for Christ and in imitation of Christ.[42] In Russia, the people often viewed fools from birth, or involuntary fools, as equally holy. In either case, the faithful believed such fools possessed the gift of prophecy.[43]

The holy fool is hardly a common occurrence in nineteenth-century Russian literature.[44] Dostoevsky's Prince Myshkin in *The Idiot* and Mar'ia Lebiadkina in *The Possessed* are notable exceptions. Evgenii is neither "foolish" nor religious. Nothing whatsoever is said about his religious beliefs or practices. But since Evgenii has insight into Peter that stems directly from his madness, his questioning of Peter's legitimacy takes on a prophetic form not unlike that associated with holy foolishness. Furthermore, like the typical holy fool, Evgenii is demented, homeless, and followed by teasing children.[45] In Greek culture, the mad do not openly challenge gods or kings; they do not tell them unpalatable truths to their faces. By contrast, the holy fool could play this role with the tsar himself, as was the case with Basil and Tsar Ivan.

The only holy fool in Pushkin's work appears in *Boris Godunov*, which deals, among other things, with the legitimacy of the tsar and the terrible crime he may have committed to gain access to the throne. Nikolka, the holy fool, approaches the tsar as he comes out of the church and requests that he kill the children[46] teasing him, just as he killed the little tsarevich (the son of Ivan the Terrible). Boris's attendants want to have Nikolka seized, but Boris intercedes and asks Nikolka to pray for him. Nikolka responds adamantly that he cannot pray for King Herod; the Mother of God will not allow it.[47] Although the boys mistreat the mad fool, he is treated with great respect by the common people and by the tsar. Nikolka is not afraid to say anything to the tsar. He is obviously not feigning madness; he is mad. Since Boris senses that Nikolka's words come indirectly from God, he does nothing to the fool.

Evgenii, in effect, carries on the tradition of the mad seer into the nineteenth century. Given the time and place of Boris Godunov, having the mad truth expressed by a holy fool is historically and artistically appropriate. Many of the characters in the play, including the tsar, see Nikolka made holy by foolishness and humiliation, and thus a vehicle for expressing the highest spiritual truths. The mad fool serves as a vessel and conduit of the truth in Russian medieval society in the same way priests at the temple served as oracles in Greek society. Plato has no doubt that secrets and mysteries are revealed to the seers when they are mad. On the other hand, a holy fool would be highly inappropriate in a poem about nineteenth-century Petersburg, especially a poem in which God, not to speak of religion, is hardly ever mentioned.[48] For Pushkin to use Evgenii as a vehicle of higher truth, he must make him mad, but he cannot make him a holy fool without discrediting his terrible visions.

We can see an intermediary stage in the representation of madness and its relation to insight into the highest matters of state in *Poltava*, which takes place more than a century after the Times of Troubles depicted in *Boris Godunov*. *Poltava* treats another rebellion against Peter the Great, that of Mazeppa—during the battle of Poltava—the site of Peter's greatest victory. Peter is glorified even more fervently in *Poltava* than in the introduction of *The Bronze Horseman*. Mazeppa's rebellion against Peter is presented as a form of madness, motivated by personal not national interests.[49] He leads many innocents to destruction, including his wife, Mariia. When Mariia finds out that her husband has had her father executed, she runs away and disappears. When she revisits Mazeppa, she is definitely mad. The visitation may be a dream but we cannot be certain, for the element of the supernatural hovers over the text. The "mad scene" is presented very much like Evgenii's vision of the Bronze Horseman, Germann's vision of the countess in *The Queen of Spades*, or the rising of the statue in the *Stone Guest*. Is it the mad Mariia talking to Mazeppa? Or is it a mad Mariia only of Mazeppa's dream? Has Mazeppa created a mad Mariia as a way of finally accepting the truth about himself? Whatever the interpretation, *Poltava* presents madness as a vehicle of psychological and spiritual truth, both for the characters and the narrator. More important, Mariia becomes a vehicle for expressing not only the truth about her husband but also the truth about Peter the Great and Russian history. Pushkin uses the same words and images from *Poltava* in the great confrontation scene in *The Bronze Horseman*.

In the following mad speech Mariia expresses her disillusionment with her husband, addressing him as though he were an imposter (a rebel usurper):

> I mistook you for another
> Old man. Leave me.
> Your mocking look is terrifying.
> You are ugly. He is beautiful:
> Love shines in his eyes,
> There is such tenderness in his speech!
> His mustaches are whiter than snow,
> On yours the blood has dried!
>
> [*Ia prinimala za drugogo*
> *Tebia, starik. Ostav' menia.*
> *Tvoi vzor nasmeshliv i uzhasen.*
> *Ty bezobrazen. On prekrasen:*
> *V ego glazakh blestit liubov',*
> *B ego rechakh takaia nega!*
> *Ego usy belee snega,*
> *A na tvoikh zasokhla krov'!*] (2:415–16)

This passage comes after a remarkably similar passage about the face of Peter the Great before the battle at Poltava, but from the point of view of the narrator and Peter's entourage.

From a tent
Surrounded by a crowd of admirers,
Peter comes out. His eyes
Are shining. His face is terrible.
His movements are quick. He is beautiful.
He is like the storm of God.

[*Iz shatra*
Tolpoi liubimtsev okruzhennyi,
Vykhodit Petr. Ego glaza
Siiaiut. Lik ego uzhasen.
Dvizhen'ia bystry. On prekrasen.
On ves' kak bozhiia groza.] (2:410)

The reader immediately sees that Mariia's mad words have even more meaning for the narrator's presentation of Peter than they do for an understanding of Mazeppa. Mariia sees Mazeppa's face now as terrifying [*uzhasen*], whereas before she saw it as beautiful [*prekrasen*]. His eyes used to shine with love. By contrast, Peter's eyes still shine among his admirers, and his face, though terrifying, is still beautiful. The war has had disfiguring effects on Mazeppa's face. Peter's terrifying face and his quick movements represent the model of martial beauty. Thus the mad Mariia, like Evgenii, the character who suffers the most and for whom the narrator shows by far the most sympathy, becomes the vehicle for expressing the truth about Peter.[50] As in *Boris Godunov*, the mad still tell us truths about tsars—here positive truths about Peter—but they need not be holy fools to do so.

Pushkin is playing a double game here, implicitly investing his heroes with the powers traditionally attributed to the holy fool, in addition to those attributed to the mad in the secular literature, while avoiding the specifically religious associations that would have been historically or textually inappropriate for the poem and that might even have detracted from, rather than added to, the valorization of Mariia's or Evgenii's mad insights. Mariia is no holy fool, but in her madness she speaks the truth about tsars. Since *Poltava* was written in 1828, at a time when Pushkin was more positively disposed to Peter, it is not surprising that her mad vision elevates Peter as it diminishes Mazeppa.

By Peter's time, the church, not to mention the state, was growing increasingly less tolerant of the phenomenon of *iurodstvo* (holy foolishness), practically and intellectually. Moreover, Peter did not suffer fools lightly, holy or otherwise. He disliked the fools traditional to medieval courts, those jesters and buffoons kept to amuse kings and tsars.[51] There were jesters at his court, but they were often members of the nobility whom Peter compelled to play the role of jester or fool against their will. Peter humiliated his jesters and employed them in his elaborate entertainments, spectacles, and practical jokes. Some were effectively employed as spies, revealing to Peter the opinions of his drunken guests. Holy fools, on the other hand, would not approach Peter, as Pushkin has Nikolka approach Godunov, for fear of being beaten. Gasiorowska writes:

> He disliked the "possessed" men [*besnovatyi*] and women [*klikusha*] and the "fools of God" [*iurodivyi*]; he considered them useless cheats who staged their epileptic seizures in public places to escape work, and favored "exorcising them with a knout, the knout's tail being longer than the devil's." There was another consideration; like the boyars, they too represented the opposition, whether raving about the coming of the Antichrist and the approaching end of the world, or predicting, among other things, the annihilation of Petersburg.[52]

Whatever Pushkin may have thought of holy fools, and we have no evidence of what he actually did think on the subject, in 1824, approximately one hundred years after Peter's death, the holy fool could have none of the power and resonance that he had in Moscow more than two hundred years earlier in the reign of Boris Godunov. Evgenii is an unlikely candidate for a holy fool, genealogically, socially, or intellectually. And Peter—the Bronze Horseman—would obviously not have reacted to a holy fool in the way that Boris did. He listens to Evgenii because Evgenii is *not* a *iurodivyi* but a previously loyal subject and supporter of the Petrine idea. Pushkin appropriates the truth-telling function of the traditional holy fool, without its specific religious context. When the hero goes mad, he goes back in time and gives voice to the increasingly discredited tradition of the holy fool, speaking terrible truths and prophesying doom to the rulers of half the world.

The Bronze Horseman's vigorous and angry response to Evgenii's threat will always remain somewhat of a mystery, as will the interplay between the supernatural and psychological in the transformation of the Bronze Horseman from monument to horseman and rider. The Bronze Horseman heeds Evgenii because his voice is prophetic, and it can be prophetic in the context of Petersburg because Evgenii is mad but *not* a holy fool. At the beginning the Word is with Peter, and the creation of the city and the empire emanate from that Word. However, it is Evgenii who speaks the last word [*uzho tebe*]. The word has passed, as it were, from Peter to Evgenii. It is the word of night, the word uttered from madness, compelled by a dark power [*sila chernaia*], and it casts a pall over everything else that has been said or done. It is a new Word, and that is why Peter must listen.

Evgenii's word, like Peter's, is tantamount to a performative; it creates action by its very pronouncement. Once the Word is spoken the world comes into existence. But the Word can also destroy. Curses, threats, and challenges are negative performatives. Because Peter acts as though Evgenii's word were prophetic, he must come down immediately from his pedestal and prevent the word from being realized. In ancient Israel, those who prophesied against the authorities were often killed because it was commonly believed that the prophecy brought on the event.[53] Most of these prophecies foretold the destruction of cities. Thus Peter must descend from his pedestal to save his city and his legacy. Evgenii does not have to be a biblical prophet for Peter to react to his prophecy. *The Bronze Horseman* is exploiting an age-old, probably universal tradition. The monument responds despite itself;[54] something forces it from its state of repose, its eternal sleep, to make the tsar act in conformance with Greek, Hebrew, and Russian models. It is not within the power of Peter, who creates by means of the Word, to ignore the Word. Peter knows the Word of destruction is as powerful as the Word of creation. The kings who do not listen to prophecy perish. Moreover, Peter is now a creature of the text, and the mad text rules.

Madness: Elevation and Punishment

Despite his validation and elevation of Evgenii's insights, Pushkin does not take a completely romantic approach to the madness of his hero. He never glosses over the terrible consequences of madness. Even the traditions that recognize the visionary potential of madness—to see as only the gods can see—often view it simultaneously as a curse: the mad, in one way or another, are destined to suffer because of their divine powers.⁵⁵ The narrator closely chronicles Evgenii's wanderings, alienation, destitution, and humiliation. And he directly ascribes them to the curse that accompanies the vision of madness. As a result of his insight, Evgenii dares to do something almost beyond the imagination of a Greek hero: not only to engage in rebellion but also to threaten a god. Thus madness leads to insight, which makes rebellion possible. Evgenii could threaten Peter only when possessed by a black power [*chernaia sila*].

Ever since the ancients, melancholia, literally black bile, has been associated with madness, anger, and violence.⁵⁶ As Rosen shows, one of the most common words for madman was *melancholon*, he who is afflicted with black bile.⁵⁷ "If you put these ideas together—invasion and eviction, plus black flooding passion—the image of madness as a black, angry, inner flood seems inevitable."⁵⁸ "The organic source of madness is black liquid."⁵⁹ "The philological basics suggest that in Greek thought, madness is indissoluble from anger."⁶⁰ In the Greek text *Problems 30*, wrongly attributed to Aristotle, but particularly influential in the Renaissance, melancholia and black bile are also considered sources of special powers, even genius. "Why are all those who become eminent in philosophy, politics or poetry, melancholics? Some so much that they are affected by diseases caused by black bile."⁶¹ But darkness and night (a common thread throughout the *povest'*) have always been associated with melancholia and madness. The Erinyes, who are responsible for Orestes' madness, are "the everlasting children of Night."⁶² "None of the successes of Zeus's bastard son [Heracles], however, escaped the ever hateful eye of Hera. Great malice welled in her heart until all at once she unleashed her pent-up ire by sending raging Madness, unmarried child of blackest Night, loathed by all the gods, upon the object of her relentless hate."⁶³ "Darkness in the Greek world had many resonances of danger and death, as for us. But it was where you might encounter gods, 'see' truths unavailable in the light.... Greek myth, literature, and cult are full of truths seen or heard in the dark: in caves, the night, the underworld. The earliest Greek oracles are shrines to Night."⁶⁴

Evgenii's response to the monument can be better understood in terms of the reciprocal relations between madness, insight, anger, darkness, and violence. Madness leads to the insight that produces anger. The anger does not undermine the insight, but it does show the underside of madness, even the underside of insight. All this is dramatized in the second part of the confrontation scene. Evgenii's glances are described as wild [*vzory dikie*, 1.167], quite different from the "fine frenzy" that Theseus evokes in *A Midsummer Night's Dream*. In addition, his eyes are filmed over [*glaza pedernulis' tumanom*, 2.171], as though he were seeing less. In the presence of the monument he becomes dark [*mrachen*, 2.173], as is perfectly appropriate for a man in the grip of madness and anger. He is possessed by a dark power [*sila chernaia*], the ancient symbol of madness. Shaking, he angrily threatens the monument.

> Possession and ecstasy characteristically manifest themselves in the following manner. An extraordinary inner tension seizes the individual, and he experiences irresistible and perhaps incomprehensible emotions. As if under compulsion of some force acting upon him, the individual feels constrained to speak or to act. In this state he may also feel fear and resist the apparent invasion of his personality. At the same time he may experience pains and seem to lose strength and breath. These internal developments are associated with external body changes. The individual's features are altered, and he begins to act as if he had lost control of his motor system. Trembling, lassitude, and drowsiness may precede the period of convulsive agitation. *Then the limbs become agitated, the gesture wild and excited, the voice changes, and what is uttered seems to be the expression of another personality.*[65] [my emphasis—G.R.]

Those who are favorably disposed to Peter's mission and interpret Evgenii's madness exclusively from a psychological perspective understandably take a dimmer view of Evgenii's "possession." Gregg sees Evgenii as a paranoid who senselessly and absurdly rebels against the great tsar. Evgenii, he argues, is subject to:

> a fully paranoid obsession which in its final phase metamorphoses the illusion of persecution into the hallucination of actual physical pursuit.... For if the distinguishing trait of the insane mind is its inability to tell illusion from reality, and if a paranoiac is by definition someone who conjures up non-existent persecutors, does not a realistic (as opposed to a romantic) reading of the scene suggest that Eugene's accusation is not a revelation of some "higher reality" (pace Merežkovskij, Lednicki), but a paranoid attempt to escape from reality?... May we not, in short, surmise that in the depths of his disordered mind there is

the uneasy perception that to have blamed Peter for his misfortunes and to have sworn personal vengeance on Russia's greatest sovereign was reckless, vain, and absurd."⁶⁶

In Greek tragedy and myth, madness either leads to punishment or constitutes punishment itself. Madness—and its concomitant insight— causes Evgenii to confront the demigod; the confrontation results in "condign" punishment. The statue comes alive because madness has expanded Evgenii's imagination. *One sees more devils than vast hell can hold; that is the madman.... Or in the night, imagining some fear, how easy is a bush suppos'd a bear?* ⁶⁷ Evgenii's anger elicits the commensurate anger [*gnev*, 2.182] of Peter, who in turn seems inflamed with wrath. It is the god "with outstretched hand" [*prostershi ruku*, 2.190] who speeds after him [*nesetsia*, 2.191]—expressions repeated from the introduction—in the form of the Bronze Horseman, externalized if one admits the supernatural, internalized if one admits only the psychological.⁶⁸

But anger thus has the same effect on Peter as it has on Evgenii. Peter abandons his godlike imperturbability and descends his pedestal. He employs the horse of state, Russia itself, to chase a common subject through the streets of Petersburg. The anger generated by madness, just like the insight generated by madness, makes Evgenii not less but more like Peter and thus continues the process whereby Pushkin decreases the distance between demigod and subject. Pushkin both elevates Evgenii and reduces Peter at the very same time.⁶⁹

The process by which madness raises Evgenii to Peter's level starts at the very beginning of section 1 of the confrontation scene (2.144), where Evgenii has a sudden insight into his fate and its connection with Peter. He recognizes the place where the flood sported [*gde potop igral*, 2.147], where the rapacious waves had crowded [*gde volny khishchnye tolpilis'*, 2.148], rioting viciously about him. The phrase "he recognized" [*On uznal*, 2.146] recalls the phrases employed to present Peter at the beginning of the poem—both "He stood" [*stoial on*] and "And he thought" [*I dumal*]—as Peter looks over the waters of the Neva. The phrases describing the monument in the first section— "What thought is upon his brow!" [*Kakaia duma na chele!* 2.156], "What power within him hidden!" [*Kakaia sila v nem sokryta!* 2.157], "And in that steed, what fire!" [*A v seme kone kakoi ogon'!* 2.158]—may also be applied to Evgenii in the second section. The fire associated with the horse in section 1 is transformed into Evgenii's mad anger in section 2. He places his burning brow [*chelo*] on the cold gate. Like his head, his blood and his heart are also afire. Like Peter's fiery steed, Evgenii seems coiled for action. By the middle of the passage, he can no longer contain himself. He utters his threat, perched, as it were, like Peter, over an abyss, and begins to run. The statue, as it rises up before Evgenii, is described in section 1 (2.151–52) as "he who motionlessly loomed / His brazen head in the dark" [*kto nepodvizhno vozvyshalsia / Vo mrake mednoiu glavoi*]. In section 2 Evgenii, rising up before Peter, "becomes dark and somber" [*on stal mrachen*]. The "power" [*sila*] hidden in Peter (2.157) corresponds to the hidden "dark power" [*sila chernaia*] that possesses Evgenii. The fire in reference to Peter's horse is transferred to Evgenii and then back to Peter. For now the statue, in its turn, erupts in anger [*gnevom vozgoria*, 2.182], threatening Evgenii [*groznyi tsar'*, 2.181].

Imagistically, symbolically, psychologically, and linguistically, Evgenii can approach Peter in a way that was inconceivable before he went mad. He can force Peter to descend his pedestal—something even the flood could not do[70]—abandon his imperturbability and turn his energy from his idea to engaging his mad subject. Peter and Evgenii have not become one, even in Evgenii's imagination; but just as Pushkin merges the consciousness of his narrator with Evgenii, so he brings his protagonists together as each turns on the other. Peter causes Evgenii's madness; Evgenii's madness elicits Peter's ire, awakening him from his eternal sleep. Evgenii emerges, if only for a moment, as a worthy antagonist of the tsar. His rash act brought on by his intense insane anger could never have been ventured had he not been both gifted and cursed by the dark power of madness.

Evgenii's elevation is short-lived, but that is perfectly in accord with the romantic notion of madness, the commonplace that a moment of insight—a variation of a moment of bliss—is worth a lifetime. After a moment of insight, Germann is confined to an asylum for the rest of his life. Evgenii is fated to wander the streets in an even more demented, destitute, and pathetic condition than before his confrontation with Peter—the curse of madness that sees too much. From a romantic point of view, Evgenii's terrible end detracts neither from his understanding nor his actions; it enhances the romantic aura of one who has paid the price for his insight and courage. He has undergone an extraordinary transformation, considering that just prior to the confrontation he was a creature almost without definition: "neither beast nor man, neither this nor that, nor inhabitant of this world" [*ni zver', ni chelovek, ni to, ne se, ni zhitel' sveta*, 2.117–18].

But what if Evgenii only imagines that the Bronze Horseman is pursuing him? In *A Midsummer Night's Dream*, Theseus implies that, although the imagined reality is not necessarily inferior to the real world, it is still an imagined and not a shared, objective world—whether the madman imagines worlds that hold more devils than hell can hold, finds Helen's beauty on every Egyptian brow, or sees a bear in every bush. For Greek tragedy and culture, the existence of the gods is a reality or a convention accepted as a reality. In the *Oresteia* Athena presides over the trial of Orestes and casts a tie-breaking vote. There may be anagogical explanations of Athena's presence, but, as one of the dramatis personae, she cannot be psychologized away. In Shakespearean tragedy and after, madness is largely psychological or psychologized. The times may aggravate the propensity to madness, if not cause it; but it is not an external force that is to blame but the individuals themselves: "The fault, dear Brutus, is not in our stars / But in ourselves, that we are underlings."[71] However, Evgenii's insight, his elevation through madness, and his threats against Peter are all presented as objective realities. The only event affecting Evgenii's madness that may be interpreted as being purely his imagination is the Bronze Horseman's descent from its pedestal and its pursuit of Evgenii, and only on the condition that we completely dismiss the possibility of the supernatural.

If we interpret this scene on a purely psychological level, then it follows that Evgenii has internalized something equivalent to the Greek idea of madness and divine punishment. In *The Queen of Spades*, Germann understands intuitively what his choice of the queen entails, but he chooses it, despite reason. It was liberation and punishment at the same time. Something similar happens to Evgenii. He understands that his rash, mad act has angered "the ruler of half the world" and that he must suffer a commensurate punishment; he has internally incorporated the certainty of his punishment, a certainty that is augmented by his madness.

The relation between anger and punishment is highlighted by the Bronze Horseman's imperturbability. Evgenii sees that the flood has altered the geography of the city, devastated the lives of numerous inhabitants, and shown the tsar's generals and the tsar himself completely helpless in its presence. Peter alone stands his ground, unmoved in every sense, as though nothing of significance were taking place. Evgenii must intuit the gravity of his rebellion, otherwise he could hardly imagine that his act would bring down the wrath of the tsar, compelling the unmoving ruler of half the world to descend from his steed and pursue a minor clerk all night through the streets of Petersburg.

Orestes knows the consequences of killing his mother. Oedipus knows what must happen, and thus what he must do, when he realizes that he has killed his father and committed incest with his mother. Orestes' punishment is imposed from the outside, the Erinyes. Oedipus's punishment is seemingly self-inflicted; Oedipus acts on the cultural codes he has internally incorporated and to which he is bound by law. Evgenii may imagine Peter pursuing him, but he is imagining and transforming an age-old pattern of infraction and retribution. Orestes flees, the Erinyes pursue; Io flees, Hera pursues. In assessing the flood, the narrator cites the point of view of the people: "the people look upon God's wrath and await punishment" [*Narod zrit bozhii gnev i kazni zhdet*, 1.104]. In the modern world, madness resurrects the oldest codes. Given the brilliance of Pushkin's rendition of the chase scene, who is to say that the imagined reality, metaphorically and poetically speaking, does not constitute or contain a truth more real "than cool reason ever comprehends." In Pushkin's world it is only the mad imagination that evokes the supernatural, but, as Dostoevsky's Svidrigailov in *Crime and Punishment* would later argue, such a statement does not disprove the supernatural; rather, it shows that only the mad have the capacity for experiencing it. Through the imagery of sound alone, Pushkin makes the mad reality of Evgenii as real as anything in the poem, as real as Peter, as Petersburg, as Russia itself. What Evgenii imagines is not the lesser for his having imagined it.

The Pushkinian text never forecloses the supernatural. It is present, or left open, in *The Bronze Horseman* as it is in *The Stone Guest*, *Poltava*, and *The Queen of Spades*. It may make the poem more convincing or acceptable to some contemporary readers if Evgenii's vision is interpreted psychologically, but the possibility of the supernatural makes the poem far richer, especially in terms of Evgenii's characterization and the power of his vision. It is one thing for Evgenii to understand the relationship between Peter and the flood; it is quite another to have the power to bring Peter back to life, to return him to history, and to confront him directly with his deeds. Although in one sense this metamorphosis reduces the Peter of the introduction, at the same time it enhances him, for it makes him, at all times, a living presence with which Russia must contend. His legacy will always call forth rebellion, for which he himself may have set the primary model.

Madness and Rebellion

Perhaps the most provocative aspect of Evgenii's madness is its relationship to rebellion. As I argued earlier, in *The Queen of Spades* Germann's potential challenge to the status quo probably constitutes one of the main reasons for Pushkin's decision to confine his hero to an insane asylum, the punishment that the persona of "God Grant That I Not Lose My Mind" portrays as a death-in-life. After having studied the Pugachev rebellion, Pushkin expressed considerable apprehension about the consequences of rebellion for Russia. He saw the effects of escalating violence, especially when rebellion lost sight of its original goals. The narrator of the ode is a firm believer in Peter, Peter's city, and Peter's idea: that is, in the necessity of reason, order, law, and imperium. His hope, even in the *povest'*, is that however terrible and inevitable the violence against Peter may be, that such madness will be temporary and thus containable.

We have seen that Pushkin treats rebellion against Peter even more harshly in *Poltava* (1828) than in *The Bronze Horseman*. Mazeppa, the Cossack hetman who turns against Peter, is unequivocally labeled, like the Neva, a villain [*zlodei*], but also a traitor [*izmennik*] and a Judas [*Iuda*]. In the end, he is thoroughly vanquished. There is no trace of his grave. In *Poltava* Peter needs no monument, no Bronze Horseman; he has raised a monument to himself through his deeds. But Evgenii is not Mazeppa. Evgenii is presented throughout as a poor victim [*bedniak*]. And since the narrator invests so much imaginative sympathy in him, at times even fusing with his hapless hero at the most dramatic point in the text, it is more difficult for him to take an unequivocal and unambiguous position against his hero's rebellion.

The text presents Evgenii's rebellious challenge to the Bronze Horseman as a dramatic convergence of all the main players: the Neva and Peter, as well as Evgenii. In the great confrontation episode in which this convergence takes place, Evgenii understands through his madness that the present-day city is not as responsible for his plight as Peter the

Great himself. This is why he rages not so much at the city as at the Bronze Horseman. When Evgenii associates Peter, the flood, and his plight, he goes back to the founding of the city, thinking of the head [*glava*] and the will [*volia*] that commanded a city be founded by the sea [*pod morem gorod osnovalsia*]. His insight is that his misfortune is directly related to Peter's original conception, which preceded the creation of the city; that is, it is related to the thought, the idea, the might, and the will that gave the city birth. When the wind howls, Evgenii then begins to see something different in his relationship with the river. He understands that the river, which seemed to be the main culprit for his unfortunate state, is, like himself, a victim of Peter: a victim of Peter's idea [*duma*], will [*volia*], power [*sila*], and fire [*ogon'*]. The river was not directing its anger at him personally but was raging against the city as the source of its own subjugation and plight. In his madness Evgenii now adopts the position of the river with respect to Peter.[72] Just as the river surrounded the guardian lions and the monument, Evgenii now circles the monument. Like the river, propelled by a dark force, he rages against the city. It is as though the river and he were now natural allies in a common cause, each justifiably rebelling against the imperious ruler who had attempted to bend them to his will, to use them for his own purposes, irrespective of the cost. Evgenii could have hardly expressed his threat against the tsar, have even thought of a real rebellion, had he not been mad, had he not been infected by the river and its mad fury.[73]

> Evgenii shuddered. Fearfully clear
> Became his thoughts. He recognized
> The place where the flood had sported
> Where the rapacious waves had crowded,
> Rioting viciously about him,
> And the lions, and the square, and him,
> Who motionlessly loomed,
> His brazen head in the dusk,
> Him by whose fateful will
> The city by the sea was founded ...
> Awesome is he in the surrounding gloom!
> What thought is upon his brow!
> What power within him hidden!
> And in that steed, what fire!

Whither do you gallop, haughty steed,
And where will you plant your hooves?
Oh, mighty potentate of fate!
Was it not thus, aloft hard by the abyss,
That with curb of iron
You reared up Russia?

[*Evgenii vzdrognul. Proiasnilis'*
V nem strashno mysli. On uznal
I mesto, gde potop igral,
Gde volny khishchnye tolpilis',
Buntuia zlobno vkrug nego,
I l'vov, i ploshchad', i togo,
Kto nepodvizhno vozvyshalsia
Vo mrake mednoiu glavoi
Togo, ch'ei volei rokovoi
Pod morem gorod osnovalsia
Uzhasen on v okrestnoi mgle!
Kakaia duma na chele!
Kakaia sila v nem sokryta!
A v sem kone kakoi ogon'!
I gde opustish' ty kopyta?
O moshchnyi vlastelin sud'by!
Ne tak li ty nad samoi bezdnoi,
Na vysote, uzdoi zheleznoi
Rossiiu podnial na dyby?]

It is impossible, after all, to exert complete control over the elements, something that Peter's heirs acknowledge. It is also impossible to exert complete control over the outbreaks of collective madness. But if the ravages of flood and the infectiousness of madness can be contained, they present no threat to Peter's city or mission. The only real danger is the potential of a much wider rebellion. It seems that the city is able to restore control in short order. After the river subsides, within the course of a day everything returns to normal. When the sun (Peter) emerges from the clouds, it uncovers no traces of the previous day's catastrophe. It is as though the flood never happened. Evgenii goes mad and takes up the life of a vagrant, hardly any threat to anyone, not to speak of Peter or Peter's legacy.

But traces of the flood remain, and that is what the poem is about. The most damaging aspect of the flood is not its immediate devastation but its more subtle, deeper, and lasting effect on the population. The people see the flood as a sign of God's wrath and thus the action of a power higher than Peter's, a power who commands a mightier outstretched hand, and who has shown his displeasure with Peter and his city. The flood thus undermines the image of Peter (the Bronze Horseman) and the legitimacy of his mission, for it seems to be a rebellion against Peter's strengths: his will, his idea, and his order. God strikes out at Pharoah, the wonder-working builder, when the Pharoah refuses to let the children of Israel go; God commands Moses to stretch out his hand and cast all of Egypt in darkness. "And the Lord said unto Moses, Stretch out thine hand toward heaven, that there may be darkness over the land of Egypt, even darkness which may be felt. And Moses stretched forth his hand toward heaven; and there was a thick darkness in all the land of Egypt three days" (Ex.10:21–22).

The confrontation between Evgenii and Peter does not occur under the immediate pressure caused by the terrible flood. Though Evgenii's sudden flash of insight into the root of his misfortune takes the reader, the narrator, and even Evgenii himself by surprise, the conditions that make the insight possible take time to mature. In fact, the rebellion comes about through their *recall*, evoked not by a flood but purely by inclement weather. There is no mention at all of any danger of a flood. But the splashing of the river onto the wharfs, the drizzling rain [*kapal dozhd'*], the doleful howling of the wind, and the blackness of night are enough to awaken Evgenii to the *memory* of that earlier November: "Evgenii jumped up; he vividly recalled the earlier horror" [*Vskochil Evgenii; vspomnil zhivo / On proshlyi uzhas*, 2.132]. Given Petersburg weather, many other days during the year might just as easily have recalled the flood. It is not the events themselves but Evgenii's recollection of the events that elicits his mad insight into Peter and spurs him to rebel. It is the maturation of those traces that must give the legacy of Peter pause and, if Evgenii is an everyman, the potential of their explosive mixture in the population as a whole. Even the narrator is not immune. For although Evgenii had made a contract with Peter, it is reasonable to assume that he harbored, like his creator, a subconscious or unconscious resentment against Peter for the demotion of his class. Madness attenuates the forces of repression, bringing out the potential rebel.

Indeed, if Evgenii were the only one so affected by the storm, the poem would become a testament to the containment of rebellion and madness, an attempt to empathize with the victims of Peter's project as a means of assuaging their anger—if not reconciling them to Peter's cause—as though empathy were the only possible and just compensation, considering the dangerous alternatives. Dostoevsky and later Merezhkovsky did not see it that way.[74] For them, Evgenii was not an isolated individual but a social type whose fate had no less profound implications for Russia's fate than Peter's idea, might, and vision. The greater danger is that whenever the wind howls and the river threatens to overflow its bank, the memory of the catastrophe will rise in the collective imagination and be associated not with the glory of Russia and the expansion of the Russian state but with the darkest aspects of Peter's might, vision, will, and idea, with the tremendous costs in human suffering that even in Peter's reign gave rise to periodic rebellions. For the mad Evgenii, Peter himself is the perfect example of the power of a mad idea imposed on an entire nation. In his madness Evgenii understands the madness of his adversary.

The confrontation scene between Peter and Evgenii focuses mainly on Evgenii's insights about Peter, on Peter's role in Russian history, and on the consequences of that history for Evgenii and the Russian people. For when Evgenii wonders where Peter is going and whether he will continue, with iron bridle, to rear Russia over the abyss, he is thinking about himself historically, including himself as part of Russia that has been raised above the abyss. He can no longer see himself alone. If he did, there is no way he could imagine being able to threaten Peter for his miraculous building enterprises. He can threaten only from the future and only from others, who, driven to extremes by Peter's idea, will eventually come to the same realization Evgenii did, but which he could imagine only when mad. Alone, Evgenii realizes he will be crushed. But it will not take another flood to awake Peter's avengers to the truth. The potential will occur whenever the waters of the Neva are roiled, whenever the wind begins to howl disconsolately.

Once Pushkin fuses Evgenii's consciousness with that of the narrator, the narrator sees with Evgenii the terrible truth that Peter "is horrible in the surrounding gloom." Now, along with Evgenii, the narrator sees that there is a Peter of darkness and that the same forces that have erected an empire and have brought glory to Russia have also taken a tremendous toll on the Russian people. The city required more than the draining of swamps; it required the sacrifice of tens of thousands of living souls. The conditions leading to Evgenii's rebellion and threatening Peter's legacy arise from the sources of Peter's greatness: from the idea, the vision, the power, the fire, the ambition, the will—all that which raises Russia over the abyss. The sad tale the narrator tells cannot be solely an unhappy *episode* about a man who loses his fiancée in a flood.

In Greek tragedy and culture, madness results from the wrath of a disrespected or improperly honored god. In *The Bronze Horseman*, the first stage of Evgenii's madness has nothing to do with angering a deity. It is only when he openly challenges Peter that the deity pursues him and drives him even more insane. But Peter is also responsible for Evgenii's madness more impersonally. Evgenii's plight and madness derive not from Peter's vigilant attention to the behavior of his subjects but simply from Peter's person and his role in Russian history. Evgenii's madness, therefore, is in some ways larger than the madness in Greek tragedy. It derives not from a critical lapse of a mortal in relationship to a specific deity but from "being" itself, specifically from being Peter's subject, from being part of Russian history, from being part of the project of the master builder. Evgenii is destroyed impersonally in Peter's personal project of nation building. Evgenii's madness and ruin are the price the Russian people must pay for entering history.

Madness, Truth, and Violence

The Bronze Horseman highlights the problematic relationship between madness, truth, and violence. "God Grant That I Not Lose My Mind" introduces us to this unsettling relationship of violence and vision in its depiction of the simultaneously creative and destructive aspects of the persona's imagined freedom. *The Bronze Horseman*, however, places this relationship at the very heart of the poem. Violence engenders Evgenii's madness, from which the truth emerges. The truth gives rise to the anger that gives Evgenii the courage to challenge the monument, to threaten Peter with rebellion. As we shall see in chapter 6, the truth that arises out of violence engendered by madness ultimately may compromise itself by that very violence. This is why, in the end, Evgenii's vision is presented ambivalently and ambiguously.

Violence and truth can be much more easily reconciled in reconstructions of the distant past. In Pushkin's version of the idealism of the medieval romance, "There Was on Earth a Poor Knight" (1835), the hero, driven by the purity of his vision and love for the Virgin, slays infidels in Palestine. The knight's vision [*viden'e*] of the truth leads to perfectly acceptable military exploits *for his time.* His possible madness at the end of the poem is attributable to the purity of his devotion to the Virgin, not to his martial acts. Cervantes undercuts Don Quixote's martial exploits because his hero is playing the knight after the Age of Chivalry has long ended. By contrast, because Evgenii's story belongs to the present, his madness elicits as much fear in the narrator as compassion. Neither the truth, nor the violence that leads to that truth or emanates from it, can be dismissed. Nor can they be resolved in a higher synthesis. Pushkin leaves the relationship between madness, truth, and violence unresolved in *The Bronze Horseman.* However, the terrible potential of that explosive mixture, which I shall explore in the following chapters, is never left in doubt.

CHAPTER 5

Madness and the River

Since Evgenii, Peter, and the river are linguistically, narratologically, and thematically woven into an intricate web, madness inevitably binds the protagonists to one another. The river is not literally mad. But metaphorically it is as mad as Evgenii. In ancient Greek culture, "the image of madness" is that of "a black, angry, inner flood."[1] "The organic source of madness is black liquid."[2] It seethes up from below, manifesting itself in uncontrolled passion, illness, and violence. It rebels against order and tradition. It wanders from its natural course. And in some instances, as in the madness of Agave and Heracles, the madness passes, and the mad are left to contemplate the destruction they have wrought.[3] The really mad even take pleasure in it. The Neva is an anthropomorphized model of this kind of violent disorder. The madness of the river becomes even more important if one argues, as A. D. Briggs has, that nature is the ultimate reality in the poem, to which both Peter and Evgenii—and humankind in general—are equally subject.[4]

The Bad River

The narrator's relationship to the river differs significantly from his relationship to Peter and Evgenii. It progresses from condescension to admiration in the introduction, and then from sympathy to outright hostility in the *povest'*. But only when the river emerges as a dark, angry, violent, and alien force does it enter into the mad universe of the poem. This process begins with the Neva's anthropomorphization in part 2.

The introduction presents the river in its primitive and thus inferior state. It flows through a dark, fog-enshrouded, desolate place. Some Finns fish there; a few houses darken its banks; the sun is hidden. Peter gives both form and meaning to the river; he drains the marshes and encloses the river in beautiful embankments. In summer and winter the Neva becomes a playground for the city's inhabitants. More important, he transforms the Neva into the site of a flourishing empire, essential to the economic and military well-being of the entire country. The narrator presents the Neva exulting in Peter's and Russia's triumph. Sensing spring, she carries the ice out to sea—commerce can begin once again—and then rejoices [*likuet*, intro. 83].

But curiously, toward the end of the introduction, the narrator addresses the elements (here he probably intends both the river and the Gulf of Finland) as though they still might pose a threat to Peter and Russia. He advises them to forget about their captive history and to reconcile themselves to their vanquished state, warning them not to disturb Peter's eternal sleep. "Let Finnish seas, in vain spite, not trouble the eternal sleep of Peter" [*Pust' volny finskie zabudut / I shchetnoi zloboiu ne budet / Trevozhit' vechnyi son Petra!* intro. 89–91).[5] The narrator recognizes the potential enmity [*zloba*] of nature, here embodied in the sea and the river. The warning obviously concerns rebellion. Later in the poem, the words *zlobno* and *zloba* are closely associated with madness, revolt, and rebellion, both in relation to Evgenii and to the river itself. The narrator intimates that, although subjugation is unpleasant, rebellion is in vain; therefore resignation is the best policy. The river ought to enjoy its new status as the major artery of the Russian imperium. If the river heeded the narrator's warning, there would be, of course, no poem. This narrative device, which Michael André Bernstein has called "backshadowing," functions more as a warning about the future than as an evaluation of the past.[6] Since I will attempt a deconstructive interpretation of the Neva's "mad rebellion" at the end of the chapter—a sort of river rehabilitation project—I would like to present a detailed description of the narrator's negative anthropomorphization of the river against which such a deconstruction must be argued.

In the beginning of part 1 of the *povest'*, the narrator seems quite sympathetic to the river. It appears as an unwilling participant in the terrible events of 1824. The rains, winds, and storm at sea are the real culprits, preventing the river from pursuing its usual course to the Gulf. It fights in vain against the elements [*no sporit' stalo ei ne v moch'*, 1.74], but, in the end, with nowhere to go, the river spills over into the city. The narrator describes the river as angry [*gnevna*], but it is not angry so much at the city or at Peter but more at the elements thwarting its path to the sea. Only when the weather worsens still further, does the river, like an infuriated wild beast, throw itself against the capital [*kak zver' ostervenias'*, 1.86].

As the narrator describes the destruction caused by the flood, his imaginative sympathies seem to change, and he begins invidiously to anthropomorphize the actions of the Neva. Now it has initiated a siege [*osada*, 1.95], an assault [*pristup*, 1.95]! The angry, or malicious, waves [*zlye volny*, 1.95] are likened to thieves climbing through windows to plunder. The flood does not even leave the dead in peace, hurtling their coffins through the streets. When the flood "attacks" Evgenii, the narrator himself begins to "rage" at the river, treating it more and more personally and negatively. In the end, it seems to be a villain whose greatest pleasure is the suffering it has visited on the inhabitants of the city. It is greedy and voracious [*zhadnyi val*, 1.134],[7] indignant, furious, rebellious, and resentful.

At the beginning of part 2 of the *povest'*, the transformation of the river from a jewel in the Russian crown to a villain and beast is virtually complete. The Neva recedes only because it has become sated with destruction and exhausted by its impudent fury. As it retreats, it admires its ravage. The narrator continues to employ the variants of the root *zlo* [angry, malicious, spiteful, angry) to characterize its behavior. Thus, on line 2.6, the Neva is described as a villain, a criminal [*zlodei*] guilty of rapine, rape, and murder. Continuing to employ the motifs of siege and plunder, the narrator portrays the river as replete with the triumph of its victory, a contrasting allusion to the introduction in which Russia is shown celebrating her victory over her enemies. The river, once a participant in these triumphs, now, like a fallen angel, revels in destruction.

INTRODUCTION (Russia)

Or Russia again
Celebrates victory over her enemies

[*Ili* POBEDU *nad vragom*
Rossiia snova TORZHETSVUET] (intro. 79–80)

PART TWO (The River)

> But, full of the ecstasy of victory
> The angry waves still boiled over.
>
> [*No,* TORZHESTVOM POBEDY *polny*
> *Eshche kipeli zlobno volny.*] (2.20–23)

The poem's last references to the river continue in this vein, emphasizing its wantonness, rapaciousness [*volny khishchnye,* 2.148], rage, anger, and rebelliousness [*buntuia zlobno vkrug nego,* 2.149]. At the end, the Neva's destruction of Parasha's little house is described as the river's play or sport. The flood, "in its play, had carried there the frail little house" [*Tuda, igraia, zaneslo / Domishko vetkhii,* 2.214–15].

Madness and the River: Peter

The negative anthropomorphization of the river brings it eerily closer, by word association alone, to the other protagonists of the drama. The more the river is associated with darkness, rage, fury, fire, resentment, revenge, and revolt, the more it emerges as a player on the fields of madness and the more it has in common, metaphorically, with those on whom it has the most lasting devastating effect: Petersburg (Peter) and Evgenii. Lines 2.20–25, referring back to the victory of the Neva cited above, emphasize an unmistakable convergence of the river and Peter—or the Bronze Horseman—and thus implicitly link rebellion and madness with Peter himself.

THE RIVER

> But, full of the ecstasy of victory
> The angry waves still seethed,
> As though beneath them smoldered a fire.
> Still covered by foam
> The Neva breathed heavily
> As though it were a steed returned from battle.
>
> [*No, torzhestvom pobedy polny*

Eshche kipeli zlobno volny
Kak by pod nimi (volnami) tlel ogon'
Eshche ikh pena pokryvala
I tiazhelo Neva dyshala,
Kak s bitvy pribezhavshii kon'] (2.20–25)

PETER

What power is concealed in him!
And what fire in that steed!
Where are you galloping, proud steed?
Where will you plant your hooves?

[*Kakaia sila v nem sokryta!*
A v sem kone kakoi ogon'!
Kuda ty skachesh', gordyi kon'.
I gde opustish' ty kopyta?] (2.157–60)

In the first passage (2.20–25), occurring near the beginning of part 2, the river is subject to villainy because it exults in a victory of destruction, in contrast to its former exultant celebration of Peter and his city (intro. 83). But a radical shift occurs here. The mad, rebellious river—which is compared to a fiery steed, covered with foam, just returned from battle—is described in almost the exact terms as the Bronze Horseman (2.157–60) in the confrontation scene. The rhyme pair *ogon'-kon'* [fire-steed] in lines 2.158 and 2.159 is exactly the same pair used to describe Peter (2.221 and 2.225). Peter becomes that fiery steed, and the narrator and Evgenii both wonder whether that steed, rearing over the abyss, might not drive Russia back into the conquered river [abyss]. The "river" horse is, of course, proud [*gordyi kon'*] because of its recent triumphs in battle (2.25)—again recalling the traditional way Peter is invoked by Pushkin himself.

Should the reader interpret the association of Peter with the river—at its most destructive and rebellious state—as essentially ironic? Peter, after all, is the master builder, the epitome of sanity, the embodiment of construction, reason, and order, whereas the river, which is attempting to destroy all that Peter and his heirs have erected, constitutes the epitome of madness—that is, destruction, anger, violence, and disorder. Like the Pharaoh, Peter is a sun god, a son of Re. In Egyptian mythology, Re is generally the personification of creation, light, and order. Every day he traverses the sky in a solar bark and then each night he passes through the underworld on another solar bark to reappear in the East each morning. His journey through the sky is uneventful, but on his journey through the underworld he confronts the giant serpent, Apep (Apophis), the embodiment of darkness, evil, nonexistence, and chaos, who lives in the celestial Nile (Nun) and attempts to destroy the created world by overturning the solar boat.[8] The snake at Peter's foot, which seems to have emerged from the Neva (the Russian Nile), is certainly the same great snake, the symbol of chaos, destruction, and darkness, intent on overthrowing and destroying Peter's ship of state. So it would seem that the fire [*ogon'*] and steeds [*koni*] of the river and Peter are directed toward entirely different goals and that their association or implied comparison further enhances the image of Peter while casting the river in a still more negative light.

But if the idea of contagious madness is applied metaphorically and without irony, the association of the mad Neva with Peter may call into question the entire Petrine project, for it suggests that the madness of the rebellious river has something important in common with Peter, something Evgenii sees in his moment of greatest insight. Pushkin employs exactly the same technique here as he does in drawing Peter metaphorically into Evgenii's mad world. When Evgenii challenges the Bronze Horseman, Peter engages the world of Evgenii and chases him through the streets of Petersburg. The words the narrator applies to the mad Evgenii become attached to Peter. The association not only brings Evgenii and Peter together, it brings them together in madness; it suggests that the madness does not belong to Evgenii alone; it is a shared disease. The association of the river and Peter also brings Peter and the Neva closer together in terms of rebellion and madness.[9] Peter and the Neva share the fire and power. Peter's fire and power, the engine of the Petrine legacy, are as potentially destructive as the mad fury of the Neva. On the one hand, Peter symbolizes order, stability, and reason; on the other, like the river, he embodies the principle of rebellion, revolt, and revolution.[10]

Once Peter's actions are likened to those of the river, then the construction of Petersburg (which in the confrontation scene is implicitly attributed to a black force, the emblem of madness and violence) may be seen as an act as violent as the flood itself. Peter's imposition of his will on nature and the Russian people, historically speaking, is no less violent than the ravages of the Neva. If the narrator presents the river's actions as mad, are Peter's any less so? The river, after all, is an elemental force, whereas Peter's actions are the direct and conscious expression of his idea and will. In order to achieve his goals, Peter had to overthrow the local gods, a traditional mythic event, but he also had to create an ideology to justify his revolution. The wonder-working builder has given the semblance of order, reason, and stability to his project, but it is a project that *The Bronze Horseman* metaphorically ties to madness. This interpretation may seem contrary to the author's point of view—at least in the introduction—but it is an interpretation and a methodology strongly supported by the *povest'*, which revels in polarities that disguise convergences. Evgenii can be a docile subject and a rebel, and Peter can be the emblem of order and revolution at one and the same time. We will expand on the revolutionary Peter later, but more deconstructive work in relation to the river still needs to be done, this time with Evgenii.

Madness and the River: Evgenii

The link between Evgenii and the river also changes our perceptions about madness and rebellion. The link between Peter and the Neva suggests that Peter and his steed may be more responsible for the destruction of the flood than the river itself. But does the black force that sets Evgenii's blood on fire and compels him to challenge Peter's city, nation, and mission differ from the fire that roils the river and drives it to rebellion? Once the Neva becomes as anthropomorphized as Evgenii, it begins to partake in the same mad universe as Evgenii. Each seems to feed on the other's anger, to be infected by the fury and madness of the other.

The river is Evgenii's sole enemy until his confrontation with Peter. But, as we have seen, by the time of the confrontation, the river has changed positions with Peter and has become linguistically and thematically aligned with Evgenii. As Peter's responsibility for the catastrophe suddenly dawns in Evgenii's mad consciousness, he reacts to the statue as the river reacts to the city. Evgenii's revolt against Peter is presented as the human counterpart of the Neva's fury against Petersburg. The narrator applies the same words to Evgenii as he applies to the river at its most willful and wanton state.

His eyes filmed over with dimness,
Flame ran over his heart,
His blood seethed. Scowling he stood
Before the prideful statue
And, teeth clenched, fingers tightened into fists,
As though possessed by some black power,
"All right then, wonder-working builder!"
He whispered with a shudder of spite,
"You'll get yours . . . !"

[*Glaza podernulas' tumanom,*
Po serdtsu plamen' probezhal
Vskipela krov'. On mrachen stal
Pred gordelivym istukanom
I, zuby stisnuv, pal'tsy szhav,
Kak obuiannyi siloi chernoi,
"Dobro, stroitel' chudotvornyi!"
Shepnul on, zlobno zadrozhav,
"Uzho tebe . . . !"] (430–35)

In a passage examined earlier, the narrator describes the waves as "*covered* with foam. Underneath angrily [*zlobno*] smolders a fire" (2.22–24). At the beginning of the poem, the river is *covered* in fog. Evgenii's eyes are *covered* as though with "fog" [*tuman*]. The river calms down after it has spent its fury. Evgenii, too, calms down after his short-lived episode of rebellion. Like Evgenii, the river boils over like a cauldron, as though possessed by a dark force, as though acting contrary to its own will. The river's fury brings on Evgenii's madness, but madness eventually leads Evgenii to understand who is primarily responsible for his plight. Once Evgenii understands this connection, he becomes mad in a more profound sense. He is no longer only the poor madman [*bezumets bednyi*], a wanderer and an alien (neither man nor beast), but a madman full of rage, fire, fury, malice, and black bile.

We need to be objective. The link between Evgenii and the Neva in terms of madness and rebellion may attenuate the narrator's sympathetic presentation of Evgenii's revolt against Peter. Linking Evgenii's madness to the fury of the river reinforces the negative implications of rebellion in general and of rebellion against Peter in particular (especially as Peter is incarnated in his city), for the poem focuses on the destruction the Neva visits on the people. Since, in part 2 of the confrontation scene, Evgenii appears as though possessed by an alien force (a black power) over which he no longer has any control—the same power that drives the river to turn on Peter—Evgenii's association with the Neva raises questions about the nature and justification of his challenge. Is Evgenii responding primarily from the anger of madness or from the insight of madness? Is he responding from "mad clarity"—"his thoughts suddenly become completely clear" [*proiasnilis´ mysli*]—or from "a dark force" [*siloi chernoi*]?

But if *The Bronze Horseman* suggests the underside of Evgenii's rebellion by establishing its link with the river, a sort of guilt by metaphoric association, can the reader reach the exact opposite conclusion: that the poem presents the river's situation more positively *because* of its link with a sympathetically drawn Evgenii? To see the river more positively, however, obviously requires some deconstruction in light of the narrator's rather explicit derogation of the Neva after the flood. Can an argument be made for a less harsh assessment of the river—in terms of madness and rebellion—against the explicit position of the narrator?

I would like to say a few words here about the value of a deconstructive approach to the river. Such an approach is especially useful here because it engenders defensible and provocative conclusions about the madness of the Neva at odds with the points of view of the omniscient narrator and implied author, which are virtually identical in *The Bronze Horseman*. The reader may need to resist the narrator's point of view the more insistently and unambivalently it is pushed. Deconstruction is not subjective speculation; it places reasonable historical and hermeneutic limits on interpretation. To be sure, in some subjective theories of reading, as exemplified by Norman Holland and Stanley Fish, readers, depending on their individual idiosyncrasies or the interpretative community to which they belong, may arrive at interpretations that the "author" could never have imagined. The classic example is Fish's experiment, in which he asked his class on religious poetry to come up with an interpretation of a poem, which, in reality, was a list of linguists' names left on the blackboard from his previous class.[11] Ideally deconstruction arrives at conclusions contrary to the rhetoric of a work of art, that is, contrary to the author's putative intentions, but only when these conclusions can be reasonably defended in terms of the facts of the work. Hypothetically the author could easily have used the same facts to arrive at different conclusions. Deconstruction is historical in that it resurrects a possibility of interpretation historically available to the author. This type of interpretative move, although in a greatly attenuated form, obviously existed long before deconstruction itself.[12] Lukács practices precisely this method on Balzac, arguing that Balzac's objective presentation of the actual world always undercuts his explicitly expressed conservative and establishment worldview.

> Engels showed that Balzac, although his political creed was legitimist royalism, nevertheless inexorably exposed the vices and weakness of royalist France and described its death agony with magnificent poetic vigor. This phenomenon, references to which the reader will find more than once in these pages, may at first glance again—and mistakenly—appear contradictory. It might appear that the *Weltanschauung* and the political attitudes of serious great realists are a matter of no consequence. To a certain extent this is true. For from the point of view of the self-recognition of the present and from the point of view of history and posterity, what matters is the picture conveyed by the work; the question to what extent this picture conforms to the views of the authors is of secondary consideration.[13]

> Yet, for all his painstaking preparation and careful planning, what Balzac really did in this novel was the exact opposite of what he had set out to do: what he depicted was not the tragedy of the aristocratic estate but of the peasant smallholding. It is precisely this discrepancy between intention and performance, between Balzac the political thinker and Balzac the author of *La Comédie Humaine* that constitutes Balzac's historical greatness.[14]

We find the same approach in Tolstoy's interpretation of Chekhov's "The Darling," in which he states that Chekhov intended to malign the type of woman who is completely dominated by her passion to love but, against his own intention and will, created a memorial to the very type that he had hoped to discredit.[15] Whether Tolstoy's interpretation is correct is irrelevant, but he probably could not have come to this deconstructive conclusion had Chekhov not provided the facts and poetry from which it could reasonably be drawn. Nor was Tolstoy the only one of Chekhov's time to read the story *otherwise*.[16] Again, this is not a case of slightly different interpretations, but interpretations contrary to what a majority of readers assume to be the author's intentions.

I would like first to exclude interpretations about the river alien to Pushkin's historical consciousness, however suggestive they might be.[17] It probably would not have occurred to Pushkin—as it clearly had to Dostoevsky—that the construction of the city on the Neva was something in and of itself evil or mad. Great cities are usually built by large rivers, which makes such cities more susceptible to flooding. Even after major floods, cities do not move; they rebuild. Nor could Pushkin have conceived the idea that building a city in these marshlands was a desecration or violation of nature. He would have been familiar with romantic poetry in which nature was romanticized and the city presented as alienating and unnatural. But there were probably few, if any, romantic works in which a devastating flood, or other natural disaster, was portrayed as *nature's* (not God's) *justifiable* revenge against a city. When the narrator turns against the river after the Neva throws itself against the city and Evgenii, his attitude seems consistent with the point of view of both the introduction and the *povest'*.

The links between the river and Evgenii may suggest, however, a counter-narrative equally supported by the metaphoric facts. Because of Evgenii's compassionately told story, the metaphoric resemblance of the river to Evgenii may attenuate the narrator's invective against the Neva, making the river's fury more like Evgenii's understandable mad rebellion and less like the wanton rage of a rapacious beast.

Before Peter, the river lived an uneventful but primeval existence. Peter harnesses it, dresses it up, and transforms it into the centerpiece of his imperium. The river is warned to accept its new role, to become reconciled to it. And it does. Like Evgenii, the Neva seems to accept the same (sane) contract that Peter has made with Evgenii and the Russian people. But when Peter's wondrous structures, the embankments that direct the river out to the sea, are unable to contain the river, the Neva overflows its artificially constructed banks and inundates parts of the city. It has no other outlet. It is not a siege or attack but a natural process that has been going on from time immemorial. Obviously the river periodically overflowed its banks even before Peter's arrival: that is why the embankments were constructed in the first place.[18] The river behaves itself in good weather. It inundates the city only when it cannot sustain the pressures from the Gulf. Like Evgenii, it cracks, boils over, and explodes. But it does not "threaten" the capital. When the winds die down, it returns to its banks and behaves like a model citizen again. The narrator needs to present the river as the epitome of wanton destruction and gratuitous rebellion so that he can make a case against all rebellions against the Petrine project. The madness is not intrinsic to the river; it is imposed on the river by the narrator in order to undercut the idea of rebellion, which he can achieve by associating the Neva with a ruthless natural force, a force allied with unreason and folly—that is, madness. The narrator is a player, a participant in the story, not an objective observer.

But even granted the violence of the Neva's rebellious behavior, the river resembles Evgenii not as an initiator of violence but as a reactant. Peter has imposed his will on the people (Evgenii) and nature (the Neva) as a means of realizing his imperialistic ambitions. He altered the course of the river by draining the swamps and containing the river within embankments. Evgenii resists only in the most extreme circumstance, when he is already mad, and the Neva does so only when it can no longer fight the winds from the Gulf. They both turn on Peter when they have no other choice. The imposition of a tremendous force will lead to a concomitant buildup of a counterforce. As in an earthquake, the forces that are gradually built up over time may explode when a critical point is reached. Both Evgenii and the river have reached that point. From this perspective, the Neva is less a villain than a beneficent, mad prognosticator (seer) presaging even greater cataclysms if Peter's revolutionary will continues to direct the course of Russian society. Here the river's howling winds, the sounds of its madness, echo Evgenii's portentous words directed at Peter, "You'll get yours" [*Uzho tebe*]. The narrator's metaphoric derogations of the Neva, so different in tone and tenor from the rest of the poem, constitute an attempt to deal with his dread of violent upheavals that have convulsed Russian society in the same frequency as the terrible floods of the Neva. The extremity of his reaction is elicited partly by his unconscious sympathies with Evgenii's rebellion, but even more so by his unconscious understanding of the river's mad fury, and of the justification and inevitability of that fury. In reviling the river, the narrator takes a stand against the mad violence that he knows is not arbitrary, wanton, or gratuitous, but arises directly out of the legacy he loves and wishes to preserve. The river in flood epitomizes the forces jeopardizing Peter's creation. It is the epitome of madness, of the terrible black force by which all the protagonists are possessed. The narrator's vilification of the river is called forth by his own ambivalence about Peter and rebellion. He must completely discredit the forces of violence in order to overcome his own temptation to listen to their rebellious, siren song, to present even more sympathetically the challenge of his poor madman, a call that, if heeded, might well destroy all that he loves.

In the end, however, the narrator's rhetoric may work against itself. Does turning the river into a ruthless villain not undermine his attempt to vilify the forces of rebellion? In fact, it gives the reader who is reading against the grain—or reading deconstructively—reason not only to see the justice of Evgenii's rebellion but to listen to the voice of the river more attentively, and perhaps pay greater heed to the justifications of an even more violent and madder rebellion.

CHAPTER 6

Madness and the Tsar

The Bronze Horseman presents Peter mostly as the target of madness. His monument is the target of Evgenii's mad warning and his city the target of the river's fury. And in some way he certainly is the cause of both. But is Peter mad himself? Is his city a mad enterprise? His mission? His idea? In the ode, Peter, his city, and his idea are presented as the quintessence of reason, order, light, progress—sanity. He is the master-builder, the antithesis of darkness, chaos, disorder, sloth—madness. To what extent does the *povest'* show that Peter has been infected by the madness of Evgenii and the Neva? Does the *povest'* necessarily imply that there was a mad Peter not only before the flood but even before the building of the capital, when the city was still only an idea in Peter's head?

Though Pushkin's most prominent successors subjected Peter to a multifaceted critical assault,[1] portraying him as cruel and barbaric, even as the personification of evil, an Antichrist, they rarely presented Peter and the city—or his idea of Russia embodied in Petersburg and its institutions—as insane.[2] For Gogol, Tolstoy, and Bely, Petersburg was the home of a soulless bureaucracy and the source of every imaginable evil. It was only Dostoevsky who fully associated Petersburg metonymically and metaphorically with madness. In *The Bronze Horseman*, Peter is clearly not insane in the same way as Evgenii or Germann. First, we know that the historical Peter was not clinically insane. Second, the historical Peter, in contrast to his role in *Poltava*, appears personally in *The Bronze Horseman* in only the first two stanzas. In the first stanza, only the first three lines, in which Peter looks over the Neva, present Peter directly; the remaining lines of the stanza describe the desolate riverscape that Peter observes. The second stanza conveys Peter's plans for founding a city by the river. By the third stanza, one hundred years have already passed. In *Poltava*, the phrase "one hundred years have passed" [*proshlo sto let*] comes only at the very end. In *The Bronze Horseman*, from the very beginning Peter is replaced by Petersburg and the realization of his idea in and through the city. When Evgenii threatens the Bronze Horseman, he is obviously not threatening the historical Peter but everything distilled in the idea of Petersburg. "Peter" is shorthand for discussing all aspects of Peter's legacy at one and the same time. Otherwise, of course, it would make no sense to speak of a mad Peter.[3] "Peter's" madness thus must differ significantly from that of Evgenii, a character in a *povest'* who goes clinically insane.

Just as the river is no person like Evgenii but nevertheless participates metonymically and metaphorically in the idea of madness, so does Peter, not as the historical figure but as the Bronze Horseman. The "imperturbability" of the Bronze Horseman is a metaphor having no more metonymic grounding in the poem than Peter's "perturbability"—his pursuit of Evgenii through the streets of Petersburg. Peter pursues the defenseless and terrified Evgenii through the very same streets as the enraged, insane river did the previous November. Thus, metaphorically, Peter participates in the action in the same way as the river does, and accordingly becomes subject to the same types of interpretative strategies. Once the poem passes beyond Peter's original conception—the idea [*duma*], the Word from which Petersburg and Russia are created—the concept of madness begins to find fertile ground and closely parallels, both in imagery and plot, the madness in which Evgenii and the Neva are entangled.

Neither the ode nor the *povest'* begins in madness. Like Peter at the beginning of the ode, Evgenii seems to be the embodiment of sanity, reconciling himself to his situation and laying out a rational plan by which he may attain his goal of peace and family happiness. Likewise, the river "accepts" the contract (glory, light, order, and beauty) that Peter offers in return for obedience. In the ode the Neva flows orderly and majestically in its magnificent embankments; only in the *povest'* does it emerge from its banks and turn on the city. Neither Peter nor Peter's idea need be mad in its conception for it to replicate years after, on a metaphoric and metonymic level, the madness of Evgenii and the Neva.

Peter enters the madness text through his association with Evgenii and the river, especially through the images of violence, anger, darkness, and gloom—the traditional metaphoric vehicles for madness. These associations all come to a head in the great confrontation scene when Evgenii threatens the monument. Evgenii links all the wonders of Peter's creation with those dark forces of madness that possess him even as he utters the threat, the same dark forces previously associated with the fury and rapine of the mad river. The association seems to take Evgenii by surprise, completely overwhelming him. Pushkin, however, prepares the reader for this surprise both linguistically and thematically, first through the contrasting imagery of the ode and the *povest'*, and then through the action and inaction of the Bronze Horseman itself/himself.

Peter and Darkness

The *povest'* presents Peter as a god of the night, a black power who hovers over his darkened city like an autumn chill. The power of this image is magnified by its stark contrast with the image of Peter in the ode where he is presented as a virtual sun god. When Peter first stands by the shores of the Neva, there is only darkness and desolation. As though by divine order, Peter dispels the darkness over the forest and the deep, and a beautiful and wondrous metropolis arises proudly from the swamp, a vibrant city of wondrous light and sound [*blesk i shum*].

When the narrator cautions the elements to subordinate themselves to Peter, he seems to be warning them against something that is self-evident, for it would be the height of insanity to return to the past, when the land and sea were desolate, when only a few poor fishermen could eke our their living by the riverbanks. Just one day after the floodwaters of 1824 recede, the sun shines brightly over the city.

> The ray of morning
> From behind tired, pale clouds
> Glinted over the silent capital
> And found no more traces
> Of yesterday's calamity; with purple cape
> Already covered was the mischief,
> Everything settled back into the former order.

> [*Utra luch*
> *Iz-za ustalykh, blednykh tuch*
> *Blesnul nad tikhoiu stolitsei*
> *I ne nashel uzhe sledov*
> *Bedy vcherashnei; bagrianitsei*
> *Uzhe prikryto bylo zlo*
> *V poriadok prezhnii vse voshlo.*] (2.69–75)

Not only is the capital quiet after the storm, it shows few traces of the devastation. The sun god reclaims his realm. The events of the *povest'* replicate the ode in which the elements have their day and then must cede to Peter and light. The sun remains the dominant reality; the storm goes off to sea; the river returns to its embankments. The Neva's madness spends itself only to give way to Peter's order. In Egyptian myth the sun god, Re, is attacked every night by his great foe, the serpent Apep, a demon of chaos and darkness, who inhabits the nocturnal abyss. And, every night, Apep is slain but, since he is immortal, he must be killed (defeated) over and over again as the sun passes through the underworld, especially at sunset and sunrise.[4] Only occasionally does Apep enjoy success, which is evident during the outbreak of storms and the roiling of the Nile. Even his greatest success, however, the swallowing of the sun (an eclipse), is rare and short-lived.[5]

But in the *povest'* section of *The Bronze Horseman*, though there is light, it is a dim reflection of the light of the ode. For when the morning rays flash out from the pale and emaciated storm clouds, a very different Petersburg emerges. It is not the Petersburg that conforms to Peter's original idea. Now that the streets are free [*svobodnye*], the people walk about with cold indifference [*s svoim beschustviem kholodnym / Khodil narod*, 2:77–78]. They seem to have been infected by the autumnal cold [*khlad*] of the first line of the *povest'* and by a darkened Petersburg. Instead of the capital's noisy gaiety, an atmosphere conducive to literary creativity and parades on the field of Mars, bureaucratic Petersburg returns to work. The hardy tradesman is already attempting to recoup his losses at his neighbor's expense. Pushkin also includes a sardonic pastiche of the verses of the "poet" Khvostov, beloved of the heavens, "singing in immortal lines of the misfortune of the Neva's banks" (2:87–88). Instead of the celebration of the ode—of the melting of the ice and the victory of Russia—the return to the previous order culminates in hack verse about the flood.

The poem suggests a diminution in both the quality and quantity of light.

But in the *povest'*, even this diminished light is the exception. Here we must distinguish, in the formalist sense, between story [*fabula*]—the chronological sequence of events—and plot [*siuzhet*]—the actual (artistic) ordering of events in the text itself. In the story [*fabula*], the flood and its attendant darkness occupy only one day. But in terms of the plot [*siuzhet*], the percentage of calm versus stormy days is less relevant than the weather on which the narrative focuses. For the plot, the rays of the sun and the morning purple are the exception. In the *povest'* the essential realities are flood, darkness, and night.

The poem begins in darkness, but the once hidden sun [*spriatannoe solntse*, intro. 10] soon dispels the darkness. However, the next four-fifths of the poem, that is the *povest'*, takes the reader back to the beginning, to the land- and seascape that Peter saw *before* he began to implement his ideas and spread his light. The river gods and the gods of the night rule the *povest'*. The first line of the *povest'*—"Over a darkened Petrograd / November breathed an autumnal chill" [*Nad omrachennym Petergradom / Dyshal noiabr' osennim khladom*, 2.1–2]—pronounces the realm of the black power [*chernaia sila*], a return to the introduction's primeval black huts and the dark forests impenetrable to the sun: [*cherneli, nevedomyi lucham, tuman, spriatannoe solntse, t'ma lesov*, intro. 7–23]. The return to night calls up all the associations of madness: black bile, internal flood, rage, fury, and violence.

To be sure, the words *night, darkness, disorder,* and *fury* do not appear in every line of *The Bronze Horseman*. But their aura and associations do. The references to rain, wind, storm, darkness, cold, haze, and inclemency regularly appear in combination with one another, until each word evokes all the others. In the first lines of part 1, a pall of darkness combines with the breath of autumn chill. A few lines down, the darkness appears with the driving rain and the blowing and plaintively [*pechal'no*] howling winds: "It was already dark and late; / Angrily the rain beat on the window, / And the wind blew, dismally howling" [*Uzhe bylo pozdno i temno; / Serdito bilsia dozhd' v okno, / I veter dul, pechal'no voia*, 1.7–9]. The epithet *pechal'nyi* [sad or sorrowful] also occurs in the last line of the ode, the real introduction to the *povest'*: "And sorrowful will be my tale" [*Pechalen budet moi rasskaz*]. A good example of this associative technique occurs in lines 1.63–72.

Thus he mused. And sad felt
He that night, and he wished
The wind would not howl so dismally   2.65
Or the rain beat on the window
So angrily ...
His sleepy eyes
He closed at last. And here is
The foul night's fog thinning,
And pale day is already drawing up ...
That day of horror!
The Neva all night
Thrust toward the sea against the gales,

[*Tak on mechtal. I grustno bylo
emu v tu noch', i on zhelal,
Chtob veter vyl ne tak unylo
I chtoby dozhd' v okno stuchal*   2.65
*Ne tak serdito ...
Sonnye ochi
On nakonets zakryl. I vot
Redeet mgla nenastnoi nochi
I blednyi den' uzh nastaet ...
Uzhasnyi den!
Neva vsiu noch'
Rvalasia k moriu protiv buri,*] (1.63–72)

In the above passage, the word *night* occurs three times, but the passage also includes the wind, the rain, the haze, the storm, the inclement weather, and the pale and terrible day. Further, it repeats exactly such phrases as the rain beating angrily at the window and the wind howling (although now *unylo* is used, not *pechal'no*) in lines 1.7–9. In line 2.128, we once more encounter drizzling rain [*dozhd' kapal*] and again the wind wails mournfully [*veter vyl unylo*]. The day appears, but it is pale and horrible [*blednyi i uzhasnyi*, 2.170]. *Uzhasnyi*, like *pechal'no* in the previous excerpt, takes us back to the beginning of the *povest'*, where the change from ode to *povest'* is marked by the change in weather: "it was a terrible time [*byla uzhasnaia pora*, intro. 92]. The word *mgla* [haze], which also can mean gloom and darkness, and which combines here with *uzhasnyi*, *unylo*, and *nenastny*, appears only twice more in the poem. The second time (2.65) it is paired with "night" and marks the moment when Evgenii goes mad: "And he burst out laughing. / The nocturnal haze (gloom, darkness) descended upon the quaking city" [*On zakhokhotal. Nochnaia mgla / Na gorod trepetnyi soshla*, 2.65–66]. Pushkin underlines the connection between his hero's madness and the pall over the city by including both in the same line. Evgenii's madness ("He burst out laughing") occupies only the first half of the line. In midline, directly after his hero's mad laughter, the nocturnal haze (gloom, darkness) descends upon the city. It is as though one had caused the other. But these lines (2.65–66) also echo the beginning of part 1 when a cold autumnal November breathes over a darkened Petersburg (2.1–2). It is as though Evgenii's madness has eclipsed Peter's sun. The third instance of *mgla* (2.155) again appears in close proximity with *uzhasnyi*, but this time it refers to Peter, who is horrifying in the surrounding darkness (gloom) [*uzhasen on v okrestnoi mgle*, 2.155].

Likewise, *mrachnyi* [morose, gloomy, dark, somber] and its variants are applied equally to Evgenii, the Neva, Petersburg, and Peter himself. "He [Evgenii] became somber" [*On mrachen stal*, 2.173]; "It was somber [in Petersburg] [*Mrachno bylo*, 2.127]; the somber wave [of the Neva] [*mrachnyi val*, 2.122]; "With his [Peter's] brazen head in the darkness" [*Vo mrake mednoiu glavoi*, 2.152].[6] The words *mgla* and *mrak* appear only four times in the entire text.

With the repetition only of a few words, a web of darkness descends upon the city and traps everything it touches. The narrator (and/or Evgenii) expresses his awe at Peter's power [*sila*], but now it is by association a dark power, the same dark power ["black power," *sila chernaia*, 2.176] used to describe Evgenii's madness and the fury of the dark and gloomy Neva [*mrachnyi val*, 2.122]. Peter, the symbol of light in the ode, has become the most terrifying example of the dark power of madness that possesses Evgenii and spurs him to rebellion [*Nad omrachennym Petrogradom / Dyshal noiabr' osennim khladom*, 2.155; *uzhasen on v okrestnoi mgle*, 2.1–2].

This gloom reaches its fitting conclusion in the last lines of the poem. The first lines of the *povest'* begin with a cold, autumn wind blowing over a darkened Petersburg. The poem ends with Evgenii's cold [*khladnyi*] corpse. As the fool in *King Lear* remarks: "This cold night will turn us all to fools and madmen." The *povest'* presents the sun in eclipse. But the poem as a whole may really be less about the absence of the sun (Peter) than about the *presence* of Peter as a black sun[7]—a traditional metaphor for madness and melancholia. A prince of darkness, untouched by the storm and the river, Peter seems even more powerful in the dark than in the light. One hundred years after the founding of Petersburg, he presides over a city for which darkness has become the most fitting metaphor. Like an inverted Moses, with an outstretched hand, the Russian Pharaoh imposes darkness on his own land.

> And the Lord said unto Moses, Stretch out thine hand toward heaven, that there may be darkness over the land of Egypt, even darkness which may be felt.

> And Moses stretched forth his hand toward heaven; and there was a thick darkness in all the land of Egypt three days. (Ex.10:21–22)

Indeed, the most disturbing aspect of the Bronze Horseman throughout the storm is Peter's outstretched arm, which turns into the symbol of oppression and, by biblical association, darkness. The image is reinforced in the poem's only virtually identical lines.

> The idol on the bronze steed *stands* with outstretched arm [*Stoit s prostertoiu rukoiu / kumir na bronzovom kone*, 1.162–63]

> The idol on the bronze steed *sat* with outstretched arm [*Kumir s prostertoiu rukoiu / sidel na bronzovom kone*, 2.142–43]

The very same image emerges once more, even more ominously, at the end of the confrontation scene, when the Bronze Horseman chases Evgenii through Petersburg on the anniversary of the flood. It is the last image the text presents of the Bronze Horseman, and it represents the final blow to the already deranged Evgenii. It is the only picture of the final terror—most of which is conveyed in sound images—and it clearly refers back to Evgenii's initial terror, when he was trapped on one of the guardian lions.[8] The outstretched hand, along with the wind and the rain, bring back the events of the preceding year and lead to Evgenii's insight and rebellion.

It seemed 180
To him that the dread tsar's face,
Instantly aflame with wrath,
Was slowly turning ...
And he runs down the empty square
And hears behind him, 185
As if it were the rumbling of thunder,
A heavily ringing gallop
Over the quaking pavement
And twilit by the pallid moon,
Arm reaching forth on high, 190
There speeds after him the Bronze Horseman
Upon the clangorously galloping steed;
And all night, wherever the wretched madman
Might turn his steps,
Behind him everywhere the Bronze Horseman 195
Was galloping with heavy clatter.

[*Pokazalos'* 180
Emu, chto groznovo tsaria,
Mgnovenno gnevom vozgoria,
Litso tikhon'ko obrashchalos' ...
I on po ploshchadi pustoi
Bezhit i slyshit za soboi, 185
Kak budto groma grokhotan'e
Tiazhelo-zvonkoe skakan'e
Po potriasennoi mostovoi.
I, ozaren lunoiu blednoi,
Prostershi ruku v vyshine, 190
Za nim nesetsia Vsadnik Mednyi
Na zvonko-skachushchem kone;
I vo vsiu noch' bezumets bednyi,
Kuda stopy on obrashchal,
Za nim povsiudu Vsadnik Mednyi 195
S tiazhelym topotom skakal.] (2.180–96)

As we recall, Radishchev wrote: "the outstretched arm shows that the great man, having eradicated the vices frustrating his efforts, now offers protection to all those worthy of being called his children." Evgenii is worthy of being called one of Peter's children, but the mighty arm provides no protection. The sounds tell him of the horse's presence; the mighty arm hovers over him as the weapon that will crush him, as it will crush all those frustrating the tsar's will.[9] But protection, or lack thereof, represents only a small part of the irony encoded into the biblical allusion to the outstretched hand.

In the panegyric literature devoted to the tsar, Peter is likened not only to God but also to Moses. It is God, Moses, and Aaron who figure in the references to the outstretched hand in Exodus and Deuteronomy. In Exodus, the outstretched arm is less a protective shield than a weapon, a means of delivering the children of Israel by striking at the evil Pharaoh. The attacks are directed at the waters of Egypt, primarily the great Nile, the source of Egyptian life and civilization. God, Moses, and Aaron stretch out their hands, smiting the waters of Egypt, infesting them with frogs, and then turning them to blood. Later Moses stretches out his hand to part the waters for the Jews to escape the Egyptians and then to drown the Egyptians in a terrible flood. Since the water is presented as the enemy of the Israelites, only when the God of Israel and his servants, Moses and Aaron, control the great river can the misfortunes of the Jews be reversed. In *The Bronze Horseman,* the tsar acknowledges that he cannot control the elements. The people see the flood as a sign of God's anger and expect punishment, for the elements are God's means of punishing the wicked: *Zrit bozhii gnev i kazni zhdet.*

This heuristic biblical analogy raises important questions about Peter's path. For Peter's eighteenth-century supporters, Peter, a modern-day Moses, promises liberation from the bondage of intellectual obscurantism and economic and military backwardness. In the poem, however, he seems more like the Pharaoh. His mighty outstretched hand does not return his people to their native land but forcibly removes them from their homes to a dark place on a forbidding river, where they perish attempting to realize the mad idea of another "wonder-working builder." The mighty arm stretches out to destroy not only foreign enemies but also all those perceived as impeding the tsar's vision and idea. There is much conflation here. Peter is not only a Pharaoh who cannot save his people from the flood, but he is also a ruler, who, in the name of liberation, and with an outstretched arm, unleashes terror against his own people.

> Or hath God assayed to go and take him a nation from the midst of another nation, by temptations, by signs, and by wonders, and by war, and by a mighty hand, and by a stretched out arm, and by great terrors. (Deut. 4:34)[10]

In every confrontation that Evgenii has with the Bronze Horseman, the outstretched arm rises above him, evoking terror and horror [*uzhas*], threatening to crush him as any other enemy of the state. The Petrine plot begins as an idea of liberation and enlightenment but concludes as a story of darkness and terror, transforming the biblical narrative into a tale of a new bondage and exile.

It is sometimes thought that *The Bronze Horseman* has no frame: Nothing sets off the ode in the beginning and nothing sets off the *povest'* at the end. The poem seems to set two monoliths side by side, ode and *povest'*, with two opposing points of view, one from above and imperially oriented, the other close and existentially engaged. But another view emerges if we pay close attention to the imagery that opens and closes the poem. Before Peter came, the text presents the reader with a poor Finn, a stepson of nature, a fisherman [*rybolov*] with a wretched skiff [*bednyi cheln*] and threadbare net [*vetkhii nevod*], eking out a living by a shore washed by desolate waves [*pustynnye volny*] and dotted with little black huts [*cherneli izby*]. Peter and Petersburg displace him. Nothing of him remains.

At the end, Evgenii, a stepson of Peter, is also displaced. All that remains of him is a cold corpse carted away for an anonymous burial. A fisherman [*rybak*] returns to visits a small desolate island [*ostrov malyi, pustynnyi ostrov*]. The adjectives return with new partners. *Vetkhii* in the "threadbare net" [*vetkhii nevod*] of the Finn now describes the "dilapidated little house" [*vetkhii domishko*]. The net [*nevod*] returns with the fisherman, just without the epithet. *Pustynnyi* [desolate], employed to describe the waves at the beginning of the ode, now modifies the little island in the Neva [*pustynnyi ostrov malyi*]. *Chernyi* [black] appears as a verbal descriptor [*cherneli izby zdes' i tam*; "black houses appeared here and there"] characterizing the houses of the Finns. It also describes the last abode of Evgenii, which is likened to a black bush [*chernyi kust*]. Does this all not suggest a history radically different from the one at the heart of the Petrine mythology of manifest destiny? Is the Peter who stands at the end really "Peter the Great, who in himself is universal history"?[11]

To answer these questions we need to go back to the difference between story [*fabula*] and plot [*siuzhet*]. From the point of view of story, the flood is a temporary setback. The Petrine project as the inexorable principle of universal history cannot be stopped or reversed. Moscow cannot return; much as the Finn, she has been eclipsed forever. The story thus tells a tale of destiny. It embodies an implied historicism, merely replacing Napoleon with Peter the Great as the embodiment of the World Spirit. All this is undoubtedly part of Pushkin's poem. But the plot, with its similar metaphoric and metonymic beginnings and endings, suggests a different view of time, especially if Evgenii and the Neva constitute the existential realities of the poem. In the end, Evgenii becomes at one with the Finn; and, as Briggs implies, the river merely plays a waiting game with Peter whom it must inevitably defeat.[12] The Bronze Horseman may then suggest less an eternal, third Rome than the "colossal wreck" of Ozymandias.

> My name is Ozymandias, King of Kings,
> Look on my Works, ye Mighty, and despair!
> Nothing beside remains. Round the decay
> Of that colossal Wreck, boundless and bare
> The lone and level sands stretch far away.[13]

For the story and for a progressive history, nothing remains of Evgenii. For the plot, and for an anti-history, nothing may remain of Peter. As we shall see in chapter 8, this resembles, in some respects, the vision that Dostoevsky took from *The Bronze Horseman* and bequeathed to his literary and cultural heirs—a Petersburg sinking back into the swamps, with nothing remaining but the Ozymandian statue of Peter, and a Russia waking up from a mad dream, the dream of Peter. From the point of view of Peter's project [*siuzhet*], this ahistorical plot [*siuzhet*]—which has firm linguistic, thematic, structural, and emotional foundation in the text—is the antithesis of light, reason, and order; it is the epitome of darkness, folly, and chaos: in a word, madness.

We need to distinguish, however, Dostoevskian and cyclical views of time from the view of time that can be extrapolated from the plot of *The Bronze Horseman*. The late Dostoevsky's view, despite appearances, is also historical; it just differs from the Petrine model. Seeing Petersburg as a historical aberration—Russian history off track—he could interpret the city's demise as the precondition for Russia's return to her proper historical path. Nor do similarities of beginnings and endings necessarily imply a grim cyclical notion of time. Cyclical views of time can convey remarkable optimism. In Ancient Egyptian culture, death is neither a final point nor nonexistence; it is the means for renewing life. The sun's journey to the underworld, where it "dies" every day, is a precarious one, but it embarks on the journey so that it can be daily reborn and rejuvenated, saving it from old age and decrepitude. *The Bronze Horseman*, however, presents a much more complicated scenario. Petersburg is not rejuvenated when the sun rises the day after the storm. Superimposed over the Petrine plot, a mad ahistorical plot emerges, a "reversionary" one, in which, despite the movement of chronological time, the existential reality not only has not changed, it has reverted to its beginnings, when Evgenii and the Finn are one. The eighteenth century saw Peter forming Russia from primordial chaos, extracting her from the state of nonbeing and bestowing existence upon her. *The Bronze Horseman* does not deny Peter and history, but its plot simultaneously also tells a different story—from the Petrine point of view, perhaps even a mad story—one that suggests a return to the original chaos that Peter saw when he first looked out over the Neva and became possessed of his terrible idea.

Peter Enters the Mad World

The last section examined the metaphoric connections of Peter (understood as monument, historical figure, city, idea, and mission) with violence and darkness—the traditional metaphors for madness. In the following section I explore how these textual figures associated with madness enter into the metonymic structure of the text, that is, how they become part of the plot, psychological or supernatural or both. Again I will be dealing not solely with Peter the Great as the historical figure but with the whole complex of issues and symbols embodied in the Bronze Horseman, including how all these are refracted in the imagination of the hero. Can the black flow of madness, the force that possesses Evgenii and the river, also be found in Peter, not only as an unintended cause of madness in others but also as an embodiment of a mad principle, *ab initio*?

In Greek tragic literature, madness is invariably associated with anger, violence, fury, and vengeance, that is, with loss of reason and control. Until the last confrontation, however, Peter remains stolid and imperturbable through the flood and Evgenii's transformation. Evgenii's threat, "You'll get yours" [*Uzho tebe*], is perhaps an attempt to rattle Peter's infuriating calm, to make him wax angry, to make him act as though he, too, were mad.[14] Evidently a mad horseman—or a mad god—chasing Evgenii through the streets of Petersburg is preferable to a deist presence, the spirit of universal history, undisturbed by the madness revolving around him. Moreover, in Evgenii's mad imagination, when Peter descends from his pedestal, responding, in kind, to his threat with passionate anger, Peter enters into Evgenii's mad world along with the river, performing an act contrary to his idea. Nothing could be madder than for Peter to abandon his position of stoic imperturbability and pursue an insignificant clerk through the streets of Petersburg.[15] Thus, both in the beginning and the end, Peter is part of a mad text. He infects the river and Evgenii with madness, and they, in turn, infect him.

> It seemed
> To him that the dread tsar's face,
> Instantly aflame with wrath
> Was slowly turning ...
>
> [*Pokazalos'*
> *Emu, chto groznovo tsaria,*
> *Mgnovenno gnevom vozgoria,*
> *Litso tikhon'ko obrashchalos'* ...] (2.180–83)

The anger of the Bronze Horseman, of course, differs significantly from Evgenii's, because, among other things, it is refracted through the historical record and Pushkin's other work about Peter. Certainly the aspect of Peter's personality most commented on was his propensity for outbursts of anger. Intimates of the tsar as well as foreign diplomats all report the terror and horror they experienced during Peter's fits of rage. "Still, the fictional image of Peter the Great would not have been complete without added glimpses of his acting under the influence of overpowering rage, not a momentary one but one lasting over a period of several weeks and culminating in his beheading a number of the Streltsy with his own hands and forcing his courtiers to do likewise."[16] And one wonders whether Pushkin was acquainted with Jacob von Stählin's accounts (96 and 83) of Peter's wrath, some of which eerily recall the confrontation between Peter and Evgenii.

> Finally, Peter had sudden outbursts of anger which, though not aggravated by convulsions, would petrify with fear those who had the misfortune of provoking them. Stählin reports that the architect Leblond, having incurred the redoubtable Tsar's terrible wrath and been threatened with his staff, was so frightened that he took to bed and died shortly afterwards (no. 90); and that an apprentice who had pulled Peter's hair while putting on his famous working cap fled in terror when the Tsar drew a dagger and brandished it over the culprit's head. *The man spent many years wandering about and living from hand to mouth before he dared to return at the news of the Emperor's death.*[17]

It was obviously dangerous to be in the presence of the giant autocrat at such times.[18] The encomiastic literature of the eighteenth century glosses over this aspect of Peter, with the occasional exception of Peter's perfectly appropriate wrath in war. Martial anger directed against the enemy rather than against one's allies (the wrath of Achilles almost dooms the Greeks in the Trojan War) is essential for victory. *Poltava* and the introduction to *The Bronze Horseman* do not focus on Peter's anger at all. In *Poltava*, Peter is magnanimous with the leaders of the defeated Swedes, and, even in war, he seems completely calm and in control. The introduction to *The Bronze Horseman* creates an impersonal, godlike presence for Peter. One hundred years later he exists only in spirit and mind through his city, his laws, and his imperialistic legacy. In the introduction, Pushkin chooses as exalted an image of Peter as he can imagine. In Greek mythology, anger motivates most of the gods' actions regarding mortals. And the Old Testament god is a god of anger as much as he is a god of justice and mercy. But, for Pushkin, Peter's greatness is not so much in the historical Peter but in the Word made city, law, and empire. Peter's calm, immobility, and imperturbability undergird his godlike unchanging presence, his "refusal," as it were, to enter into "private history."[19] He is above anger.

But as soon as Peter waxes angry at Evgenii, he leaves the world of the encomiastic literature—and the world of the introduction—and reverts to a specific instantiation of his historical personality, the wrathful tsar. History and *petites histoires* take the place of myth. Peter is a man like Evgenii, possessed by the same forces and subject to irascibility like any other man. He enters a world where he is vulnerable to the same infectious forces of madness as Evgenii and the Neva.

When Evgenii threatens the Bronze Horseman, he is responding to Russian history possessed by a dark, pagan power [*chernaia sila*]—perhaps by an insane idea that began in darkness and never fully emerged from it. The flood shows that truth manifests itself fully only in disaster. Only in its fury does the Neva reveal the abyss over which the city and Peter's idea are precariously perched. Similarly Evgenii sees the truth not when he is a law-abiding civil servant with hope and faith in the future but only when he loses everything and goes mad. Peter's goal, of course, is to subordinate and tame the abyss. The city—a monument to order, reason, harmony, and control—gives the impression of its victory over the forces that once threatened it. But what if all this, as Dostoevsky came to think, was but a veneer that covered up a much darker and truer reality: that the city itself was the mad vision of Peter, who imposed that vision upon the place and the people who were transplanted there, and, in the process, unleashed the very forces he had hoped to contain.

The great confrontation scene brings the Neva, Evgenii, and Peter together. All three seem to converge metaphorically as they engage one another. Each is enmeshed in the same images of darkness, anger, violence, reprisal, chaos, and disorder. All seem possessed by a dark power [*Kak obuiannyi siloi chernoi*, 2.177]. The word *sila* [power or force] is used only three times in the entire poem—once with the elements: "But by the *force* of the winds from the Gulf" [*No siloi vetrov ot zaliva*, 1.79]; once with Peter: "What *power* is concealed in it [his brow]" [*Kakaia sila v nem sokryta!* 2.157]; and once with Evgenii: "as though possessed by a dark power" [*Kak obuiannyi siloi chernoi*, 2.176]. In section 1 of the confrontation scene, the power or might [*sila*] is associated with Peter. It is the power behind the will, mind, daring, and ambition [*duma, sila, ogon', gde ty opustish' kopyta*] responsible for the founding of the city. But this figure appears terrible to Evgenii and the narrator, whose consciousnesses here are fused by *erlebte Rede*. "How terrible he appears in the surrounding gloom" [*Uzhasen on v okrestnoi mgle*, 2.155].

The word *uzhas* is just as significant here as in the passages discussed earlier. It introduces the *povest'* and sets its tone of horror: "It was a horrible time" [*Byla uzhasnaia pora*, intro. 92]; "It was a terrible day" [*Uzhasnyi den'!* 1.71]. It then occurs five times in the next one hundred or so lines (2.40–156). The first of these instances describes what Evgenii sees when he arrives at the place where Parasha's house used to stand: "A horrible sight. He could not recognize [it]!" [*Uznat' ne mozhet. Vid uzhasnyi!* 2.40]. The next is Evgenii's recalling of the "past horror" [*proshlyi uzhas*, 2.132]. The word also describes the effects that the events had on Evgenii's mind: "Alas, his confused mind could not bear these terrible shocks" [*Uvy! ego smiatennyi um / Protiv uzhasnykh potriasenii / Ne ustoial*, 2.89–92]. In lines 2.94–95 Evgenii is described as "silent but full of horrible thoughts" [*Uzhasnykh dum bezmolvno polon*, 95–96], an almost direct echo of the beginning of the ode where Peter is described as "full of great thoughts" [*polon velikikh dum*, intro. 2]. But in the *povest'* we have a different Peter. To be sure, Peter still has a great idea [*duma*] imprinted on his brow, but it is a Peter who is now horrifying because of it. This is when Evgenii, in the light of his madness, understands the madness of Peter's idea, specifically its realization in the idea-city Petersburg. Peter is possessed by a terrible black power, and his creation, Petersburg, is the monument to that power. The text performs this association through rhyme and metonymy.

> As though possessed by a dark power
> "All right, wonder-working builder!"

> [*Kak obuiannyi siloi chernoi*
> "*Dobro, stroitel' chudotvornyi!*"]

The rhyme words comment on, and supplement, each other emotionally and semantically. Their power is further enhanced by the consonance of the words directly preceding them: *siloi, stroitel'* [power, builder]. The ungrammatical rhyme pair *chernoi* [black] and *chudotvornyi* [miracle- or wonder-creating] directly associates Peter's idea with a black force—and thus madness. Peter becomes the great builder who has created his wondrous works with the aid of a black power—and, even more ominously, he becomes the "creator" of "darkness." For Evgenii, the wonder-working builder and the dark force have become identical. Peter's power [*sila*], fire [*ogon'*], will [*volia*], and idea [*duma*] are all manifestations of this force. It is what makes Peter rear Russia over the abyss. But ultimately it is also the power that possesses the river and Evgenii. Evgenii can recognize the madness of the idea, because, being in the thrall of madness himself, he is moved by a similar dark force. He has become in some ways like Peter. The tsar, the river, and Evgenii are all locked in a mad embrace. For Pushkin, this is the tragedy of all rebellions: Evgenii's, the Neva's—and Peter's.

Greek tragedy and culture often associate the undertaking of rash and dangerous ventures with the behavior of the mad. For Evgenii, Petersburg is the epitome of such a mad enterprise. It can only end in what, for the Greeks, was the most heinous and revolting of all deeds—the murder of one's own comrades or children. And so the mad Bronze Horseman pursues Evgenii through the streets of Petersburg, just as the mad waters of the Neva had pursued the inhabitants of the city one year earlier. And therein lies the answer to the question of the proud steed's direction and destination. In Evgenii's imagination, the horse's energies have all been diverted at him, against one of Petersburg's children, a former supporter of the Petrine idea. The idea has turned against itself. The confrontation scene presents Peter as a modern-day, deluded Hercules turning on and destroying his own children in a fit of horrific madness.[20]

CHAPTER 7

Madness, Narrator, and Author

The Narrator and Home

In the introduction the narrator figures as a character in his own production. Although he remains a disembodied presence in the *povest'*, he plays an equally crucial role there, now anthropomorphizing the river, now melding with Evgenii, now revealing a decided ambivalence toward Peter and his legacy. What is more, he is not immune to the madness he so brilliantly depicts. Madness in *The Bronze Horseman* is a contagious disease. Evgenii is infected by the madness of the river, and Peter by both the river's and Evgenii's madness. The narrator stands above neither the ode nor the *povest'*. He may not be "infected" by madness in the same way as the other actors in the poem, but he is radically altered by it.

The narrator's attitude toward Peter and his legacy seems to change in the *povest'*, as his sympathy, compassion, and distress for his hero increases. Just as Evgenii's life and ideas are transformed by his encounter with the mad fury of the river, so the narrator's point of view begins to change under the influence of Evgenii's misfortune. He begins to see truths about Peter made possible by Evgenii's madness. He also begins to see truths about himself. The more he takes Evgenii's position imaginatively, the more alienated he becomes morally and intellectually from the capital he eulogizes in the introduction. He realizes that Evgenii's alienation and madness are not aberrations but rather the inevitable consequences of Peter's idea, and that his own introduction, like countless other adulatory literary representations of the capital, participates willy-nilly in an erasure of madness, the darkest side of Peter's legacy. As a genre, the ode, like the sun, erases the traces of previous storms and floods. Evgenii's madness sows doubts in the narrator's mind about his Petersburg home.

The ideal of Greek culture is to be at home. The madman is invariably a wanderer and a vagabond, driven from his home and alienated from his environment. He is someone whose mind exists elsewhere, whose wits are not at home. In the introduction, the narrator is perfectly at home in Petersburg. He defends Peter's decision to abandon the old Russian home, Moscow, in favor of a more modern and Europeanized capital, an "imperial seat" [*tsarskii dom*], from which the tsar can defend Russia, attack his enemies, and celebrate his victories. The narrator delights in writing and reading at home in his room without benefit of a lamp during the white nights. He takes pride in the city's military might; its fantastic summers and dazzling winters; its effervescent nightlife; and the harmony and beauty of its river, palaces, gardens, and bridges. The introduction presents an unambiguously positive Peter and Petersburg, concluding with a glorification of triumphant Russia and a warning to those who stand in her way. Pushkin is working within a long cultural and literary tradition of exalting Peter and the Petrine legacy.

The *povest'*, however, tells a different tale, a tale of wandering and dispossession. The *povest'* ends not in imperial Petersburg at all but on a desolate island eerily similar to the one that Peter looked over one hundred years before. Neither Parasha nor Evgenii receives a proper burial place—the quintessential signifier of home. The flood washes away Parasha, and Evgenii's body is quickly buried right where he is found, on that desolate island in the Neva. Evgenii's dream was to be buried by his grandchildren, his Petersburg descendants, in a new Russian home. But not only are there no grandchildren, there are no descendants, no burial sites.

Unlike his hero, the narrator is literally neither mad nor homeless. But he reaches the *other* truth about Petersburg not through his own madness but through the madness of his hero. In Evgenii, madness leads to truth; and truth to the wrath, fury, and reckless challenge almost always associated with the mad. The narrator, however, need not go mad to understand and appreciate the truth Evgenii comes to only after terrible suffering. Nor does he need to become a wanderer to experience the alienation—the not-at-homeness—associated with madness. Just as the narrator uses the mad river to explore his fear of rebellion, he uses his mad hero to confront his own alienation from Petersburg, his doubts about the new Russian home. As he follows Evgenii through the streets of Petersburg, especially when he merges with his hero, he becomes, as it were, a mad wanderer himself. He need not utter Dostoevsky's "I hate you, Peter's creation" to reveal his alienation; he need not be chased by Peter to hear the hoof beats of his steed.

The narrator's disillusionment and fear come to a head in two of his interpolations in the *povest'*. The first occurs the day after the storm, when the waves have somewhat abated. Evgenii, not yet mad but fearing the worst, is on his way to find out what has happened to Parasha. The narrator, both transcribing Evgenii's thoughts and commenting in his own person, asks: "Or is all our life nothing but an empty dream, a mockery of heaven at our earth?" [*il' vsia nasha / I zhizn' nichto, kak son pustoi , / Nasmeshka neba nad zemloi?* 1.151–53].[1] In the introduction the narrator warns Russia's enemies not to disturb the eternal sleep [*son*] of Peter. The statement has no literal interpretation. In the *povest'* the word *son* is associated with Evgenii's dream [*mechta*], his ideal, which he fears he has lost in the flood. The eternal sleep, by analogy, becomes Peter's dream-idea and the realization of that idea in city and empire. When that idea is challenged, the Bronze Horseman is roused from his sleep (or meditation) to confront the threat. But in this passage it is not only Evgenii who questions whether his dream [*mechta*] is an empty dream [*pustoi son*] but the narrator himself. Along with his resignation in the presence of forces that man cannot control, the narrator's statement expresses bitter disillusionment with the Petrine project. The narrator imagines the disparity between the Petrine promise and the Petrine reality to be a mockery of the gods, with whom, of course, Peter is associated. It is now an empty dream, not an eternal one. It is not the highest manifestation of reason, light, harmony, beauty, and order, but a cruel joke and, if a cruel joke, a deception.

The narrator's comments in the famous confrontation scene are just as challenging—although admittedly more ambiguous. Here Pushkin fuses the point of view of the introduction and the *povest'*. On the one hand, the narrator expresses his admiration or awe of Peter's might, idea, fire, and daring; on the other, he experiences the same terror that his hero does in the presence of Peter, who may be leading Russia not to greater glory but into the abyss, over which his steed seems precariously perched. "How horrible he appears in the surrounding gloom" [*Uzhasen on v okrestnoi mgle!* 2.155]. The narrator projects his own doubts and fears about Peter onto his mad hero, who, because he is mad, can act on them and express them in a form that the narrator cannot and will not do in his own person.

The end of part 1 of the *povest'*, which finds Evgenii in a parodic position stranded on a guardian lion, provides an important key to understanding how much further Evgenii's alienation and madness can be seen as a metaphoric vehicle for expressing the narrator's doubts and fears about Peter, Petersburg, and the Petrine idea. The narrator again uses *erlebte Rede* simultaneously both to transcribe Evgenii's consciousness and to introduce his own point of view.

> And he, as though bewitched,
> As though on the marble riveted
> Cannot get down! About him
> Is water and nothing more!
> And, with his back turned to him,
> In unshakable eminence
> Over the tumultuous Neva
> Stands with outstretched hand
> The idol on his bronze steed.
>
> [*I on kak budto okoldovan,*
> *Kak budto k mramoru prikovan*
> *Soiti ne mozhet! Vokrug nego*
> *Voda i bol'she nichego!*
> *I obrashchen k nemu spinoiu*
> *V nekolebimoi vyshine,*
> *Nad vozmushchennoi Nevoiu*
> *Stoit s prostertoiu rukoiu*
> *Kumir na bronzovom kone.*] (1.155–63)

The reader does not know for sure whether Evgenii is aware of the Bronze Horseman; on the other hand, he seems transfixed by it. For the first time he has come to intuit Peter's responsibility for his fate. Peter could not stop the flood, and he could not protect the city's inhabitants; he reneged on his contract. Peter is now not so much the historical Peter the Great, or the narrator's imaginative construct in the introduction, but an idol [*kumir*].

But the narrator's point of view is equally devastating. For he, too, gives us a Peter different from the one in the introduction; in fact, he gives us the very same idol, referring again and again to the Bronze Horseman as *kumir* or *istukan*. In this passage of *erlebte Rede*, the narrator expresses his own point of view at the same time as he transcribes the consciousness of his hero. Infected by his hero's feelings, ideas, and situation, the narrator now also sees the great tsar as a terrible and alien presence. The Petersburg that was the epitome of home to him in the introduction turns out to be an inhospitable place ruled over by a terrifying idol (a pagan god) possessed by a dark force—a madman. The narrator finds himself, along with his hero, alone and homeless in what he thought was his home.

Perhaps even more frightening, the narrator finds himself sympathetically representing Evgenii's rebellion. And here I would like to press further the somewhat psychoanalytic approach of the previous paragraphs. The words with which Evgenii threatens the Bronze Horseman seem to be borrowed from the narrator. If these bitterly ironic words, especially "wonder-working builder" [*stroitel' chudotvornyi*], belong to the narrator as much as they do to Evgenii, they mark a reversal of the narrator's view of Peter found in the introduction The words echo the narrator's earlier interpolation in which he viewed the inability of the city to withstand the flood as a deception, a mockery of the gods. Moreover, this mad mockery now comes not *from above* but *from below*, from the narrator as well as from Evgenii. It is a madder, more surprising challenge than Evgenii's, for it comes not from someone who has begrudgingly reconciled himself to Peter's agenda (Evgenii), but from a worshiper of Peter, a voice that stood with Peter on the side of order, light, harmony, and reason in the introduction and that ominously warned all the forces of unreason, chaos, disorder, and madness that dared to threaten Peter's idea. It is an ingeniously disguised challenge; though the words are the narrator's, Evgenii utters them. In fact, it is the only direct quotation from Evgenii in the entire poem (the voice of Evgenii elsewhere is rendered almost entirely through *erlebte Rede*). It is almost as though, at least here, the narrator was trying to divorce himself from being associated with the challenge. He gives freer reign to his challenge precisely because he can ascribe it entirely to the deranged Evgenii, as a challenge justified by Evgenii's circumstances, as a challenge that only a madman would undertake: the challenge of the madman Radishchev! The narrator imagines the consequences of the challenge for himself personally without making the challenge in his own person. The same procedure is applied in "God Grant That I Not Lose My Mind," where the persona imagines being locked up in an asylum, chained, and teased like an animal. Horrified at his own imaginings, he prays that he not go insane. In *The Bronze Horseman*, he imagines an even more terrible consequence for madness because it has wide-reaching historical, political, and social consequences; it is linked to the worst of all crimes: rebellion. And is it really only Evgenii who imagines being chased by the Bronze Horseman? If the narrator plays as important a role in the *povest'* as he does in the introduction, it is his story that is told in *The Bronze Horseman* as much as Evgenii's.

When read retrospectively, the narrator's warning in the introduction—not to disturb Peter's eternal sleep—has a dual function. It is a warning to Russians as well as to Russia's traditional enemies in Finnish waters; but it is also a warning to the narrator himself. Like Evgenii, the narrator disturbs Peter's sleep and must also pay the price of his intellectual rebellion (albeit only imagined) as he recognizes the truth of Evgenii's vision and echoes Evgenii's challenge to Peter. The tsar pursues not only Evgenii; he pursues all those who imagine rebellion. The narrator can challenge Peter only from the position of madness, not his own madness but the madness of *the Other*. But at the end of poem, "the poor madman" [*bednyi bezumets*] and "my Evgenii" [*moi Evgenii*] fuse into "my madman" [*bezumets moi*, 2.220]. Here Evgenii and the narrator have become one. Imaginatively the narrator has become the mad *Other*. Whose cold corpse lies in that little house at the end of the poem? "God Grant That I Not Lose My Mind" asks that the narrator be preserved from insanity, figuratively speaking, from being buried alive. In *The Bronze Horseman* Evgenii dreams, with God's help, of his grandchildren burying him. The last line describes the burial of Evgenii's cold corpse on an island in the Neva. Ironically a poem entitled *The Bronze Horseman* must serve as Evgenii's only monument. If the poem describes the interment of Evgenii's dream, it also describes the interment of the narrator's dream and his estrangement from the city he still passionately loves.

It is tempting to see *The Bronze Horseman* as a diptych, representing simultaneously held antithetical views about Peter of equal power and validity. But a narrative poem is an event in time, with a beginning and an end. The ode is not present in the same way at the end as it is at the beginning, not only because it is now counterbalanced by the *povest'* but because the *povest'* comes later and, in some sense, supersedes it. The poem has no epilogue, no concluding frame. Peter and his city do not remain the impregnable and immovable presences that they were in the ode. Once the Bronze Horseman descends from his horse and enters the world of the *povest'*, Peter, Petersburg, and Peter's legacy are changed. The Peter of the ode can never be restored. After the *povest'* the narrator cannot return to the same home again, just as Evgenii could no longer return home after he threatened the monument. At the end, the narrator returns to the beginning, but it is not to Peter, but to the time before Peter—and to a cold corpse. It ends with a madman destroyed by an idol—by another madman. The ode and reason belong to the eighteenth century, the *povest'* and madness to the nineteenth. Dostoevsky and Bely made sure to take up where *The Bronze Horseman* left off.[2]

Madness and the Demonic

In the confrontation scene the protagonists are united and driven by a black or dark power. I have shown how the text integrates many of the associations of darkness that have been traditionally ascribed to madness, but, because of the relative paucity of textual evidence, I have not made much of the connection between madness and the demonic, pagan, or Satanic. Almost all primitive cultures consider madness as possession by demons, evil spirits, or dark forces of the underworld. And the same idea pervades classic Greek and Latin literature and culture. "Possession by unclean or evil spirits and demons is a frequent cause of illness, especially of madness, in the New Testament."[3] Jesus performs cures by casting out violent spirits (Matthew 8:28–34; Mark 5:1–13; Luke 8:2, 26–33). Though *The Bronze Horseman* seems dominated by series of polar oppositions, the text contains few references to God or religion to which the pagan, demonic, or satanic can be explicitly opposed.[4] Going outside the text does not help. Though Pushkin respected religion, especially as he grew older, it played little role in his life and art, and he had strong reservations about the state of the Russian clergy.[5] A deconstructive reconstruction of the religious depends on proving the "presence of an absence," because nothing in the text supports a reconstruction of a religious idea opposed to the pagan and demonic.

I have reserved the discussion of the pagan and demonic for the section on the narrator because they manifest themselves as important aspects of the narrator's alienation and disillusionment with Petersburg. Again I have the narrator in mind and not necessarily the author. Though Pushkin uses "God Grant That I Not Lose My Mind" as a means of imaginatively exploring the consequences of going mad, he obviously did not plan to go mad or feign madness. The same may be said about *The Bronze Horseman.* Though the poem confronts the issue of alienation simultaneously in the narrator and his hero, Pushkin had no intention of seriously abandoning Petersburg after writing the poem. The poem is an imaginative exploration of his attitude toward the city conditioned by the genre(s) in which he is working. *The Bronze Horseman* reflects a similar imaginative exploration of the anxieties or superstitions or both about pagan Petersburg and its possession by natural and demonic forces.

The introduction represents an encomium to an essentially pagan capital. One pagan world has displaced another. The bogs and dark forests give way to modern European buildings, many based on Greek and Roman models. Beautiful palaces, towers, bridges, gardens, and embankments embellish the city, which hosts a seemingly perpetual round of balls and parties. It is a military capital engaged in martial exercises and the celebration of great victories.

> Flaunt your beauty, Peter's city, and stand
> Unshakable, like Russia.
>
> [*Krasuisia, grad Petrov, i stoi*
> *Nekolebimo, kak Rossiia.*] (intro. 84–85)

Alternatively, if the primary change is not from one pagan world to another but involves Petersburg eclipsing Moscow, then one might see the transformation as a form of paganizing: that is, displacing a religious civilization by a pagan one. Religious Moscow, the third Rome, is described as an old faded widow. The new empress, the young tsaritsa, the queen of the northern city, presents a son to the imperial Petersburg house, the new Russian home. Given that in the very next line Russia celebrates her victory over her enemy, it seems that the vanquished include Moscow as much as Sweden.

But Moscow is not only summarily dismissed in the introduction;

it does not even enter the *povest'* as a contending force in the manner of either Evgenii or the Neva. Nor does sculpture play a significant antireligious role in the text, despite Iakobson's contention that the attitude of the Orthodox Church toward statuary suggested to Pushkin that statues were closely "associated with idolatry, with devilry, with sorcery."[6] The problem with Iakobson's view of the Orthodox association of statuary with the demonic—however interesting per se—is that it finds little support in the text. Pushkin actually advances the very opposite point of view in his criticism of Russian Orthodoxy. Attributing Gogol's views on plastic arts to Pushkin further undercuts Iakobson's argument. Pushkin was not a provincial like Gogol, nor was he from a deeply religious family from Moscow like Dostoevsky: Gogol and Dostoevsky were overwhelmed by the capital and by its many monuments. Although born in Moscow, Pushkin grew up not in the Orthodox tradition but in the carefree and pagan atmosphere of his socialite parents. At twelve he left Moscow for Petersburg to attend school, where he was surrounded by statues and monuments, which probably seemed no more pagan to him than the gardens and squares they occupied. The clergy was certainly more alien to him than the Bronze Horseman. Many religious interpretations of Petersburg attribute the flaws of Peter and his legacy to the influence of the Devil or to possession by evil spirits. Petersburg could be saved, then, only by Christian exorcism, by causing the devils to inhabit the swine that presumably would throw themselves over the embankments. But this is Dostoevsky's vision, not Pushkin's.

But if indeed *The Bronze Horseman* presents the displacement of one pagan world by another—the displacement of the pre-Petrine river gods by the Bronze Horseman—and if indeed the poem presents the bright, beautiful, harmonious, and ordered city as a facade and the city possessed by a mad black power as the real Petersburg, then how does *The Bronze Horseman* relate the pagan to the demonic and assess its significance for Russia's future? "Whither do you gallop, haughty steed?" Two pagan, demonic scenarios suggest themselves: one in which the poem presents disparate pagan forces in contention with each other, the other in which the pagan forces presented in the *povest'* represent the underside or dark side of the same "bright" pagan forces in the introduction. This is an important distinction. The poem shows how much more difficult it is to conquer the demons within than those without. Petersburg's original raison d'être was to counter an external threat, not an internal one.

In the first alternative involving disparate contending forces, the *povest'* presents quiescent or subdued pagan powers rising up against other pagan powers embodied in the imperial Petersburg of the introduction. The water gods of the river and the sea will always contest Peter's victory. The narrator's hope that the Neva will accept its subjugated role is vain. Nor does his warning have much force. But the flood does not represent the only pagan or natural danger; Evgenii offers an equally serious "pagan" threat, a threat from the people within the imperium, a resistance from Peter's rebellious sons disillusioned with the disparity between promise and reality, between the Word and the Deed.

The other pagan alternative suggests a different disposition and opposition of forces, one in which antagonistic pagan forces represent not disparate contending entities but reciprocal sides of each other. The *povest'* does not so much present a new Petersburg to the reader as it reveals the dark underside or alter ego of the Petersburgian harmony, beauty, order, and reason of the introduction. It ties the failure of the Petrine project to a mysterious, nocturnal, black power, something intrinsic—not extrinsic—to Petrine ambition, will, power, and imagination, something intrinsic, in fact, to all pagan projects, Peter's or otherwise. Now that Petersburg has superseded Moscow, not only can nothing interfere with the development of the magnificent capital but there is also nothing to keep in check the demonic, pagan spirit that animates it.

The introduction creates a sun god, an obedient river, and a docile populace; the *povest'* shows us a prince of darkness, a rampaging river, and a rebellious son. The sun god and the prince of darkness are not distinct, contending forces but different incarnations of the same entity. Peter's creative and destructive powers are manifestations of the same force [*sila*]. When the sun is shining, all is order; when night sets in, chaos and madness reign, and Evgenii and the Neva revolt. *The Bronze Horseman* dramatizes the narrator's fears about the consequences of a pagan victory. He does not fear sheer nothingness—that below the surface there is a void—but that a dark pagan force has displaced the Christian civilization that preceded it. In *The Devils*, Dostoevsky's vision of what will happen when devils take over the world is partly based on his reading of Pushkin's poem "Devils" [*Besy*], and he uses the first lines of the poem as the epilogue to the novel.

In Pushkin's lyric, the narrator's carriage loses its way in a snowstorm at night. Neither the driver nor the horse can find the way, for a devil is drawing them off course. But it is evident that it is not one devil but an infinite number of them [*beskonechny*] ("My name is Legion: for we are many"). The plaintive whining and howling of these swarms of devils wrench the narrator's heart. This lyric evokes precisely the pagan demonic that *The Bronze Horseman* shows is undermining the Petrine legacy. The presence of the pagan demonic, the black force [*sila chernaia*], is embodied in the same monument that serves as a tribute to the pagan sun god. The only opposition to the Bronze Horseman is the Bronze Horseman. Orthodoxy no longer constitutes a viable opposition. Zachariah will no longer work. "On that day, says the Lord, I will strike every horse with panic and its rider with madness" (Zachariah 12:4). One might posit an absence—an abyss or black hole rather than a black force—at the root of the Petrine project, but this is to impose a twentieth-century view on Pushkin's time and artistic universe. For *The Bronze Horseman*, the absence of the religious demonic (Satan) as an explanation for Petrine darkness and madness compels the substitution of an equally powerful pagan demonic. And this demonic must be invested with sufficient life and power so that it can challenge the pagan edifice constructed by the master builder of the introduction. This is why the monument—the pagan idol—must come to life and become embodied as the "double" of Peter the Great and his state (the steed). As the Bronze Horseman—the idol [*kumir, istukan*]—overcome by a dark power, rouses itself from its eternal sleep, descends from its pedestal, and proceeds to chase Evgenii through the streets of Petersburg, it undermines the aura of imperturbability and law that sustain the imperial, pagan Petersburg of the introduction.

Both the conclusion of part 1 and the introduction to the confrontation scene begin with the suggestive lines of the idol on the bronze steed with outstretched arm. Here at last the reality of Petersburg, the black force, reveals itself in all its pagan might and splendor. The idol, not God, wields the power of the outstretched arm. In a moment of mad vision, Evgenii sees Peter as an idol who—as the rhyme pair *kumira/polumira* indicates—rules half the world. Through the mad eyes of his hero, the narrator becomes party to the same vision. Only in the darkness—and through madness—does it become possible for both the narrator and Evgenii to see the true pagan, demonic Peter, horrible and terrifying, rising up as an idol in the November night, to see beyond the solar splendor of the introduction.

> Round the idol's pedestal
> The poor deranged man walked
> And cast fierce glances
> Upon the countenance of the ruler of half the world.
>
> [*Krugom podnozhiia kumira*
> *Bezumets bednyi oboshel*
> *I vzory dikie navel*
> *Na lik derzhavtsa polumira.*] (2.165–66)
>
> His blood seethed. Scowling he stood
> Before the prideful idol.
>
> [*Vskipela krov'. On mrachen stal*
> *Pred gordelivom istukanom.*] (2.173–74)

Zachariah speaks of God striking the rider and the steed with madness. As Bethea shows, the Western tradition often portrays horse and rider as separate entities. The rider, with strong and steady hand, controls a horse whose energy and power can be potentially destructive to the state if not properly harnessed. "Hence in Western literature as in statuary it was essential *to keep distinct* the notions of horseman and horse, rider and ridden.... In Russia, however ... this Western formula could not be so easily transported."[7] Despite some positive images of horses in Russian folklore, the Russian literary and cultural imagination often associates the horse with the Mongol hordes that invaded Russia from the East, devastating the country and effectively enslaving it for more than two hundred years. The horse and rider thus symbolize not only pagan emperor and empire but also pagan destruction.[8] This is the horse out of control, driven by a rider under the influence of a dark power. In *The Bronze Horseman* it is also the horse (associated with water) that Neptune calls from the waves, a symbol of the blind forces of primordial chaos and madness.[9] Bethea correctly cites Borges to emphasize that the idea of wanderlust associated with the horseman is not unique to the Russian experience. Borges's image of horse and rider, however, goes far beyond wanderlust; it encapsulates the narrator's fear that all that the pagan Peter—the horse and rider, the Bronze Horseman—has built up contains within itself the seeds of its own destruction, that the horse perching precariously over the water will return to its origins in the waves of the Neva, as it joins with the black force that has rebelled against the city, paradoxically uniting with itself against itself. Borges writes: "The figure of the man on the horse is, secretly, poignant. Under Atilla, the "Scourge of God," under Genghis Kahn, and under Tamarlane, the horseman tempestuously destroys and founds extensive empires, but all he destroys and founds is illusory. His work, like him, is ephemeral. From the farmer comes the word "culture" and from cities the word "civilization," but the horseman is a storm that fades away."[10] The *povest'* of *The Bronze Horseman* presents not only a clerk in the grip of insanity but a whole world ravaged and possessed by a pagan dark force, a force that from ancient times has been the domain of madness. This is the other side of the paganization of Russian society. This is the truth the narrator works out for himself imaginatively in the *povest'*. It was left to Dostoevsky to take the implications of *The Bronze Horseman* to their extreme conclusions by populating all Petersburg with mad demons (*The Double*) and then by tracing the spread of these demons to the Russian heartland (*The Devils*).

Madness and Rebellion: Narrator and Author

At the end of an unpublished chapter of *The Captain's Daughter*, the narrator, recalling the events of the Pugachev rebellion many years afterward, warns about the terrible dangers of Russian rebellions.

> They did not know whom to obey. There was no lawful authority anywhere. The landowners were hidden in the forests. Bands of brigands were ransacking the country. The chiefs of separate detachments sent in pursuit of Pugachev, who was by then retreating toward Astrakhan, arbitrarily punished both the guilty and the innocent. The entire region where the conflagration had raged was in a terrible state [*bylo uzhasno*]. God save us from seeing a Russian revolt [*russkii bunt*] senseless and merciless. Those who plot impossible upheavals [*perevoroty*] among us,

are either young and do not know our people or are cruel men who do not care a bit about the lives of others and even hold their own lives cheap.

Although the narrator who writes these lines is a man in the spirit and mind of the eighteenth century—he is presumably writing a memoir for his descendants—he is probably expressing views quite close to Pushkin's. The first plans of *The Captain's Daughter*, dating from 1833, coincide with the composition of *The Bronze Horseman*. What makes the rebellion so terrible [*uzhasno*] is that it engulfs everyone. Unspeakable crimes are committed on both sides. In typical understatement, Pushkin writes: "The chiefs of separate detachments sent in pursuit of Pugachev, who was by then retreating toward Astrakhan, arbitrarily punished both the guilty and the innocent."

In *The Bronze Horseman*, Pushkin ties all types of rebellion with madness. The narrator presents the objective reasons for the river's fury, but he becomes explicitly and vehemently hostile to the river when he relates the destruction it wreaks, especially on his poor hero. Although far more sympathetic to Evgenii's rebellion than to the Neva's, the sympathy is somewhat undercut by the association of Evgenii's rebellion in thought and deed with the dark power of madness, a power that illuminates and blinds Evgenii at the same time. Peter's metaphoric identification with the madness and fury of both the river and Evgenii equally ties Peter to rebellion.

These revolts correspond to the three forms of rebellion that Pushkin cites as having occurred throughout Russian history. In *The Bronze Horseman*, the river most closely corresponds linguistically and thematically to the senseless and merciless rebellion of the people during the Pugachev rebellion—as described in both *The Captain's Daughter* and *The History of Pugachev*—and to the many rebellions that periodically devastated large areas of the country before, during, and after the reign of Peter the Great. These are the revolutions from below. Perhaps Evgenii's rebellion, however, can best be characterized as a middle rebellion or a rebellion from the side, that is, a rebellion or revolt of the dissatisfied or disillusioned from various classes of the nobility. Boris Godunov might be placed in this loosely defined class as well as the participants in palace revolutions, including the Decembrists. In *The Bronze Horseman*, Evgenii may represent the remnants of the old nobility whose fortunes and place in society, according to

Pushkin, suffered a significant decline when the service nobility superseded it.[11] But it was the third rebellion, the Petrine rebellion, the rebellion from above—which Pushkin was wont to call revolutionary—that most preoccupied Pushkin personally, since it was the rebellion responsible for the decline of the class to which he belonged and the class he believed was the best hope of preserving and promoting the values essential to the health of the Russian state.[12]

The quotation from *The Captain's Daughter* clearly shows that Pushkin *most feared* revolution from below, and his hope was that, although the embankments could not prevent periodic floods, some of them catastrophic, these floods could be contained, and that the empire could and would recover from them quite quickly. The hope, however, that they would not leave a trace the following day represents wishful or metaphoric thinking and not Russian reality, as the *povest'* implies. The Pugachev rebellion posed a far greater danger to the Russian state than the flood did to the inhabitants of Petersburg. Interestingly Pushkin argues that the most dangerous revolution experiment from below was actually taking place in his own time: it was Jacksonian democracy in America, which promised all free males, irrespective of property holding, equal voting rights.[13] For Pushkin this was tantamount to political insanity.

Despite his admiration for certain aspects of Peter's reign and accomplishments—he had an almost Hegelian view of Peter as the incarnation of human history[14]—Pushkin accused Peter of being the real Russian revolutionary, a sort of Russian Andrew Jackson, *avant la lettre*. In the first years of the reign of Nicholas I, Pushkin had hoped that the Petrine revolutionary tide could be stopped if not reversed, that the new tsar, Nicholas I, could initiate a counterrevolution from above. Shaw writes: "Freed from exile, he hoped for reforms 'from above,' and during the first years of the reign of Nicholas I he eagerly interpreted the Tsar's acts and gestures as harbingers of reform. Pushkin was almost rapturous at the rumor that Nicholas would 'by a counter-revolution to Peter [the Great's] reforms, restore the ancient nobility to its former position of influence and responsibility in government and society.'"[15] On 16 March 1830 Pushkin wrote to Viazemsky: "When the Sovereign departed, he left in Moscow a plan of a new organization, a counter-revolution to Peter's revolution."[16] Later he would write Chaadaev:

[Peter the Great] tamed the nobility by promulgating the *Table of Ranks*, and the clergy by abolishing the patriarchate (N.B.: Napoleon said to Alexander: "You are *Pope* at home; that is not so stupid"). But it is one thing to make a revolution, and another to enshrine the results. Up to Catherine II, Peter's revolution was continued among us, instead of being consolidated. Catherine II was still afraid of the aristocracy; Alexander was a Jacobin himself. The *Table of Ranks* has already been doing away with the nobility for 140 years, and the present emperor was the first to place a dike (very feeble, so far) against inundation by a democracy worse than that of America.[17]

Several points are noteworthy here. First, Pushkin sees the revolution of Peter the Great as something continuing into the present. In fact, until Nicholas, the Romanovs were spearheading the revolution. Pushkin has in mind the practice of granting entry to the hereditary nobility to more and more commoners on the basis of their rank in the civil, military, and court service.[18] Catherine was too timid to continue the revolution, but Pushkin calls Alexander I a Jacobin—a Robespierre—that is, someone willing to use extreme violence (the Reign of Terror is implied) against the aristocracy in order to promote and protect an extreme egalitarian or leveling program.[19] This may seem blown out of all proportion; yet the meaning is clear. Most important for *The Bronze Horseman* is the metaphoric expressions Pushkin uses to convey his idea about the rebellion. He likens the egalitarian policy of Peter—which he presents as being prosecuted even more vigorously by Peter's heirs than by Peter himself—as a "flood" [*le débordement*], which only the present tsar Nicholas has begun to stem. Nicholas has started to build a dike [*une digue*], which, from the context, Pushkin views as the first step in the counterrevolution. He explicitly associates democracy with a flood and all its excesses [*débordement*]. *The Bronze Horseman* suggests that the Petrine egalitarian project was at its height during the last flood in 1824, at the end of Alexander's regime. Alexander had let loose the waters, which, in the end, he found himself helpless to control: the greatest danger of all revolutions. But for Pushkin there can be nothing worse than revolution from below that is aided, abetted, and led from the very top, by the tsar himself. Can this be understood as anything but the epitome of insanity? The Romanovs were destroying the nobility, the only class that could resist, if not reverse, the revolution; they were undermining their own position. As one of Nicholas I's police chiefs formulated this idea: "The Landowner is the most reliable bulwark of the sovereign.... If his power is destroyed, the people will become a flood, endangering in time even the Tsar himself."[20] In a note about a work that he was contemplating about the nobility, Pushkin emphasizes that, paradoxically, Peter both started and consolidated the revolution, implying that the present-day Romanovs are essentially reincarnations of Peter the Great, doing Peter's work. Thus Peter is just as present as he was in the past. "The means by which one carries out a revolution are not the same as those by which one consolidates it—Peter I is at one and the same time Robespierre and Napoleon—the Revolution incarnate" [Les moyens avec lesquels on accomplit une révolution, ne sont plus ceux qui la consolident—Pierre I est tout à fois Robespierre et Napoléon—La Révolution incarnée (12:205)].

But when seen in the larger political context, neither is Evgenii's rebellion entirely innocent. When considered a representative of his class, he cannot be viewed only as a victim of the revolution from below (the river, the flood, the people) and from above (Peter and his heirs). The nobility is as deeply involved in the revolution as the forces from below and above. Pushkin, in other words, finds these revolutionary forces endemic in the very class that should be the bulwark against revolution. After all, among the most prominent members of the Decembrist uprising were Pushkin's own friends, many from his own class.[21] However much Pushkin may have been in sympathy with some of the goals of the Decembrists, after 1825 he became increasingly disillusioned with radical change, especially brought about by the nobility. After having told Grand Duke Michael that the duke's family were Jacobins, Pushkin proceeded to rail against the Russian nobility [*dvorianstvo*]. "There is no more explosive revolutionary material in all Europe. Who was on the Senate Square on 14 December? Only the nobility. How many of them will be present during the very next uprising? I don't know, but it seems to me there will be many" (8:60). Statements like these about the Russian nobility sound eerily like Dostoevsky's statements about the Russian intelligentsia.

For the "historical" Pushkin, rebellion and revolution were the height of madness; they were violent, destructive, merciless, infectious, and destructive of family and home. He found elements of precisely this black angry flood in all strata of the Russian population, seemingly sometimes in unconscious, cross-purposed collusion. In *The Bronze Horseman* itself, the same black force [*sila chernaia*] overcomes all the representatives of madness. This is why they all are enmeshed in darkness. The river cannot overcome the force from the Gulf, Evgenii cannot control his anger, and the Bronze Horseman cannot maintain its immobility and calm. Given how Pushkin understands the political context of rebellion, it is easy to see how Evgenii can both be the victim of the flood and align himself with the flood, be the victim of an elemental uprising and be in league with it. The Decembrists had, after all, support among the people because of the promises the Decembrists made to them. But from wherever the rebellion arises, it will engulf all and infect all with madness. No one will escape. The river turns on Peter and Evgenii; Evgenii turns on Peter; Peter turns on Evgenii. If Peter is the ultimate revolutionary, it is not really a question of the embankments being unable to contain the Neva, of his being unable to control the flood. Peter himself has opened the floodgates and thus, like Evgenii, is in collusion with the river. He is the flood. When, as the result of his reforms, there will no longer be a *dvorianstvo* [nobility]—for everyone will be *dvorianstvo*—there can be no effective embankment to contain the river, the people, the revolution. Then true madness must surely reign.

Conclusion

Deconstructing *The Bronze Horseman*

Dostoevsky, *The Double*, and the Pushkinian Legacy on Madness

---

Tracing the Russian literary legacy of Pushkin's portrayal of madness would obviously require another book. Because the theme of madness, especially in *The Bronze Horseman*, is so tied to the theme of "Petersburg," the task becomes even more complex, involving some of the most important works and novelists of the nineteenth century, including, among others, Dostoevsky, Gogol, Tolstoy, Pisemsky, and Bely. Fortunately Dostoevsky's *The Double* (1846), more than any of his other later works—or those of any other writer—provides us with an ideal tool for examining the implications of Pushkin's work on madness for his Russian successors.

In his discussion of *The Double*, Joseph Frank remarks that Dostoevsky's decision to change the original subtitle from *The Adventures of Mr. Goliadkin* [*Prikliucheniia Gospodina Goliadkina*] to *A Petersburg Poem* [*Peterburgskaia poema*] had, among other things, the "advantage of correctly assigning *The Double* its place in the Russian literary tradition initiated by *The Bronze Horseman*."[1] But Dostoevsky does much more than just place *The Double* in a "tradition," especially since *The Bronze Horseman* first appeared posthumously only nine years earlier. *The Double* directly takes on *The Bronze Horseman* on the Petersburg theme, tying it inextricably to the issue of madness.[2] Dostoevsky consciously reworks the plot, imagery, and characterization of *The Bronze Horseman* to his own deconstructive ends. And paradoxically, although *The Double* appeared only a few years after the publication of *The Bronze Horseman*, it, arguably, represents the most radical transformation of Pushkin's text ever attempted, far more imaginative and radical than Dostoevsky's own later attempts in the 1860s and 1870s.

Since, before Pushkin, Petersburg had been presented almost entirely positively, Pushkin's ambiguous treatment of Petersburg represented a turning point in the portrayal of the city in Russian literature.[3] "Pushkin was the last bard of the bright side of Petersburg. Every year afterward the image of the northern capital grew dimmer and dimmer."[4] Dostoevsky's early work, *The Double*, represents not the chronological but the "aesthetic" end point of this tradition, for it takes the negative implications of *The Bronze Horseman* regarding madness to their absolute extreme conclusions, foreshadowing, if not including, almost all the elements of the anti-Petersburgian tradition in Russian literature of the second half of the nineteenth century.

Dostoevsky's strong animus toward Petersburg comes out equally in both his early and later works about the city. But there is a significant difference between them. However ambivalently and ambiguously Pushkin presents Peter and Evgenii, he poeticizes and mythologizes them throughout; he bathes them in his most moving poetry, incorporating them in a mythological universe in which empire and individual are inextricably bound. In his later works Dostoevsky inverts the adulatory mythology that dominated the portrayal of Petersburg before Pushkin, but by demonizing it, he ultimately remythologizes—and repoeticizes—his subject. Dostoevsky's later works, then, are similar to *The Bronze Horseman* in that in these, too, he mythologizes the city and the tsar, but remythologizes only Pushkin's negative representations. In *The Double*, however, Dostoevsky engages in a far more radical operation: he completely depoeticizes and demythologizes Peter, Peter's legacy, and Peter's victims, emptying his subject—in a negative kenosis—of all mythological and sacred significance.

The dark vision of Petersburg in Dostoevsky's later work derives from his Slavophile–Pochvennik agenda, with its rejection of much of Peter's legacy and its revulsion at the ills of the modern metropolis.[5] For Dostoevsky, Petersburg is the new Babylon, the window through which Western evils—rationalism, individualism, and socialism—continue to enter and poison the Russian land. Even more, it is the most fantastic, alien, and unnatural of Russian cities. According to the Underground Man, it is also the most rational and abstract place on earth.[6]

But Peter and his city loom no less large in the mature Dostoevsky than they do in *The Bronze Horseman*; they are just negatively reproblematized—and demonized. Raskolnikov, the hero of *Crime and*

Punishment, dreams of becoming a world historical figure, who can, in good conscience, sacrifice thousands of human beings to achieve his mission; in other words, he is a sort of nineteenth-century Peter the Great. For the late Dostoevsky, Peter the Great is still alive in his city, still directing the course of Russian history. In the epilogue of *Crime and Punishment* Peter's legacy is represented in apocalyptic terms: men possessed of will and intelligence engage in internecine warfare that nearly results in the destruction of the human race.

Both the animus and apocalypticism associated with Peter and Petersburg are reflected in the few references Dostoevsky later makes to *The Bronze Horseman*, particularly in his nonfiction. Most of these references, alluding to line 16 of *The Bronze Horseman* ["To hack a window through to Europe," *V Evropu prorubit' okno*], are derogatory.[7] Dostoevsky presents the *okno* not as Russia's window to Europe but as a hole [*dyr'ia*] through which much that was bad [*durno*] and harmful [*vredno*] entered Russia, and he characterizes Petersburg as a Finnish bog [*chukhonskoe boloto*] separating the educated classes from the people. In an 1862 article he writes that Peter's reforms introduced German bureaucracy [officialdom, *chinovnichestvo*] into Russia and initiated the most horrible corruption of morals.[8] In the notes for a section of *A Diary of a Writer* for 1876, referring to Pushkin's lines, "I love you, Peter's creation" [*Liubliu tebia, Petra tvoren'e*], he remarks: "I confess, I do not love it" ["*Vinovat, ne liubliu ego*"].[9] Peter has played an enormous role in Russian history but one that Dostoevsky hopes has played itself out. For only the end of Peter's influence can usher in the next, higher stage in Russia's spiritual and historical development. But this Peter is still an apocalyptical Peter, a devil who has finally been defeated—or will be defeated. In *The Double*, by contrast, Peter's status itself is radically reduced, even nullified.

Correspondences

Both *The Bronze Horseman* and *The Double* tell a story of aborted love resulting in the insanity of the *chinovnik* hero. At the end of *The Bronze Horseman*, Evgenii is found dead on one of the islands devastated in the flood of 1824; in *The Double*, the incurably insane Goliadkin is taken away to an asylum, where he will probably spend the rest of his life. The "love" plots are divided into three parts, each developing the hero's progressive derangement as he faces his unhappy fate. In the first episode of *The Bronze Horseman,* the flood forces Evgenii to take refuge on one of the marble lions. He is terrified less by his own precarious situation than by his fears for his fiancée, Parasha, who lives on an island severely battered by the storm. After braving the Neva to find her his worst fears are confirmed, and he goes mad on the spot [*zakhokhotal,* 2:265]. As we have seen, this episode does not mark a complete transformation from sanity to madness. Evgenii enters the third and last stage of his derangement when he threatens the statue of Peter in word and gesture and then imagines the statue pursuing him all night through the streets of Petersburg. Eventually he is found dead on an island he had wandered to.

Dostoevsky's Goliadkin suffers three mishaps in courting his superior's daughter, Klara Olsuf'evna. After each, his psychological condition seriously deteriorates. After Goliadkin's first unsuccessful attempt to court Klara Olsuf'evna, he is barred from her house. He is so shaken that he visits a doctor to seek help. Despite the apparent hopelessness of his amatory prospects, Goliadkin makes another attempt to win over Klara by going to her birthday party uninvited, from which he is forcibly and humiliatingly ejected. Returning home from the party, he experiences a mental breakdown; he sees for the first time the double that will haunt him to the end of the novel.[10] As in *The Bronze Horseman,* the third episode shows the hero in the final stage of madness. He returns to the scene of his final humiliations (just as Evgenii finds himself for the third time by the marble lions and the Bronze Horseman) in an attempt to abduct Klara. This time he is taken, raving mad, to the insane asylum.

Each work consists of three main episodes in which the hero becomes increasingly deranged—mutatis mutandis—as a result of his growing awareness of, and responsibility for, the loss of his beloved. Evgenii makes a valiant effort to visit Parasha as soon as the flood subsides; Goliadkin makes several attempts to "rescue" Klara, including a plan to elope with her or abduct her. But there are even more striking parallels. Evgenii's madness is closely linked to the flood: his imagination of its ravages (episode 1, his fear for Parasha); its actual destruction (episode 2, the trip to the island where Parasha lives); and his thoughts about those—the one—responsible for his loss (episode 3, his confrontation of the monument). In addition to the fury of the flood, in the second episode Pushkin emphasizes the gloomy, autumnal

Conclusion 185

cold of November, the nocturnal darkness, and the plaintive wailing of the winds. Nouns and epithets of darkness, gloom, and horror [*mrak, t'ma, mgla, mrachnyi, unylyi,* and *uzhasnyi*] dominate the atmosphere of the poem proper—all perfectly in accord with the madness that is soon to descend on the hero as inexorably as the flood.[11]

It is precisely on such a night that Goliadkin, in the second main episode, loses Klara Olsuf'evna. "It was a horrible [*uzhasnaia*] November night—damp, foggy, rainy, snowy, teeming with swollen faces, colds in the head, fevers, swollen faces, quinsies, ailments of all kinds and descriptions: that is to say, with all the gifts of a Petersburg November. The wind howled in the deserted streets, lifting up the black water of the Fontanka canal above the rings on the bank, and fitfully brushing against the lean lamp-posts which echoed its howling in a thin, shrill creak, constituting, as it were, an endless squeaky, jangling concert so familiar to every resident of Petersburg" (509; 1:138).[12] After being ejected from Klara's birthday party, Goliadkin "suddenly set off again like mad and ran and ran without looking back, as though he were pursued, as though he were fleeing from some still more awful calamity. His situation was, indeed, horrible [*uzhasnoe*]" (510; 1:139).[13] Bemoaning the terrible weather, Goliadkin asks himself "whether there is going to be a flood" [*ne budet li navodneniia,* 512; 1:140]; he thinks the water has risen so violently. At this moment Goliadkin meets not the Bronze Horseman but something far more frightening: himself, his double. Just like Evgenii (404), Goliadkin shudders [*On vzdrognul,* 1:141] after he hears "steps" behind him: "Suddenly through the howling of the wind and the uproar of the storm, the sound of steps very close at hand reached his ears again. He started and opened his eyes" (512; 1:141). We should not be surprised that he does not hear "a heavy ringing gallop" [*tiazhelo-zvonkoe skakan'e*], for, after all, it is Goliadkin's double, not Peter, behind him. But, like Evgenii, he soon begins to run. Here Dostoevsky echoes almost exactly the text of *The Bronze Horseman* at perhaps the most critical point in Evgenii's story—immediately after he threatens the monument: Evgenii "suddenly full tilt set off running" [*vdrug stremglav / Bezhat' pustilsia* (438–39)]; "Goliadkin suddenly, without looking back, set off running" [*vdrug pustilsia bezhat' bez ogliadki* (1:142)].

Although not quite so severe, the weather on the second crucial night (596; 1:213), just as in *The Bronze Horseman,* closely resembles that of the first.[14] It reminds Evgenii of the flood; it makes Goliadkin imagine that he is being pursued through the streets of Petersburg by innumerable copies of himself. After his confrontation with Peter, Evgenii spends his days wandering around the city. Likewise, Goliadkin spends his last day at large wandering around town, confused, disheveled, bedraggled, and deranged. When he is finally taken to the asylum, he is a completely broken man, hardly more alive than Evgenii's cold corpse at the end of *The Bronze Horseman*.[15]

Peter

Dostoevsky uses these structural similarities not to show his affinity with Pushkin but to establish the point of reference from which he can more easily dramatize the differences between his vision of Peter and Petersburg and Pushkin's: specifically, to deflate Peter's image, legacy, and vision by emptying them of their aura and grandeur. Peter's legacy has not been and will not be superseded because there is no longer anything monumental, substantial, or historically significant to be superseded. Aside from the inclement weather associated with the flood, Dostoevsky shows little, if any, of Pushkin's Petersburg. Pushkin's "I love you, Peter's creation" [*Liubliu tebia, Petra tvoren'ie*], his magnificent paean of Peter and Petersburg in the introduction to *The Bronze Horseman*, is completely absent from *The Double*. Further, Dostoevsky reproduces almost none of Petersburg's grandeur, beauty, and dynamism: the reader sees neither the white nights of summer nor the pinching frosts of winter. Whereas Evgenii ventures outside to the city's great squares and monuments—especially to the marble lions and the monument of Peter—Goliadkin confines most of his activities to his dingy, dirty apartment in Shestilavochnaia Lane; the reader sees only the inside of a few shops, restaurants, apartments, and offices. The Bronze Horsemen is conspicuous by its absence from *The Double*, which includes not a single reference to the Falconet statue. The only praise of Petersburg comes from the lips of a mimicked Goliadkin. In one of his conversations with himself, Goliadkin Senior entertains his double, Goliadkin Junior, with anecdotes about the glories of the capital—an indiscriminate mélange, at best—concluding with readings from Baron Bambreus. Goliadkin singles out the iron railing of the Summer Garden as Petersburg's greatest architectural attraction.

> When in good spirits, Mr. Goliadkin was sometimes fond of telling an interesting anecdote. Being now in such spirits, he told the visitor a great deal about the capital, about its entertainments and attractions, about the theater, the clubs, about Brülov's picture, and about the two Englishmen who came from England to Petersburg just to look at the iron railing of the Summer Garden, and then immediately returned home; about the office; about Olsufii Ivanovich and Andrei Filippovich; about the way that Russia was progressing, hour by hour, toward perfection; that "Arts and Letters flourish here today"; about an anecdote he had recently read in the *Northern Bee* concerning a boa-constrictor in India of extraordinary strength; about Baron Bambreus, and so on and so forth. (531; 1:156–57)

In the introduction and the *povest'*, Peter the Great dominates *The Bronze Horseman*, whether as the incarnation of tyranny[16] or of Russian manifest destiny.[17] Neither of these Peters appears in *The Double*.[18] Civil servants of the fifth and sixth rank, which seem infinitely above his own ninth rank, rule Goliadkin's world.[19] If Peter exists for Iakov *Petrovich* Goliadkin, for this "son of Peter," he takes the form of His Excellency, whom Goliadkin sees as the ultimate representative of the government, and therefore as his true father. The narrator, however, treats all these civil servants—especially their presence at Klara Olsuf'evna's birthday party—with mock-heroic irony: "Oh, if I were a poet! of course, I mean, like Homer or Pushkin; with any lesser talent one would not venture; ... I would describe for you ... how the father Olsufii Ivanovich, a hale-looking old man and a state councilor, who had lost the use of his legs in his long years of service and been rewarded by fate for his zeal with investments, a modest house, some small estates, and a beautiful daughter, began to sob like a child and announced through his tears that His Excellency was a beneficent man" (499; 1:128–29). *The Double* singles out these officials because it treats Peter primarily through his successors (the Russian officials described above) and his legacy (the bureaucratic order). Moreover, these officials hardly play the same role in Goliadkin's imagination as Peter does in Evgenii's. His Excellency does not emerge as a world historical personality, a "mighty figure," as Hegel described the type, who "must trample down many an innocent flower and crush to pieces many things in its path."[20] Peter's descendants, the department heads and His Excellencies, do not ride horses over the abyss; they do not command armies and navies to realize Russia's manifest destiny: they walk from one office to another, commanding at best a detail of timorous civil servants.

Dostoevsky focuses most of all on Peter's true legacy, the bureaucracy, which receives little attention in *The Bronze Horseman*. While Pushkin concentrates on the cataclysmic events of the flood and the dramatic confrontation between his antagonists, Dostoevsky underscores the prosaic and undramatic: the bureaucratic "adventures" of a minor copy-clerk. For Pushkin and Evgenii, Peter still lives; "his will remains alive in the city";[21] he has become an integral part of the consciousness of all Russian subjects. The poet in *The Bronze Horseman* is no less a son of Peter than Evgenii is. The tragic exists in Petersburg only because Peter, the spirit of Russian imperialistic history, is still destroying those who stand in his way. The dominating presence of the Bronze Horseman, the amplification of Peter in Evgenii's mind, and all Peter's antagonists—the rage of wind, rain, flood, and sea—engender a monumental Peter. In Dostoevsky's demythologized representation of the city, Peter lives—or rather survives—only through an aborted legacy, a soulless bureaucracy that parodies, if not mocks, his vain ambitions. *The Double* thus stands in a kenotic relationship to *The Bronze Horseman*: it enacts a desacralization—a humiliation—of Peter. Peter's city is a city of dead souls.[22] This bureaucracy of "merit," with its attendant table of ranks, takes a higher toll than the ravages of nature (flood) and will (the Bronze Horseman). The institution has long stopped serving the interests of Peter's vision; it lives on despite, not for, Peter.

The Clerk [*Chinovnik*]: The Narrative Stance

Pushkin's work concentrates on his little hero, Evgenii; but *The Double*, which goes to extremes in everything, focuses almost exclusively on Goliadkin. Therefore Dostoevsky has to get at Peter entirely through his clerk, his *chinovnik*. Pushkin maintains Peter's monumentality at the same time that he reduces him; he maintains Evgenii's relative insignificance at the same time that he elevates him. In *The Double*, Dostoevsky not only reduces Peter, either by eliminating him or representing him through his failed institutions, he also reduces his hero much beyond Pushkin and never even hints at any redeeming features. In his previous work and first novel, *Poor Folk*, Dostoevsky, in contrast to Gogol in *The Overcoat*, attempted thoroughly to humanize his clerk, Devushkin, by endowing him with love, compassion, humor, and sentiment. In *The Double*, he reduces his clerk by stripping him of all those traits that he employed in the characterization of his earlier hero.[23]

Dostoevsky underlines his departure from Pushkin by radically transforming the narrator's attitude toward his hero, especially his madness and its relation to protest and rebellion. He obviously takes a much less sympathetic approach toward Goliadkin than Pushkin does toward Evgenii.[24] Goliadkin is not young, hale, and hearty but is old and balding, and, from the very beginning of the novel, mentally ill. His name is not pleasing to the ear. He has neither family nor a real dream. Unlike Evgenii, he does not think of marrying, having children, and being buried by his grandchildren. He has only himself, his servant, and, later, his double(s). His "romantic" attachment to Klara Olsuf'evna, similar to Poprishchin's in Gogol's "Notes of a Madman," constitutes a travesty of the sentimental romance. Further, the Klara Olsuf'evna that the reader sees is not the real person but a distorted image of Goliadkin's deranged imagination. Dostoevsky removes from *The Double* not only Pushkin's Peter with his "great thoughts" but also Evgenii with his more modest, but sympathetically presented, dream. Peter's monumental plans for empire destroy Evgenii's dream and drive him insane; in a scene as comic as it is pathetic, the butler of Goliadkin's superior throws Goliadkin down the stairs.[25]

Indeed, the narrator even presents his hero's movements and speech as ridiculous. As Viktor Vinogradov and others have remarked, Goliadkin's abrupt movements make him appear more like a puppet on a string than a human being.[26] Goliadkin is too timid to say anything briefly and directly; he makes endless, exasperating circumlocutions. Mikhail Bakhtin and Vinogradov remark that in transcribing Goliadkin's consciousness and speech the narrator at times seems to fuse with his hero,[27] but Terras and M. F. Lomagina demonstrate that the narrator distances himself from his hero even in those passages where the narrative voice seems to fuse most closely with that of Goliadkin or his double. In fact, Dostoevsky's use of *erlebte Rede*, which at best gives the impression of false camaraderie, in most cases verges on depreciating mimicry—all of which only deepens the ironic divide between narrator and hero.[28]

Whereas Pushkin suggests the possibility of the "little man" achieving an insight commensurate with the dream of his epic antagonist and arising even to challenge his enemy at the very center of his creation (Petersburg), Dostoevsky presents the prosaic adventures of Goliadkin in deflationary mock-epic style—a device that is far more obvious in the work's original journal form than in the revised version, from which Dostoevsky deleted the mock-epic headings for all the chapters.[29] We see Goliadkin on a shopping expedition, eating pies in a restaurant, riding in his carriage, trying to join a party, being ejected from the party, and waiting in the rain to carry away an imagined fiancée—at best a series of nonadventures. The only Peter that Goliadkin ever meets is his servant, Petrushka, a drunkard who, as in Gogol, occupies an even lower plane of social and moral being than his master or his double—both sons of Peter [*Petrovichi*].[30]

The poet of *The Bronze Horseman* sings of Evgenii as much as he sings of Peter; it behooves him to remember with compassion history's tragic casualties. Dostoevsky focuses on a diminished Goliadkin because he represents, both as Petrovich, the son of Peter, and as Russian everyman, what has remained of Peter's legacy in nineteenth-century Russia. Dostoevsky seems to withdraw sympathy for Goliadkin even when his misfortunes increase. Even in suffering Goliadkin remains petty and unsympathetic.

There is a limit, however, beyond which Dostoevsky cannot reduce Goliadkin without compromising his hero's national and universal significance. He cannot turn Goliadkin into a Gogolian Akakii Akakievich. Goliadkin differs markedly not only from Dostoevsky's own Devushkin in *Poor Folk* but also from innumerable down-and-out comic *chinovniki* of the 1830s and 1840s. He occupies a responsible position as the assistant clerk in his office. He is literate, financially secure, ambitious, and for all we know, until his descent into madness, quite competent. Had his chief's nephew not worked in his office, he might even have received the promotion he desired. He has relationships with women. At times he cuts a ridiculous figure, but he is not nearly as ridiculous as Akakii Akakievich or Poprishchin. As Terras has shown, Goliadkin speaks more correctly than Devushkin; he is familiar with a good number of historical facts and anecdotes; and he has read quite a few journal articles and novels.[31] Konrad Onasch maintains that Goliadkin has even been affected by the ideas of the French Enlightenment and Jean-Jacques Rousseau.[32] The terrible significance of Goliadkin is that he is not a subhuman, or even atypical in a Dostoevskian higher sense, but precisely a Russian everyman.

The Clerk: Madness and Rebellion

Pushkin's sympathy for Evgenii increases as Evgenii descends into madness; but he also valorizes his madness. That the humble Evgenii could have threatened Peter only when he was mad points, as we have seen, to a distinctly romantic conception of madness: only in madness can the truth break through the constraints of fear and reason and challenge ultimate authority.[33] When Evgenii faces the Bronze Horseman for the first time after the flood, he is terrified precisely by the clarity of his thoughts—a clarity made possible by madness ["*proiasnilis' / V nem strashno mysli*," 404–5).[34] Moreover, Evgenii's madness elevates him to Peter's level. He, too, now sees historically; he understands the goals for which the rights of individuals—his rights—have been sacrificed. He also becomes, for the reader, so much a part of Peter's story and the story of the Russian state that Peter seems almost inconceivable without him. If Evgenii's illumination, his insight into Peter and his creation, reflected nothing more than paranoia—as Richard Gregg argues[35]—both Peter's achievement and the terrible cost of that achievement would be severely diminished. Diminishing Evgenii seriously diminishes Peter.

Dostoevsky, on the other hand, depoeticizes, deromanticizes, and devalues Goliadkin's madness in *The Double*. In nineteenth-century works featuring autoscopic doubles,[36] the double (even if it is exclusively a projection of the more negative or evil side of the self) often emerges as more interesting and venturesome, even more vital, than the original self. Goliadkin's double, however, is the very opposite of a higher self; it does not transform him into a seer; it does not even give him insight.[37] On the contrary, Dostoevsky empties Goliadkin's madness, like madness in the Age of Reason, of all that is vital and elevating. It is a depoeticized madness as prosaic as Goliadkin himself. "Goliadkin's very madness," according to Terras, "is ridiculous in its wretched pettiness, its lack of spirituality, its shallowness of feeling. Goliadkin's folly is a travesty of madness for really, there is nothing, but nothing at all, to go mad from."[38] Dostoevsky wisely did not invent for Goliadkin anything as imaginative as Poprishchin's King of Spain (in Gogol's "Notes of a Madman"), for "people who are dull and commonplace when sane remain just that when they become insane."[39] Petersburg has so reduced the spirit of man that "true" madness, the romantic last resort of protest and opposition, can no longer exist. Evgenii's crazed perception of the Bronze Horseman chasing him through the streets of Petersburg constitutes a magnificent flight of visionary madness worthy of Peter himself; it is the very antithesis of seeing oneself chased through these same streets by exact replicas of one's shabby and repugnant self. As Donald Fanger writes: "Here is not even Gogolian *poshlost*, but nothingness, raised by the quality of attention it receives to a higher power, where it becomes terror."[40]

> "Bow or not? Answer or not? Recognize him or not?" our hero wondered in indescribable anguish. "Or pretend that it is not I, but somebody else, strikingly like me, and look as though nothing were the matter. It is simply not I, not I—and that's all there is to it," said Mr. Goliadkin, taking off his hat to Andrei Filippovich and keeping his eyes fixed upon him. "I'm ... I'm entirely all right," he whispered with an effort; "I'm ... quite all right. It's not I at all, Andrei Filippovich. It's not I at all, not I—and that's all there is to it." (481; 1:113)

Much like Merezhkovsky, Dostoevsky probably saw not only truth but also the seeds of an effective rebellion arising out of Evgenii's mad visions.[41] What is so potentially threatening to Peter—to the state—about Evgenii's madness (his higher sanity) is that it calls forth rebellion from one of Russia's most docile citizens, from a man whose ideal was to distance himself from affairs of state—to live a life, as it were, outside historical time.[42] Thus Dostoevsky not only deprives Goliadkin of Evgenii's visionary madness and sympathetic character but also his status as a serious rebel; he presents Goliadkin's rebellious thoughts as petty, conventional, and ridiculous, that is, no different from his other ideas and concerns. In the revised version of *The Double*, the elimination of many passages relating to rebellion attenuated Dostoevsky's polemic with *The Bronze Horseman*.[43] But these cuts also obscured the reasons for Goliadkin's rebellious thoughts and his preoccupation with "freethinking" and imposture. As one of the deleted letters (a reflection of Goliadkin's guilty conscience) makes clear, complaints were soon going to be made—or already had been made—against Goliadkin; everyone, even his chief, would know about his disgraceful behavior toward Karolina Ivanovna. Goliadkin imagined that he would not only be publicly humiliated but would probably lose his position, his place of residence, and, like Evgenii in *The Bronze Horseman*, be forced to wander the streets of Petersburg. All this is made explicit in a passage cut from the 1846 version, in which Vakhrameev, an intermediary through whom Goliadkin is conducting a correspondence concerning his enemies' plots, excoriates Goliadkin for his scandalous behavior. (It is, of course, really Goliadkin writing to himself.)

> In conclusion, I must tell you that Karolina Ivanovna's petition regarding your affair [*delo*] has been submitted a long time ago, and that our mutual friend, Nikolai Sergeevich Skoroplekhin, has been busy working in Karolina Ivanovna's behalf. As a result of this affair being made public knowledge, you will no longer be able to find a place to live; you will be deprived of all credit and trust; and you will lose your position at work. For all your machinations have been anticipated and nullified by the petitions and supplications of Karolina Ivanovna before your chief. Finally, all your hopes and nonsensical ravings about Izmailovskii Bridge and thereabouts will come to naught all of themselves when your dissolute life is made fully public. Rejected by everyone, tormented by pangs of conscience, you will not know where to lay your head; you will be forced to wander the earth, nurturing in vain in your heart the viper of your own debauch and vengefulness. (1:414)

In *The Bronze Horseman*, the loss of his beloved unhinges Evgenii and eventually leads to his protest, his revolt—all of which the narrator presents with great sympathy.[44] But in *The Double*, rather than ennobling his hero by a deeply moving relationship with a young girl, as he had done with Devushkin in *Poor Folk*, Dostoevsky involves Goliadkin in a rather shady relationship with a German woman.[45] Furthermore, Goliadkin's madness, in contrast to Evgenii's, is brought on not by the loss of his beloved but by fear of public exposure. By "depriving" Goliadkin of love and showing him to be the primary cause of his own misfortunes, Dostoevsky undercuts not only Goliadkin's intrinsic worth but also the justification for Goliadkin's rebellion against his fate. Moreover, Evgenii's rebellion is engendered and inspired by madness. Madness gives him the possibility of understanding the causes of his misfortune and thus the raison d'être of rebellion. His rebellion arises out of and is inspired by his madness. Goliadkin's rebellion does not arise from his madness at all. On the contrary, his madness is caused by his rebellious thoughts, by his fear of rebellion, which is anathema to him and which he tries to suppress. By reversing the relationship between madness and rebellion in *The Bronze Horseman*, Dostoevsky once again depreciates Goliadkin's madness.

Having an inordinate, servile respect for authority, Goliadkin experiences enormous guilt whenever he thinks disrespectfully of his superiors, when, for example, he begins to feel envious, angry, and bitter after being passed over for promotion. But for Goliadkin to question the decisions of the authorities, to think that one has the right to a position occupied by a rival, constitutes nothing less than a challenge to the entire system. Furthermore, Goliadkin's rebellion manifests itself not in outright defiance, as in Evgenii's case, but in a debased form of imposture [*samozvanstvo*].[46] *Samozvanstvo* has always constituted one of the most serious threats to the state in the Russian political consciousness, for it calls into question the legitimacy of those who rule.[47] But Dostoevsky turns the theme of *samozvanstvo* into travesty.[48] In his little world Goliadkin views any challenge to the existing order—albeit only the bureaucratic order—as the delegitimation of all authority and of "the place" of everyone who depends on that authority, including his own. Inevitably it is not Peter who descends from his pedestal to squelch the rebellion of one of his sons; it is Goliadkin himself in the person of his own double.

By questioning the legitimacy of those in higher positions, Goliadkin lays himself open to the claims of those who occupy lower positions. In contrast to Evgenii, Goliadkin begins to experience the challenge from *below* far more acutely than the one from *above*. He now comes to see himself—in the person of his double—as a pretender who has neither religious nor social legitimacy for the position he presently occupies. It is thus not the mighty Peter who descends from *above* to crush Goliadkin but petty demons—Goliadkin's own doubles—who rise from *below* the earth to undermine Goliadkin's legitimate place as titular councilor, a middling rank at best in the Russian civil service: "But with every step, with every thud of his foot on the granite of the pavement, there would leap up as though from beneath the earth an exactly identical Mr. Goliadkin, perfectly alike, and of a revolting depravity of heart" (566; 1:186–87). Peter is absent from the Petersburg text partly because he is no longer needed to crush such a paltry challenge to his authority; it is left to Goliadkin, or his impostor double-devil, to do it himself. As Uspenksii has argued, in the Russian cultural consciousness the royal impostor owes his power to the devil, to the Antichrist; but, by analogy, so do all who engage in role playing and the donning of masks [*samozvanstvo*]. Goliadkin's perception of being conducted to the underworld by the devil is thus condign punishment, in his own mind, for his imagined imposture.[49]

Many nineteenth-century doubles are suicidal. To preserve its "legitimate" self, to crush the rebellion raging inside, the self must destroy its alter ego; but to do so necessarily entails the destruction of the "legitimate" self as well. Whereas for Evgenii rebellion is the greatest act of self-affirmation—for it is through his rebellion that Evgenii comes, willy-nilly, to play a role in Peter's story—for Goliadkin, the crisis of self—and the madness it generates—not only stifles rebellion [*samozvantsvo*]—it is in fact a defense mechanism that leads not to rebellion but to the suppression of rebellion.[50]

What is most unusual about Dostoevsky's disparaging diminution of Goliadkin's madness and its relationship to freethinking and rebellion—and not only in terms of *The Bronze Horseman* but also in terms of Dostoevsky's later work—is that it undercuts the notion of rebellion from below. Evgenii could, at least in madness, threaten Peter. He sees the threat as something outside and alien, and thus something that, *at some time*, can be confronted, even challenged, as his threatening gesture and words symbolize. In Goliadkin, both rebel and avenger are so completely internalized that they become two sides of the same self. What possible challenge can the Goliadkins of Russia, or of the world, offer when they internalize their own punishment and go mad? From the pessimistic point of view of *The Double*, *The Bronze Horseman* presents a gross exaggeration of the human potential for rebellion in the modern world.

In his attempt to demythologize and deromanticize *The Bronze Horseman*, Dostoevsky has to dethrone Peter and radically to reduce Evgenii. Goliadkin's madness from beginning to end is divorced from truth and insight. One can hardly imagine a more depressing work than *The Double*—a view expressed, as we have seen, even by some of Dostoevsky's contemporaries. *The Double* shows in bold relief the relatively romantic portrayal of madness in *The Bronze Horseman* and Pushkin's other works on madness. It also reveals, by contrast, the ambiguities of Pushkin's masterpieces. It is these ambiguities regarding both Petersburg and madness, and not Dostoevsky's deconstructions and demythologizations, that held sway over Russian literature of the nineteenth and early twentieth centuries. In his later works Dostoevsky himself "retreated" from his maximalist positions, remythologizing—even reromanticizing—Petersburg, the rebellious hero, and madness. Only Dostoevsky could take these themes as far as Pushkin, but neither in *The Double* nor in any of his later works could he present them in the perfect tension that Pushkin achieved in prose, lyric, and narrative poetry in, yes, the annus mirabilis—1833. Pushkin, then, not only defines madness for Russian literature, he erects the greatest monument to it in the language. In contrast to Dostoevsky, he presents it more ambivalently and ambiguously and thereby opens up the theme to continual exploration—an unusual achievement, especially regarding madness, for the poet of reason, harmony, light, balance, and good sense.

The Double attempts to undercut the romantic connection in *The Bronze Horseman* not only of truth and madness but also of madness, truth, and violence. Thus Dostoevsky's presentation of prosaic madness is ultimately far less radical than Pushkin's. For Plato and the Greeks, the madness associated with violence is not the madness associated with truth. Don Quixote is sometimes "violent," but whether his exploits are true is subject to doubt, and the exploits themselves are always related with humor. The mad Lear attains greater wisdom only with the loss of power. But when the narrator of *The Bronze Horseman*, with the eyes of his mad hero, looks up in horror at the terrible monument and recognizes the relationship between the "dark power" and the will, the idea, the mission—and the truth—of Peter the Great—and when he further associates that dark power with the truth and the rebellion of Evgenii—he has formulated perhaps the most explosive idea of madness and truth in Western literature. *The Bronze Horseman* objectifies the horror of Pushkin's vision into madness, ironically vouchsafed to the sanest of Russian poets.

To conclude, I would first like to say a few words about Pushkin's works on madness taken together. In my introduction and elsewhere in this book I have emphasized their different emphases, scopes, and approaches. Many of these differences are obviously conditioned by genre. The generic differences between "God Grant That I Not Lose My Mind" and the two narrative works, *The Queen of Spades* and *The Bronze Horseman*, are obvious. But the differences between the narrative pieces are also striking. In contrast to *The Queen of Spades*, *The Bronze Horseman* is not only in verse, it comes from a different tradition in Pushkin's own work: the romantic verse tale, of which it is the culmination. Furthermore, *The Bronze Horseman* is itself a hybrid text, comprising an unusual introductory ode and a tale in verse as much *prosaic* as romantic. It is impossible to assess how much the original idea of a work determines the genre in which it is embodied and how much the genre determines the shape of the idea. But we know that genre played a significant role in Pushkin's writings on Pugachev. Pushkin wrote most of *The History of Pugachev* in the autumn of 1833. A few years later he penned a fictional account of the same historical events in *The Captain's Daughter*. The different representation of Pugachev in the two works reflects far more the "poetics" of different genres—history and the romantic tale of adventure à la Walter Scott—than Pushkin's evolving or changing view of Pugachev. The fiction demanded a Pugachev different from the rebel that Pushkin had portrayed in the history. Undoubtedly Pushkin uses different genres to explore different aspects of madness, but the genre he chooses significantly shapes what he can say.

In *The Bronze Horseman*, Pushkin uses madness as a vehicle for exploring possibilities inherent in his earlier romantic verse tale, *Poltava*, though he obviously focuses less on the historical Peter than on the contemporary significance of Peter's legacy. But *The Bronze Horseman* is also a subversive text that takes us in surprising directions, cutting across, if not subverting, genre expectations, especially with regard to the narrator. The mad hero, Evgenii, appears almost as a means, a subterfuge, by which the narrator can explore the most terrifying aspects of Peter and his mission. Occasionally his voice fuses with that of his mad hero, permitting him to speak unspeakable madness without uttering it in his own name. But the mad text also goes deeper; it speaks the language of the unconscious and the repressed. The portrait of the Neva appears at times less about the flood's devastation than about the narrator's animus toward the river and its threat of rebellion. Given the highly ambivalent portrait of Peter in the *povest'*, one is tempted to see the introductory ode as a classic example of reaction-formation, animus disguised as excessive love. If *The Bronze Horseman* is about the narrator as much as it is about Evgenii, Peter, or the Neva, madness becomes the primary device for revealing the narrator to himself, for composing, in effect, his innermost autobiography, which can only be realized in terms of Peter the Great. In the end, the most historical of texts turns into the most personal. The verse tale touches the lyric. *The Bronze Horseman* becomes a variation of "God Grant That I Not Lose My Mind." Madness may provide an essential key—if not the most essential key—to the life of both the citizen and the poet.

If, alongside its historical and political concerns, *The Bronze Horseman* reveals through madness an intensely personal, "lyric" side, then "God Grant That I Not Lose My Mind," Pushkin's most intensely personal lyric, appropriates madness to explore a larger world. In *The Bronze Horseman*, universal history masks the personal story of the narrator; in "God Grant That I Not Lose My Mind," the persona's imagined confinement masks the larger universal concerns of the creative imagination and the journey of the personality through crisis and rebirth. Despite the great generic differences between this verse tale and lyric, madness makes it possible for each work to expand far beyond its ostensible focus—and to embrace its generic antithesis. "God Grant That I Not Lose My Mind" appears both to begin and end as a poem about loss of freedom and confinement, resulting first from social constraints and then from madness itself. But Pushkin also presents madness as a vehicle of infinite expansion. The poem does not take us into Russian history, but it embraces the land, the sea, and the sky, and explores the innermost depths of the human psyche, a place that can be reached only by madness. *The Bronze Horseman* begins with the universal (the inevitable conflict between society and the individual) and ends with the personal; "God Grant That I Not Lose My Mind" begins with the personal (the persona's fear of madness) and ends with the universal. In each case the long journey is made possible by madness.

The Queen of Spades, in some ways, is the odd man out. One expects the prose of the poet to be less personal than his poetry. But Pushkin seems to make impersonality in prose an artistic goal in itself. By comparison to *The Bronze Horseman* and "God Grant That I Not Lose My Mind," the narrator in *The Queen of Spades* seems detached and distant from his hero. It is not easy to imagine Germann as the narrator's alter ego. And yet, perhaps even because of the story's impersonality, *The Queen of Spades* emerges as the most universal of the mad texts of 1833, and Germann as the most convincing everyman. The narrator exposes all Germann's spiritual, moral, and imaginative deficiencies,

Conclusion

including his materialism, vulgarity, and willingness to use others as a means to further his ambition. But madness permits Pushkin to open up the other side of Germann, who turns out to be much more than a creature imprisoned and limited by ambition; in fact, he becomes a creature who lives for adventure and risk, a creature, in the end, of imagination. Pushkin almost begrudgingly reveals this side of Germann, virtually waiting to the end to render his hero in his completeness. But herein lies Pushkin's genius, to see the potential in a character that he obviously has little affection for. To force Germann to be fully exposed, Pushkin has to take him to the extreme; he has to make him mad. In the end, Germann's madness, his breakdown (madness), turns into a breakthrough, and it is precisely this breakthrough that ties *The Queen of Spades* to the other works on madness of 1833. Pushkin forces even Germann to see what the narrator of *The Bronze Horseman* and the persona of "God Grant That I Not Lose My Mind" were forced to see. In all the works of 1833 truth comes at a high price. It is not only the unsympathetic Germann who is compelled to pay a high price for it. In strange contradistinction to the Greek tradition, madness is at one and the same time punishment and reward. It may represent the moment of truth for which we must all be willing to sacrifice our lives. But if the truth of the unconscious always arrives, as Lacan argues, by surprise, *The Queen of Spades* does not cede anything, in terms of the representation of madness, to its brilliant companion works of 1833. In the end, madness trumps genre.

Notes

Preface

1. "A Pushkin—nashe vse," in *Literaturnaia kritika* (Moscow: Izdatel'stvo khudozhestvennaia literatura, 1967), 166. The eminent Russian poet Vladislav Khodasevich wrote that his homeland was contained in eight small volumes of Pushkin's works. See his unfinished poem, "Ia rodilsia v Moskve. Ia dyma," in *Sobranie sochinenii*, 4 vols. (Moscow: Soglasie, 1996), 1:345.

2. D. S. Mirsky, *A History of Russian Literature* (New York: Knopf, 1966), 98–99. Dostoevsky's famous Pushkin speech, in which he lauded Pushkin's unique and universal genius, played a major role in the early stages of the cult. See F. M. Dostoievsky, *The Diary of a Writer*, trans. Boris Brasol (Santa Barbara, Calif.: Smith, 1979), 978–80. For the original, see F. M. Dostoevskii, *Polnoe sobranie sochinenii*, ed. V. G. Bazanov et al., 30 vols. (Leningrad: Nauka, 1972–90), 26:147–48. Nikolai Gogol's famous statement about Pushkin, though written almost fifty years earlier than Dostoevsky's, strikes a similar chord: "Pushkin is an extraordinary phenomenon, and perhaps the truest manifestation of the Russian spirit: he embodies the Russian man as he may appear in two hundred years." See his "Neskol'ko slov o Pushkine," in N. V. Gogol', *Sobranie sochinenii*, 7 vols. (Moscow: Izdatel'stvo khudozhestvennaia literatura, 1967), 6:68. But as Andrzej Lazari has shown, Dostoevsky's ideas about Pushkin may still be very much alive today. See his "Dostoevskii kak ideologicheskii avtoritet v politicheskoi bor'be nashikh dnei," *Dostoevsky Studies* 2 (New series), no. 1 (1998): 104–13. William Hazlitt and John Keats, among others, applied similar ideas about universality to Shakespeare. See M. H. Abrams, *The Mirror and the Lamp* (Oxford: Oxford University Press, 1953), 245.

3. The other two pieces are "Kirdzhali" (1834) and *Egyptian Nights* (1835).

Introduction

1. Even if we had had as much information about Shakespeare's life as we do about Pushkin's, the reason why Shakespeare wrote *Hamlet, King Lear,* and *Macbeth*

in five years beginning in 1601 would be as inexplicable as why Pushkin wrote *The Queen of Spades, The Bronze Horseman,* and "God Grant That I Not Lose My Mind" in approximately one year.

2. *The Queen of Spades* does not have a Byronic hero; Germann is more of a parody of a Napoleonic hero.

3. I have in mind the works of prominent literary figures. Undoubtedly madness plays a more important role in popular fiction and melodrama, especially the Gothic novel of the late eighteenth and early nineteenth centuries.

4. It is curious that in many ways Tolstoy, Turgenev, and Goncharov—Dostoevsky's contemporaries—took more from Pushkin than Dostoevsky but, in contrast to Dostoevsky, they rarely if ever wrote about madness.

5. On the other hand, the category of typological romanticism has even greater limitations than the category of period romanticism. Writing about madness may seem more conducive to the "romantic" than to the "classical" temperament, but Aeschylus, Sophocles, Euripides, Cervantes, Shakespeare, and Pushkin are not typical romantics, in even the broadest definition of typological romanticism. In *Madame Bovary,* Flaubert thought he was writing in the anti-romantic spirit of Cervantes.

6. Michel Foucault, *Madness and Civilization: A History of Insanity in the Age of Reason,* trans. Richard Howard (New York: Vintage, 1988), 107–16. "Confinement is the practice which corresponds most exactly to madness experienced as unreason, that is, as the empty negativity of reason; by confinement, madness is acknowledged to be *nothing*" (116). The Gothic novel of the late eighteenth century might seem to constitute an important exception in the Age of Reason, but Gothic novelists exploit madness for sensational effect rather than exalt it as a higher form of perception and knowing.

7. See "The Great Confinement," in Foucault, *Madness and Civilization,* 38–64. For a defense of Pinel against Foucault, see Lillian Feder, *Madness in Literature* (Princeton, N.J.: Princeton University Press, 1980), 31–33. Most of the scholarship devoted to madness in literature between the sixteenth and nineteenth centuries deals not so much with new conceptions of mental illness as with the rise of public, secular institutions first to keep, and then to treat, the mentally ill. Since mental illness was often seen as a spiritual illness, one that God visited on an individual, few even thought of cure. But as hospitals or institutions arose for housing the homeless, vagabonds, criminals, and the physically ill, they also became natural places for containing, restraining, and managing the mentally ill. Since governments wished primarily to maintain order and to ensure public security, they attempted to keep undesirables, of all kinds, off the streets. Mental patients were not to be treated but to be separated from the rest of the population for the sake of public safety.

8. From a Foucaultian point of view, the romantics would seem to have had a great deal to lose from the desacralization of madness. But the destigmatization of madness—the debunking of the idea of madness as curse, plague, and divine punishment—was probably more beneficial than detrimental to the romantic

cause, for it made it more possible to present madness as a vehicle to higher truth. Though Hoffmann occasionally links madness with the demonic, he is more apt to present the everyday world of bourgeois reality—the normal—as the true realm of the devil. Gogol obviously took this idea to an extreme conclusion.

9. Ruth Benedict, "Anthropology and the Abnormal," *Journal of General Psychology* 10 (1934): 59–80.

10. For a discussion of the relationship of madness and prophecy in the Old Testament and in Near Eastern religions in general, see George Rosen, *Madness in Society: Chapters in the Historical Sociology of Mental Illness* (New York: Harper, 1969), 21–70. Karl Jaspers attempted to prove that Ezekiel was a schizophrenic. See citation in Rosen, *Madness in Society,* 60.

11. *The Works of Plato,* trans. Benjamin Jowett, 4 vols. (New York: Random House, 1928), 3:401–2.

12. Though a rationalist as he is, Plato makes an important distinction between the source of prophecy and its interpretation. Identifying the source of divination in human beings with the organ of the liver, Plato comments on the nature of divination:

> And herein is a proof that God has given the art of divination not to the wisdom, but to the foolishness of man. No man, when in his wits, attains prophetic truth and inspiration; but when he receives the inspired word, either his intelligence is enthralled in sleep, or he is demented by some distemper or possession. And he who would understand what he remembers to have been said, whether in a dream or when he was awake, by the prophetic and inspired nature, or would determine by reason the meaning of the apparitions which he has seen, and what indications they afford to this man or that, of past, present or future good and evil, must first recover his wits. But, while he continues demented, he cannot judge of the visions which he sees or the words which he utters; the ancient saying is very true, that "only a man who has his wits can act or judge about himself and his own affairs." And for this reason it is customary to appoint interpreters to be judges of the true inspiration. Some persons call them prophets; they are quite unaware that they are only the expositors of dark sayings and visions, and are not to be called prophets at all, but only interpreters of prophecy.

(*The Dialogues of Plato,* trans. B. Jowett, 4 vols. [New York: Scribners, 1901], 563)

13. *The Works of Plato,* 3:402.

14. For a discussion of Cassandra's madness and its relation to prophecy, see Ruth Padel, *Whom Gods Destroy: Elements of Greek and Tragic Madness* (Princeton, N.J.: Princeton University Press, 1995), 25–28. "But in her frenzy Cassandra expresses a wisdom beyond conscious or reasoned logic; the images she sees convey the inevitable emotional and moral relationships among past, present, and future" (Feder, *Madness in Literature,* 88).

15. Rosen, *Madness in Society*, 63.

16. "And he went up from thence unto Bethel: and as he was going up by the way, there came forth little children out of the city, and mocked him, and said unto him, Go up, thou bald head; go up, thou bald head.

And he turned back, and looked on them, and cursed them in the name of the Lord. And there came forth two she bears out of the wood, and tare forty and two children of them" (2 Kings 2:23–24).

17. The persona in Pushkin's "The Wanderer" [*Strannik*] (1835) comes closest to evoking this image of the prophet. His relatives and friends shun him as though he were a raving madman in urgent need of a physician.

18. Paul probably did not have in mind the kind of foolishness practiced in medieval Russia but, rather, the "foolish" wisdom of the Gospel as opposed to the wisdom of the Greek philosophers, the wisdom that believed because it was absurd: "Credo quia absurdum."

19. Jeremiah was not afraid of predicting that terrible events would befall the kings with whom he was conversing. Though, in the end, friends in high places saved him, he was often beaten and imprisoned.

20. Alan Sheridan, *Michel Foucault: The Will to Truth* (London: Tavistock, 1980), 16–17.

21. For a discussion of Lear's "reason in madness," see Robert Bechtold Heilman, "Reason in Madness," in *This Great Stage: Image and Structure in King Lear* (Seattle: University of Washington Press, 1963), 173–224; and Feder's chapter also entitled "Reason in Madness," in her *Madness in Literature*, 98–146.

22. In Pushkin's famous interpolated poem from "Scenes from Knightly Times" (1835), "There Was on Earth a Poor Knight," the hero, driven by the purity of his vision and love for the Virgin, slays infidels in Palestine. When he returns home, he locks himself up in his castle. Isolated, silent, sad, he dies possibly having gone mad. Pushkin leaves the relationship between religious devotion, zeal, vision [*viden'e*] and madness tantalizingly ambiguous.

23. *Hamlet* presents a very different problem. Although issues of madness are raised in the play, Hamlet is obviously not mad in the same sense as Quixote, Lear, or the heroes of Greek myth and tragedy. In fact, on occasion, Hamlet is able to exploit to his own advantage the perception of others that he is mad.

24. F. M. Dostoevskii, *Polnoe sobranie sochinenii*, ed. V. G. Bazanov et al., 30 vols. (Leningrad: Nauka, 1972–90), 28.2: 251. Hereafter, *PSS*.

25. In *The Idiot*, Aglaia, referring indirectly to Myshkin, says that he is "the same as Don Quixote, but only serious and not ridiculous." Aglaia recites Pushkin's entire poem in front of family and friends. See Dostoevskii, *PSS*, 8:207.

26. Ibid., 7:214, 188.

27. Dostoevsky did not shy away from the flattering association of epilepsy and prophecy.

28. Feder argues that the English poet Thomas Hoccleve concluded that madness "is a condition that deprives a man of self-control only to lead him to a deeper apprehension of reason" (*Madness in Literature*, 110).

Chapter 1. Choosing the Right Card

1. M. L. Gofman writes that Pushkin's formulation of the problem of madness is the most successful in Russian literature, indeed that all Russian literature may be said to derive from it ("Problema sumasshestviia v tvorchestve Pushkina," *Novyi zhurnal* 51 [1957]: 62). Although he sees *The Queen of Spades* as the culmination of Pushkin's work on madness, he devotes only four pages to the story (82–86). For additional discussions of madness in the story, see Gareth Williams, "The Obsessions of Madness of Germann in 'Pikovaja dama,'" *Russian Literature* 14, no. 4 (1983): 383–96; E. M. Taborisskaia, "Svoebrazie resheniia temy bezumiia v proizvedeniiakh Pushkina 1833 goda," in *Pushkinskie chteniia: Sbornik statei* (Tallinn: Eesti Raamat, 1990), 81–87; G. P. Makogonenko, *Tvorchestvo A. S. Pushkina v 1830-e gody: 1833–1836* (Leningrad: Khudozhestvennaia literatura, 1982), 249–55. For a review of the Russian reception of the story, see N. O. Lerner, *Rasskazy o Pushkine* (Leningrad: Priboi, 1929), 141–42.

2. F. M. Dostoevskii, *Polnoe sobranie sochinenii*, ed. V. G. Bazanov et al., 30 vols. (Leningrad: Nauka, 1972–90), 30.1:92. Hereafter, *PSS*. Many have agreed with Dostoevsky's praise of Pushkin's remarkable ability to efface the line between the realistic and the fantastic. For one of the earliest and most convincing demonstrations of Pushkin's technique of combining the realistic and the fantastic, see A. L. Slonimskii, "O kompozitsii 'Pikovoi damy,'" in *Pushkinskii sbornik pamiati Professora S. A. Vengerova* (Moscow: Gosudarstvennoe izdatel'stvo khudozhestvennoi literatury, 1923), 171–80.

3. Caryl Emerson, "'The Queen of Spades' and the Open End," in *Pushkin Today*, ed. David Bethea (Bloomington: Indiana University Press, 1992), 35–36.

4. Germann is actually playing Stoss, a German variation of faro. The player (or punter) picks a card of his choice from one deck and places it face down on the table. (If Germann did not have the right to choose the cards he wanted, the story about learning which cards to play would make no sense.) Then, from the top of his own deck, the dealer turns up a card on his right and then on his left. If the card on the dealer's right equals the value (the suit is irrelevant) of the player's card, then the dealer wins; if the card on the dealer's left equals the value of the player's card, the player wins. The three, seven, and ace all come up on the left. German, however, chose a three, seven, and queen. Because on the last day the queen came up on the right and the ace came up on the left—and Germann was holding a queen—the dealer won. Had Germann chosen an ace, as he was supposed to have done, he, of course, would have won. The dealer has the edge, for if the card on both the dealer's right and left matches the player's, the dealer wins, and, in the case of faro, he usually takes half the player's bet; however, in Stoss, as in *The Queen of Spades*, the dealer takes the player's entire bet. For a detailed description of this card game as played in Pushkin's time, see Vladimir Nabokov's commentary to Aleksandr Pushkin, *Eugene Onegin* (Princeton, N.J.: Princeton University Press, 1975), 2:258–60.

5. Diana Lewis Burgin, "The Mystery of 'Pikovaia dama,'" in *Mnemozina: Studia*

litteraria russica in Honorem Vsevolod Setchkarev, ed. Joachim T. Baer and Norman W. Ingham (Munich: Fink, 1974), 46–56; M. Iu. Lotman, "Tema kart i kartochnoi igry v russkoi literature nachala xix veka," in *Trudy po znakovym sistemam* (Tartu: Tartuskii gosudarstvennyi universitet, 1975), 7:122–42; Nathan Rosen, "The Magic Cards in 'The Queen of Spades,'" *Slavic and East European Journal* 19 (1975): 255–75; Murray M. Schwartz and Albert Schwartz, "'The Queen of Spades': A Psychoanalytic Interpretation," *Texas Studies in Literature and Language* 17 (1975): 275–88; Williams, "Obsessions of Madness," 383–96.

6. Ia. L. Levkovich, "Stikhotvorenie Pushkina 'Ne dai mne Bog soiti s uma,'" in *Pushkin: Issledovaniia i materialy* (Leningrad: Akademiia nauk SSSR, 1982), 10:176–92.

7. "*Plamennyi nedug*," "*plamennyi vostorg*," "*vikhor' buinyi*" ("Conversation of a Bookseller and the Poet") (1824; 2:325); "*smiaten'e*" ("The Poet") (1827; 3:65); "*goriachka*," "*sviashchennyi bred*" (*Eugene Onegin*, 1832; 6:29; 1:58).

8. But it would be incorrect to conclude that madness was a concern only of Pushkin's poetry. As D. Blagoi shows, in *Sotsiologiia tvorchestva Pushkina: Etiudy* (Moscow: Federatsiia, 1929), 311–28, madness was perhaps Pushkin's most frequently used metaphor for describing, individually and collectively, all things socially and politically unsound, destabilizing, and dangerous. For a discussion of German views of madness during the late Enlightenment, both in literary and nonliterary texts, see Theodore Ziolkowski, *German Romanticism and Its Institutions* (Princeton, N.J.: Princeton University Press, 1990), 144–80. For similar analyses of unreason and madness in the Age of Reason, see Max Byrd, *Visits to Bedlam: Madness and Literature in the Eighteenth Century* (Columbia: University of South Carolina Press, 1974); Lillian Feder, *Madness in Literature* (Princeton, N.J.: Princeton University Press, 1980), 147–202; Michel Foucault, *Madness and Civilization: A History of Insanity in an Age of Reason* (New York: Random House, 1965); Jutta Osinski, *Über Vernunft und Wahnsinn: Studien zur literarischen Aufklärung in der Gegenwart und im 18. Jhdt.* (Bonn: Bouvier, 1983); Georg Reuchlein, *Bürgerliche Gesellschaft, Psychiatrie und Literatur: Zur Entwicklung der Wahnsinnsthematik in der deutschen Literatur des späten 18. und frühen 19. Jahrhunderts* (Munich: Fink, 1986); and George Rosen, *Madness in Society: Chapters in the Historical Sociology of Mental Illness* (New York: Harper, 1969), 151–71. See also L. I. Vol'pert's comparison of Pushkin and Stendhal, "Tema bezumiia v proze Pushkina i Stendalia: 'Pikovaia dama' i 'Krasnoe i chernoe,'" in *Pushkin i russkaia literatura: Sbornik nauchnykh trudov* (Riga: Latviiskii gosudarstvennyi universitet imeni P. Stuchki, 1986), 46–58. For works in Pushkin's library indicating his familiarity with the contemporary literature on madness, see B. L. Modzalevskii, *Biblioteka A. S. Pushkina* (St. Petersburg: Akademiia nauk, 1910), 53, 246, 273, 346. Vol'pert (54) also notes, in relation to "The Queen of Spades," that Pushkin cut just those pages in Leuret's *Fragments psychologiques sur la folie* devoted to hallucinations.

9. For the most detailed discussions of Batiushkov's life and his madness, see M. P. Alekseev, "Neskol'ko novykh dannykh o Pushkine i Batiushkove," *Izvestiia*

Akademii nauk SSSR: Otdelenie literatury i iazyka 8, no. 4 (1949): 369–71; Viacheslav Koshelev, *Konstantin Batiushkov: Stranstviia i strasti* (Moscow: Sovremennik, 1987), 276–340; L. Maikov, *Batiushkov: Ego zhizn' i sochineniia*, 2nd ed. (St. Petersburg: Marks, 1896), 222–40.

10. Typical of Odoevsky's view are statements like the following, made by one of his artist-heroes in *Russian Nights* [*Russkie nochi*], Odoevsky's most famous work: "Doesn't the state of a madman resemble the state of a poet?... Isn't the exalted state of a poet ... closer to what is called insanity than insanity is to an ordinary animal-like stupidity?" (Vladimir Odoevskii, *Russkie nochi* [Leningrad: Nauka, 1975], 25–26).

11. The more serious works patterned after Hoffmann by Gogol ("The Portrait") and the young Dostoevsky ("The Landlady") are clearly not their most successful endeavors.

12. As Ralph Tymms shows, in *The Double in Literary Psychology* (Cambridge: Bowes, 1949), even before Hoffmann's death in 1822, parodies were being written on Hoffmannian doubles. "So the romantic tale ends by parodying itself; with the self-destructive irony of the whole movement, the German Romantic, having, over a period of a decade or two, elaborately hoisted up a bizarre image of his own self-division, now turns upon his *Janus bifrons*, and bowls over the puppet he had himself glorified into 'super-reality'" (71).

13. N. V. Gogol', *Sobranie sochinenii*, 7 vols. (Moscow: Izdatel'stvo "Khudozhestvennaia literatura," 1957), 3:45–75.

14. Ibid., 3:191–214.

15. Dostoevskii, *PSS*, 1:109–229.

16. Roberta Reeder, "*The Queen of Spades*: A Parody of the Hoffmann Tale," in *New Perspectives on Nineteenth-Century Russian Prose*, ed. George J. Gutsche (Columbus, Ohio: Slavica, 1982), 95.

17. Pushkin places great emphasis on Germann's imagination throughout the story. In the narrator's formal introduction alone, he calls attention, three times, to the effect the story had on Germann's imagination. Germann "had strong passions and a fervent imagination" [*"imel sil'nye strasti i ognennoe voobrazhenie"*] (8:235); the anecdote about the three cards "had exerted a strong influence on his imagination" [*"sil'no podeistvoval na ego voobrazhenie"*] (8:235); and, somewhat later, the amazing anecdote "again represented itself to his imagination" [*"snova predstavilsia ego voobrazheniiu"*] (8:236).

18. Liza is an ambiguous figure in the tale. The narrator describes her unfortunate situation as a ward of the demanding old countess with great sympathy. But she has things in common with Germann. She is proud [*samoliubiva*], a dreamer [*mechtatel'nitsa*], and possesses a lively imagination [*voobrazhenie*]. She reads the latest sentimental and romantic literature. She wants radically to change her situation. She is looking for a savior [*izbavitel'*]. The tryst she arranges with Germann—a tremendous risk—may arise from desperation but also from reading romantic fiction. Experience soon makes her more practical. She comes to her senses after learning that Germann has caused the countess's death. By contrast,

the death of the countess makes Germann even more reckless. He starts off with only a small fortune [*malen'kii kapital*] and loses everything; Liza starts off with nothing and achieves, through marriage, his ideal: a considerable fortune [*poriadochnoe sostoianie*] (8:252). The narrator does not seem to begrudge her success. In the epilogue the reader learns that Lizaveta is bringing up a poor relative. Is she trying to do a good deed, acting against the example of her former tormentor? Or is she about to assume, with her own ward, the very role the old countess played? Pushkin leaves the question open. For several less positive assessments of Liza's actions and fate, see W. J. Leatherbarrow, "'The Queen of Spades,'" in *The Voice of a Giant: Essays on Seven Russian Prose Classics*, ed. Roger Cockrell and David Richards (Exeter: University of Exeter, 1985), 1–14; Joseph T. Shaw, "The 'Conclusion' of Pushkin's 'Queen of Spades,'" in *Studies in Russian and Polish Literature in Honor of Waslaw Lednicki*, ed. Zbigniew Folejewski et al. ('S-Gravenhage: Mouton, 1962).

19. See, for example, the studies of Lauren Leighton, "Numbers and Numerology in 'The Queen of Spades,'" *Canadian Slavonic Papers* 19 (1977): 417–43; Lauren Leighton, "Gematria in 'The Queen of Spades': A Decembrist Puzzle," *Slavic and East European Journal* 21 (1977): 455–69; Harry B. Weber, "'Pikovaia dama': A Case for Freemasonry in Russian Literature," *Slavic and East European Journal* 12 (1968): 435–47; Sergei Davydov, "The Ace in 'The Queen of Spades,'" *Slavic Review* 58, no. 2 (1999): 309–28.

20. Gogol', *Sobranie sochinenii*, 3:401–45.

21. Vladimir Nabokov, *Lectures on Russian Literature* (London: Weidenfield, 1982), 106.

22. Although psychoanalytic interpretations presuppose latent desires, they often do not, as romantic psychology is wont to do, admit the possibility of other selves. For the more psychoanalytically oriented interpretations of the story, see chapter 2 and the following: M. M. Schwartz and A. Schwartz, "A Psychoanalytic Interpretation"; Rosen, "The Magic Cards"; and Burgin, "The Mystery."

23. The odds of Germann's winning at Stoss three times in a row are one in eight ($\frac{1}{2} \times \frac{1}{2} \times \frac{1}{2}$). It is a tremendous risk because he is betting his entire fortune. The odds that the very first cards the dealer turns over on the left are three, seven, and ace ($\frac{1}{13} \times \frac{1}{13} \times \frac{1}{13}$), are one in over two thousand (2,197 to 1). That is what is "improbable."

24. This may very well be Pushkin's code for indicating the complexity of Germann. In comparing the superiority of Shakespeare's characters to those of Molière in terms of their passions, Pushkin writes: "The characters created by Shakespeare are not, as in Molière, basically types of such and such a passion, such and such a vice, but living beings filled with many passions, many vices; circumstances develop their varied and many-sided personalities before the viewer. In Molière, the miser is miserly—and that's all; in Shakespeare, Shylock is miserly, acute, vindictive, philoprogenitive, witty" (Carl R. Proffer, ed., *The Critical Prose of Alexander Pushkin* [Bloomington: Indiana University Press, 1969], 240).

25. "*Net! Raschet, umerennost' i trudoliubie: vot moi tri vernye karty, vot chto*

utroit, usemerit moi kapital, i dostavit mne pokoi i nezavisimost´!" (8:235). Shaw, in "The 'Conclusion'" (119), has shown that the ace [*tuz*], which has the additional meanings of a portly man or a man of rank and wealth, often fills in the series—three, seven, ace—when the ace is not actually mentioned. In the series just alluded to, the expression "peace and independence" "provides" the missing ace.

26. A. L. Siniavskii, in *Progulki s Pushkinym* (London: Collins, 1975), if I understand him correctly, argues that, for Pushkin, chance and risk are perhaps our only guarantee of attaining something eternal (39). Siniavskii has in mind the famous line from "The Feast in Time of the Plague": "perhaps is our guarantee of immortality." [*"Bessmertiia, mozhet byt´, zalog."*]

27. Healthy gambling in context of the story would mean risk without risking everything. It also implies a kind of gambling that permits one to walk away so that one may play again.

28. Dostoevskii, *PSS*, 14:5–508, 15:5–197.

29. Vladimir Nabokov, *Despair* (New York: Vintage, 1965), iii.

Chapter 2. Madness and Psychoanalysis

1. See the discussion of madness in the story by M. L. Gofman, "Problema sumasshestviia v tvorchestve Pushkina," *Novyi zhurnal* 51 (1957): 82–86; Gareth Williams, "The Obsessions of Madness of Germann in 'Pikovaja dama,'" *Russian Literature* 14, no. 4 (1983): 383–96; E. M. Taborisskaia, "Svoebrazie resheniia temy bezumiia v proizvedeniiakh Pushkina 1833 goda," in *Pushkinskie chteniia: Sbornik statei* (Tallinn: Eesti Raamat, 1990), 81–87; G. P. Makogonenko, *Tvorchestvo A. S. Pushkina v 1830-e gody* (Leningrad: Khudozhestvennaia literatura, 1982), 249–55. For a review of the Russian reception of the story, in general, see N. O. Lerner, "Istoriia 'Pikovoi damy,'" in *Rasskazy o Pushkine* (Leningrad: Priboi, 1929), 141–42.

2. The narrator of *A Raw Youth* speaks of Pushkin's Germann as "a colossal figure, an unusual, completely Petersburg type—a type from the Petersburg period" (F. M. Dostoevskii, *Polnoe sobranie sochinenii*, ed. V. G. Bazanov et al., 30 vols. [Leningrad: Nauka, 1972–90], 13:113; hereafter, *PSS*).

3. Most of the previous psychological and psychoanalytic interpretations of the story are based on variations of the Oedipal triangle, with either Germann coveting the countess or being punished for rebelling against his father or both. See, for example, Diana Lewis Burgin, "The Mystery of 'Pikovaia dama,'" in *Mnemozina: Studia litteraria russica in honorem Vsevolod Setchkarev*, ed. Joachim T. Baer and Norman W. Ingham (Munich: Fink, 1974), 46–56; Nathan Rosen, "The Magic Cards in 'The Queen of Spades,'" *Slavic and East European Journal* 19 (1975): 255–75; Murray M. Schwartz and Albert Schwartz, "'The Queen of Spades': A Psychoanalytic Interpretation," *Texas Studies in Literature and Language* 17 (1975): 275–88; Iu. M. Lotman, "Tema kart i kartochnoi igry v russkoi literature nachala XIX veka," in *Trudy po znakovym sistemam* (Tartu: Tartuskii gosudarstvennyi universitet, 1975), 7:122–42; Williams, "Obsessions of Madness," 383–96. My approach

does not at all deny the importance of Oedipal factors (I will later make use of them myself), but, as will be evident, I treat them for analytical purposes as the imaginative correlatives of more primal personality structures.

4. There are many widely diverging interpretations of Lacanian psychoanalysis, partly because Lacan intended his psychoanalysis to be more of an exploration of unconscious truth than a body of information or doctrines. He has said, "I don't have a conception of the world. I have a style" (quoted in Sherry Turkle, *Psychoanalytical Politics: Jacques Lacan and Freud's French Revolution*, 2nd ed. [New York: Guilford, 1992], 232). Turkle argues that Lacanian theory gives us a "compelling cast of inner agents and games to play with ... of possibilities ... for concrete manipulation" (xviii). For the best discussion of the developments of Lacanian psychoanalysis in France, see Turkle's *Psychoanalytical Politics*.

5. Several works in the last few decades have dwelt at length on the ubiquitousness of the numbers three, seven, and one, and their various combinations and permutations. See, for example, A. L. Slonimskii, "O kompozitsii 'Pikovoi damy,'" in *Pushkinskii sbornik pamiati Professora S. A. Vengerova* (Moscow: Gosudarstvennoe izdatel'stvo khudozhestvennoi literatury, 1923), 174–77; V. V. Vinogradov, "Stil' 'Pikovoi damy,'" *Pushkin: Vremennik Pushkinskoi komissii* 2 (1936): 87–91; Harry B. Weber, "'Pikovaia dama': A Case for Freemasonry in Russian Literature," *Slavic and East European Journal* 12 (1968): 435–47; Andrej Kodjak, "'The Queen of Spades' in the Context of the Faust Legend," in *Alexander Pushkin: A Symposium on the 175th Anniversary of His Birth* (New York: New York University Press, 1976), 91–92; Lauren Leighton, "Numbers and Numerology in 'The Queen of Spades,'" *Canadian Slavonic Papers* 19 (1977): 417–43; Lauren Leighton, "Gematria in 'The Queen of Spades': A Decembrist Puzzle," *Slavic and East European Journal* 21 (1977): 455–69; Paul Debreczeny, *The Other Pushkin: A Study of Alexander Pushkin's Prose Fiction* (Stanford: Stanford University Press, 1983), 219–22; Sergei Davydov, "The Ace in 'The Queen of Spades,'" *Slavic Review* 58, no. 2 (1999): 309–28.

6. Sigmund Freud, *New Introductory Lectures on Psychoanalysis*, trans. James Strachey (New York: Norton, 1965), 80.

7. Sigmund Freud, *Civilization and Its Discontents*, trans. James Strachey (New York: Norton, 1961), 39–41.

8. E. M. Forster, *Howard's End* (London: Edward Arnold, 1973), 57.

9. Caryl Emerson, "'The Queen of Spades' and the Open End," *Puškin Today*, ed. David Bethea (Bloomington: Indiana University Press, 1992), 35; Anthony Boucher, "Of Fortune and Faro," *Opera News* 30, no. 11 (1966): 12.

10. In chapter 4 of Dostoevsky's *The Gambler* (1865), the narrator, Aleksei, contrasts the Russian and German attitudes toward money and work. "The Russian is not only incapable of acquiring capital, but squanders it in a reckless and indecent way." Russians use roulette as a means of growing "rich all at once, in two hours, without working." But if they ever win, they are bound to lose their winnings as quickly as they won them. Germans, on the other hand, work like oxen, piling up money, which is passed on, intact, from one generation to another. "The

eldest son is likewise transformed into a virtuous *vater* and the same story [of sacrifice and accumulation—G.R.] begins all over again. In that way, in fifty or seventy years, the grandson of the first *vater* really amasses significant capital, and he leaves it to his son, and he to his, and he to his, till in about five or six generations one of them actually turns out to be a Baron Rothschild or Goppe and Co. or the devil knows who." Aleksei says that he would rather live his entire his life "in a Kirgiz tent ... than bow down to the German idol" (Dostoevsky, *PSS*, 5:225–26).

11. Vinogradov, "Stil'"; Slonimskii, "O kompozitsii," 175–76.

12. For the implications of *tuz*, see Joseph T. Shaw, "The 'Conclusion' of Pushkin's 'Queen of Spades,'" *Studies in Russian and Polish Literature in Honor of Wacław Lednicki*, ed. Zbigniew Folejewski ('S-Gravenhage: Mouton, 1962), 119.

13. For a discussion of the occurrence of three and seven as bets in faro, see Vladimir Nabokov, trans., *Eugene Onegin*, 2 vols. (New York: Random House, 1964), 2:261; Rosen, "The Magic Cards," 255–57. See also Debreczeny's discussion, in *The Other Pushkin*, 199, 325, of Tomashevskii's observations on this point. Also see B. V. Tomashevskii, "Istorizm Pushkina," in *Pushkin: kniga vtoraia, Materialy k monografii, 1824–1837* (Moscow: Akademiia nauk SSSR, 1961).

14. Of course, we—and Germann—learn about Germann's passionate nature only through the course of the story, only when he attempts to realize the object of his obsession.

15. Freud, *Civilization*, 72.

16. Julia Kristeva, "Revolution in Poetic Language," in *The Kristeva Reader*, ed. Toril Moi (New York: Columbia University Press, 1986), 152.

17. Neil Cornwell (*Pushkin's Queen of Spades* [London: Bristol, 1993], 66) advances perhaps the most novel interpretation of Germann's mental state on the last few days. He speculates that when Germann fell at the countess's funeral, he hit his head on the stone floor and suffered a concussion, which precipitated his madness and caused him to hallucinate all the succeeding events, with the exception of the epilogue.

18. For Kristeva, woman represents the desire that is repressed, both in women and men, in patriarchal culture. "Woman is a specialist in the unconscious, a witch, a bacchanalian, taking her *jouissance* in an anti-Apollonian, Dionystic orgy" (ibid., 154).

19. Since Germann is often seen as a rebel, it is not surprising that his gambling is seen as an unconscious rebellion against his father, the superego (Debreczeny, *The Other Pushkin*, 110–12). But the most common psychological explanation of Germann's choice of the wrong card is that of self-punishment for the guilt he experiences for the death of the countess (Rosen, "The Magic Cards," 265–70).

20. Disparaging remarks about American ego psychology are common in Lacan: "The academic restoration of this 'autonomous ego' justified my view that a misunderstanding was involved in any attempt to strengthen the ego in a type of analysis that took as its criterion of 'success' a successful adaption to society—

a phenomenon of mental abdication that was bound up with the ageing of the psychoanalytic group in the diaspora of the war, and the reduction of a distinguished practice to a label suitable to the 'American way of life'" (Jacques Lacan, *Écrits*, trans. Alan Sheridan [New York: Norton, 1977], 306–7).

21. Jacques Lacan, *The Four Fundamental Concepts of Psychoanalysis*, trans. Jacques-Alain Miller (New York: Norton, 1977), 44.

22. Lacan, *Écrits*, 314.

23. Lacan, *Four*, 45.

24. See also Lacan, *Écrits*, 128–29, 171, 299–300, 313–14, 164–65.

25. As we shall see, in contrast to Lacan, anti-psychiatrists, such as Kristeva, Deleuze and Guattari, Cixous, and Laing, seek liberation in the idealization of desire associated with the pre-Symbolic (sometimes called the semiotic or pre-Oedipal) stage of development—Lacan's imaginary stage. Kristeva, as a feminist, sees the phallocentric, symbolic order as the antithesis of truth. Representation itself, since it is part of the Word, the symbolic order, tends to undermine unconscious truth, which is "an unrepresentable form beyond true and false, and beyond present-past-future" (*Kristeva Reader*, 155).

26. Rosen, "The Magic Cards," 260–70.

27. Ibid., 257–58.

28. Hélène Cixous, *Readings: The Poetics of Blanchot, Joyce, Kafka, Kleist, Lispector, and Tsvetayeva* (Minneapolis: University of Minnesota Press, 1991), 112.

29. Ibid., 113.

30. R. D. Laing, *The Politics of Experience* (New York: Ballantine, 1967), 138.

31. Ibid., 143.

32. For the argument that General Epanchin, in *The Idiot*, is Dostoevsky's deromanticized projection of a successful Germann, a man who slowly gains his fortune, see I. Masing-Delič and Pandora King, "General Epanchin as Germann: A Travesty on Pushkin's 'Queen of Spades' in Dostoevsky's *The Idiot*," *Dostoevsky Studies* 9 (1989): 171–91.

33. In Hades, in the less exalted *Odyssey*, Achilles seems to have had a change of mind. He tells Odysseus that he would rather be a day laborer on Earth than an immortal hero in Hades. "By god, I'd rather slave on earth for another man— / Some dirt-poor tenant farmer who scrapes to keep alive— / than rule down here over all the breathless dead" (*The Odyssey*, trans. Robert Fagels [New York: Penguin, 1996], 265).

34. Giles Deleuze and Félix Guattari, *Anti-Oedipus: Capitalism and Schizophrenia* (Minneapolis: University of Minnesota Press, 1983), 87.

35. There is some evidence that the choice Germann makes was one that—again unconsciously—he had decided on quite a bit earlier. When leaning over the countess's body at her funeral, Germann imagines that she winks at him. While moving backward, he stumbles [*ostupilsia*] and takes a very bad fall, landing flat on his back. Is this not the same type of "accident" he later has when he chooses the wrong card and sees the countess, again, winking at him? Alan Sheridan describes the real in Lacan as "that over which the symbolic stumbles, that

which is refractory, resistant, ... [that] which is lacking in the symbolic order, the ineliminable residue of all articulation, the foreclosed element, which may be approached, but never grasped: the umbilical cord of the symbolic" (Lacan, *Écrits*, x).

36. Lacan contrasts, in his L-Schema, the symbolic relationship (S–O), based on unconscious communication, that exists between the subject (S) and object/Other (O) with the imaginary relationship (o–o′) that exists between the ego (o) and its object/other (o′) (*Écrits*, 193–94).

37. Lacan distinguishes pleasure [*plaisir*], an imaginary desire, from [*jouissance*], a more symbolic desire. Since Germann's obsession with the queen seems to oscillate between these two forms of desire, I have sometimes used the word *pleasure* and sometimes *desire*, depending on the context (Lacan, *Écrits*, 319–24).

38. An example of this is his description of the unbelievable relationship—in all respects—between Saint-Germain and his grandmother.

39. Lacan, *Écrits*, 58.

40. In other words, imaginary desire, however flawed, seems to be far more in touch with unconscious desire than Germann's ego ideal. Further, its greater association with unconscious desire may even prepare the reader for the unconscious "mistake" at the end against the ego ideal.

41. Williams, in "Obsessions of Madness," has written interestingly about Germann's equal fascination for the countess and the secret of the cards. He presents Germann's attraction, however, as a perversion. As Germann watches the countess undress, Williams states that Germann already "may be considered to be insane" (391). Only in the last sentence does he seem to realize that it is not the countess herself but the age she symbolizes that so attracts Germann (394). Germann "looks back with nostalgia to the financially non-competitive, almost feudal society of the last years before the revolution, in his hopeless love for the image of the countess" (394). See also Slonimskii, "O kompozitsii," 179.

42. "What is repeated, in fact, is always something that occurs ... *as if by chance*" (Lacan, *Four*, 54).

43. Sigmund Freud, "The 'Uncanny,'" *Collected Papers*, 5 vols. (New York: Basic Books, 1959), 4:389–91.

44. Ibid., 2:399.

45. It seems probable that Germann's mother is Russian (not unusual for the time) and that he derives his passionate side from her. Saint-Germain, his alter ego, shows him the possibility of overcoming the "German" side of himself, the side of control and indefinitely delayed gratification. "German" and "Russian" are meant in the story only as conveniences of thought; they refer to universal characteristics within us all. Tom Shaw has speculated that Germann may be the point of departure for Goncharov's Shtolts in *Oblomov*. Goncharov explicitly states that Shtolts derives his more "feeling" side from his Russian mother, his more practical and rational side from his German father.

46. Lacan, *Four*, 25.

47. Psychotics were interesting to Lacan, especially because of the way they used language. But Germann's madness results in the virtual loss of all language.

48. Lacan, *Écrits*, 215.

49. "The psychoanalytic experience has rediscovered in man the imperative of the Word as the law that has formed him in its image.... May that experience enable you to understand at last that it is in the gift of speech that all the reality of its effects resides; for it is by way of this gift that all reality has come to man and it is by his continued act that he maintains it" (Lacan, *Écrits*, 106). The real order exists outside the symbolic order and therefore can never be reached by language.

50. Lacan, *Écrits*, 214.

51. Ibid., 215.

52. Ibid., 199.

53. See the previous chapter for a detailed discussion of Pushkin's deflation of Germann's imagination throughout the story.

54. Since the early 1930s Soviet critics have fairly consistently seen Germann as a representative of a new class, the money- and power-hungry bourgeoisie, fated to displace the older and weaker nobility as embodied in the decrepit countess. See, for example, D. P. Iakubovich, "'Pikovaia Dama': Stat´ia i kommentarii," in *A. S. Pushkin: Pikovaia dama* (Leningrad: Gosudarstvennoe izdatel´stvo khudozhestvennoi literatury, 1936); A. G. Gukovskii, *Pushkin i problemy realisticheskogo stilia* (Moscow: Gosudarstvennoe izdatel´stvo khudozhestvennoi literatury, 1957), 340–53, 364–65; Tomashevskii, "Istorizm Pushkina," 198–99; N. L. Stepanov, *Proza Pushkina* (Moscow: Akademiia nauk SSSR, 1962), 76–79.

55. For others who have seen Germann as a Faust, a romantic rebel, or a challenger of the social order, see Weber, "A Case for Freemasonry," 435–47; M. M. Schwartz and A. Schwartz, "A Psychoanalytic Interpretation"; Kodjak, "The Faust Legend," 87–118; F. Falchikov, "The Outsider and the Number Game: Some Observations on 'Pikovaia Dama,'" *Essays in Poetics* 2, no. 1 (1977): 96–106; and V. Esipov, "Istoricheskii podtekst v povesti Pushkina 'Pikovaia dama,'" *Voprosy literatury* 4 (1989): 193–205.

56. Lacan, *Écrits*, 68.

57. Turkle's *Psychoanalytical Politics* ascribes the politically radical direction of psychoanalysis in France in the 1960s and 1970s to Lacan's erasure of the division between the personal and social in the definition of the subject. Once the personal and the social could be seen as two sides of the same coin, a political psychoanalysis became possible.

Chapter 3. Freedom and the Prison House of Madness

1. The lyric was published in 1841 posthumously. The Academy edition states that it was probably written between October and November 1833 (3:1248–49). For a long time most scholars dated the poem sometime between 1830 and 1833, as there were no facts on which to justify a more exact date. For a discussion of the problems of dating the poem, see M. P. Alekseev, "Neskol´ko novykh dannykh o

Pushkine i Batiushkove," *Izvestiia Akademii Nauk SSSR* (Otdelenie literatury i iazyka) 8, no. 4 (1949): 369–72. Recently, however, several scholars have advanced a later date, basing their arguments on the similarity of the poem to later works concerned with escape, flight, liberty, and peace, such as "Strannik" ["The Wanderer"] and "Iz Pindemonti" ["From Pindemonti"]. I. V. Izmailov prefers 1835–36 ("Liricheskie tsikly poezii Pushkina 30-kh godov," in *Pushkin: Issledovaniia i materialy*, vol. 2 [Leningrad: Akademiia nauk SSSR, 1982], 37); Ia. L. Levkovich argues for November 1835 ("Stikhotvorenie Pushkina 'Ne dai mne Bog soiti s uma,'" in *Pushkin: Issledovaniia i materialy*, vol. 10 [Leningrad: Akademiia nauk SSSR, 1982] 183–92).

2. Although "God Grant That I Not Lose My Mind" is often acknowledged to be one of Pushkin's "greatest short poems" (Vladimir Nabokov, trans., *Eugene Onegin* by Aleksandr Pushkin, 4 vols. [New York: Pantheon, 1964], 3:74), it has received relatively little critical attention. The most detailed commentaries are those of M. Gershenzon, *Mudrost' Pushkina* (Moscow: Pisateli v Moskve, 1919), 25–26; Levkovich, "Stikhotvorenie Pushkina," 176–92; E. Étkind, *Simmitricheskie kompozitsii u Pushkina* (Paris: D'Institut d'études slaves, 1988), 67–68; and Andrei Bitov, *Pushkinskii dom* (Moscow: Sovremennik, 1989), 238–39; E. M. Taborisskaia, "Svoeobrazie resheniia temy bezumiia v proizvedeniiakh Pushkina 1833 goda," *Pushkinskie chteniia: Sbornik statei* (Tallinn: Eesti Raamat, 1990), 74–75. Bitov's comments on the poem are actually his narrator's, but Bitov also published this section as literary criticism in *Voprosy literatury*. Bitov compares Pushkin's "God Grant That I Not Lose My Mind" and "The Prophet" [*Prorok*] with Tiutchev's "Madness" [*Bezumie*].

3. Walter Arndt, *Pushkin Threefold* (New York: Dutton, 1972), 253, 255. I use the Arndt translation because of its attempt to be as literal as possible. I have occasionally retranslated words where secondary meanings needed to be brought out.

4. For convenience, I have divided the poem into three sections. Section 1 contains stanza 1; section 2, stanzas 2 and 3; and section 3, stanzas 4 and 5.

5. Gershenzon, who emphasizes the dark side of Pushkin's works, considers that the poem "God Grant That I Not Lose My Mind" demonstrates that Pushkin's genius [*isstupleniie i sovershenstvo*] lies precisely in the extinction of reason [*ugashenie razuma*] (*Mudrost' Pushkina*, 24–27). It is dangerous to generalize on the basis of "God Grant" alone. When confronted with a poem like "*Bakhicheskaia pesnia*," in which both *um* [mind] and *razum* [reason] are identified with inspiration, Gershenzon is compelled to modify his equation of *razum* with *rassudok*—the cold, lifeless eighteenth-century rationality—and propose two forms of *razum* in Pushkin: the good *razum* associated with inspiration, and the bad (*ushcherbnyi*) *razum* associated with *rassudok*. Likewise, Gershenzon, in "Sny Pushkina," speaks of *dnevnoi rassudok* (day reason) and *nochnoi razum* (night reason) (*Stat'i o Pushkine* [Moscow: Gosudarstvennaia akademiia khudozhestvennykh nauk, 1926], 110). But, in fact, most instances of *razum* in Pushkin's later lyrics have rather positive connotations.

6. The hypothetical is foregrounded by the repetition of the hypothetical particle *by (b)* seven times.

7. After the passive "I was left" (*ostavili menia*) in line 6 (technically an indefinite "they" construction echoing the meaning of line 1), every sentence is expressed in the active voice.

8. Many of the ideas and much of the diction of stanzas 2 and 3 and the first three lines of stanza 5 can be found in Pushkin's poems about the poet and poetry. "The Poet" (*Poet*) is a good example. It includes a "wild" [*dikii*] poet running off; the same rhyme as lines 13–14, *poln/voln* (full of/waves), though reversed; and *shirokoshumnye dubrovy* [broadly rustling oak groves] in place of *shum glukhoi dubrov* [the rustling murmur of oak groves, line 27]. "Arion" (*Arion*) also has *poln/voln*, as well as *vikhor′ shumnyi* [a rumbling whirlwind]. The desire to escape to nature is a recurrent theme in Pushkin, but it is also a commonplace of romantic poetry. In Keats's "Ode to the Nightingale," which focuses more on the relationship between death and poetry than madness and poetry, the poet, as in Pushkin's poem, fusing with the nightingale, similarly dreams of flight for the sake of poetry: "That I might drink, and leave the world unseen, / And with thee fade away into the *forest dim*: / Fade far away, dissolve, and quite forget / What thou among the leaves hast never known" (John Keats, *Complete Poems*, ed. Jack Stillinger [Cambridge: Harvard University Press, 1982], 280). Also romanticizing "home" in his "To a Skylark," Wordsworth writes somewhat polemically: "Leave to the nightingale her *shady wood*" [my emphasis] (*The Complete Poetic Works of William Wordsworth* [London: Macmillan, 1928], 648).

9. O. S. Murav′eva, "Ob osobennostiakh poetiki pushkinskoi liriki," in *Pushkin: Issledovaniia i materialy*, vol. 13 (Leningrad: Nauka, 1989), 25.

10. Étkind, *Simmitricheskie kompozitsii*, 67.

11. Those who see these "empty skies" as godless do not explain why the persona would be so happy to gaze into godless skies. Perhaps the persona is imagined as having taken God's place or assumed His powers, both in terms of creativity and destructiveness.

12. S. A. Kibal′nik argues that the image of flight or escape [*pobeg*] links "God Grant That I Not Lose My Mind" with a cycle of poems that Pushkin wrote in the last years of his life, all of which reflect a strong influence of literary romanticism associated with the poets of the "Lake School" [*Ozernaia shkola*] ("Tema izgnaniia v poezii Pushkina," *Pushkin: Issledovaniia i materialy*, vol. 14 [Leningrad: Akademiia nauk SSSR, 1991], 50).

13. E. M. Taborisskaia, who tends to see the poem as an abstract exercise, implies that the destructive principle in the poem does not imply action: it is only a metaphor for the poet's subjective feelings ("Svoeobrazie resheniia temy bezumiia v proizvedeniiakh Pushkina 1833 goda," *Pushkinskie chteniia: Sbornik statei* [Tallinn: Eesti Raamat, 1990], 74–75). This interpretation, of course, begs the question of what constitutes real action in a poem and what is *not* an expression of the poet's subjective consciousness.

14. As we have seen, madness and poetry have been linked since ancient times. For more modern examples, see Michel Foucault, *Madness and Civilization: A History of Insanity in an Age of Reason* (New York: Random House, 1965); George

Rosen, *Madness in Society: Chapters in the Historical Sociology of Mental Illness* (New York: Harper, 1969), 1–225; Max Byrd, *Visits to Bedlam: Madness and Literature in the Eighteenth Century* (Columbia: University of South Carolina Press, 1974), xi–xv; and Lillian Feder, *Madness in Literature* (Princeton, N.J.: Princeton University Press, 1980), 3–201. Pushkin's "God Grant That I Not Lose My Mind" recalls Shakespeare's lines from *Midsummer-Night's Dream*: "The lunatic, the lover, and the poet, / Are of imagination all compact ... The poet's eye in a fine frenzy rolling / Doth glance from heaven to earth / From earth to heaven" (William Shakespeare, *The Complete Works*, ed. G. B. Harrison [New York: Harcourt, 1952], 2.1: 7–113. All references to Shakespeare are to this edition.) And Michael Drayton writes of Marlowe: "For that fine madness still he did retain / Which rightly should possess a poet's brain" (*Poems of Michael Drayton*, ed. John Buxton, 2 vols. [Cambridge: Harvard University Press, 1953], 1:154). For the quintessential Russian formulation of the similarity between the madman and the poet, see "The Second Night" of V. F. Odoevsky's *Russian Nights*. "Doesn't the state of a madman resemble the state of a poet?... Isn't the exalted state of a poet ... closer to what is called insanity than insanity is to an ordinary animal-like stupidity" (*Russian Nights*, trans. Olga Koshansky-Olienikov and Ralph E. Matlaw [New York: Dutton, 1965], 55–56). Pushkin undoubtedly was acquainted with much of the material that would eventually be incorporated into *Russian Nights*, in which the relationship between madness and artistic genius is often underscored.

15. Étkind, *Simmitricheskie kompozitsii*, 67. However prosaic, the last line is wonderfully powerful, with its striking sound symbolism in the phrase *Da vizg; da zvon*.

16. In the eighteenth century the equation of poverty and insanity was quite common, according to Foucault (*Madness*, 46–64), and vagrants were frequently locked up in the same place as the clinically insane.

17. Ibid., 68–69.

18. For the most detailed discussions of Batiushkov's life and his madness, see M. P. Alekseev, "Neskol'ko novykh dannykh o Pushkine i Batiushkove," *Izvestiia Akademii Nauk SSSR: Otdelenie literatury i iazyka* 8, no. 4 (1949): 369–71; Viacheslav Koshelev, *Konstantin Batiushkov: Stranstviia i strasti* (Moscow: Sovremennik, 1987), 276–340; and L. Maikov, *Batiushkov: ego zhizn' i sochineniia*, 2nd ed. (St. Petersburg: Marks, 1896), 222–40.

19. After 1840 Batiushkov calmed down considerably, making no further attempts on his life. He painted, sculpted, and loved spending time with children. During the Crimean War he became especially preoccupied with politics, reading the journals and newspapers, and making copious notes. He was well dressed, had exquisite manners, and was always respectful to women. He ate and slept well, and exercised regularly. With his excellent constitution, he might have lived considerably longer had he not contracted typhus in 1855. Even so, he outlived many of his younger confreres, including Pushkin, Lermontov, and Gogol.

20. Nabokov has noted a reference to Batiushkov—a mad poet—in the bright voice [*iarkii golos*] of the nightingale in the last stanza of the poem (3:60–61, 74–75).

21. Because of Pushkin's wide reading, it is virtually certain that he knew something about the treatment of the mentally ill in the late eighteenth and early nineteenth centuries, especially since the issue was made extremely topical by the reforms of Phillipe Pinel and William Tuke, initiated in the early 1800s. According to Georg Reuchlein, at the end of the eighteenth century the description of visits to insane asylums constituted "almost a literary genre unto itself" (*Bürgerliche Gesellschaft, Psychiatrie und Literatur: Zur Entwicklung der Wahnsinnsthematik in der deutschen Literatur des späten 18. und frühen 19. Jahrhunderts* [München: Fink, 1986], 68–69). Jutta Osinski describes this literature in German in some detail in *Über Vernunft und Wahnsinn: Studien zur literarischen Aufklärung in der Gegenwart und im 18. Jhdt* (Bonn: Bouvier, 1983), 59–66. Although there are no easily discovered "smoking guns" to be found in Pushkin's own library, some of the titles attest the probable discussion of the insane and Pushkin's definite interest in the subject. The library includes, for example, an 1836 copy of Thomas Taylor's biography of John Howard (1726–1790), the great English prison reformer who made extensive visits to hospitals as well as prisons. See B. L. Modzalevskii, *Biblioteka A. S. Pushkina* (St. Petersburg: Akademiia Nauk, 1910), 346. There is also a portrait of William Tuke in Hazlitt's *Spirit of the Age* from 1825 (Modzalevskii, *Biblioteka*, 246) and a copy of *Fragments psychologiques sur la folie* of François Leuret (a student of Pinel) from 1834 (Modzalevskii, *Biblioteka*, 273). L. I. Vol'pert has noted, in relation to *The Queen of Spades*, that Pushkin had cut just those pages in Leuret's work that were devoted to various types of hallucinations ("Tema bezumiia v proze Pushkina i Stendalia: 'Pikovaia dama' i 'Krasnoe i chernoe,'" *Pushkin i russkaia literatura: Sbornik nauchnykh trudov* [Riga: Latviiskii gosudarstvennyi universitet imeni P. Stuchki, 1986], 54). Furthermore, the library contains numerous memoirs and ethnographical studies of Russia and other countries; journals devoted to the arts and sciences; and a good number of books on medicine and on prisons, which often housed mentally deranged persons (Rosen, *Madness in Society*, 168–69). These writings often contained descriptions of visits to hospitals in which the mentally deranged were kept (Osinski, *Über Vernunft*, 59). Charles Dickens, who made a point of investigating every city he visited, wrote about his visit to Paris in 1847: "I have been seeing Paris—wandering into hospitals, prisons, dead-houses, operas, theatres, concertrooms, burial-grounds, palaces, and wine-shops.... [E]very description of gaudy and ghastly sight has been passing before me in a rapid panorama" (*The Nonesuch Dickens: Letters* [Bloomsbury: Nonesuch, 1938], 2:9).

22. The Russian *beda* (line 19) is not only misfortune, it is also poverty.

23. For discussions of the attitude toward madness in the Classical Age, see Foucault, *Madness*; Byrd, *Visits to Bedlam*; Rosen, *Madness in Society*, 151–71; and Feder, *Madness in Literature*, 147–202.

24. G. Glebov, "Filosofiia prirody v teoreticheskikh vyskazyvaniiakh i tvorcheskoi praktike Pushkina," in *Pushkin: Vremennik Pushkinskoi komissii*, vol. 2. (Moscow, Akademiia nauk SSSR, 1936), 206; Wacław Lednicki, *Pushkin's Bronze Horseman: The Story of a Masterpiece* (Berkeley: University of California Press,

1955); V. Nepomniashchii, "Dvadtsat' strok: Pushkin v poslednie gody zhizni i stikhotvorenie 'Ia pamiatnik sebe vozdvig nerukotvornyi,'" *Voprosy literatury* 9, no. 4 (1965): 132–35; S. G. Bocharov, *Poetika Pushkina* (Moscow: Nauka, 1974), 21; Catharine Theimer Nepomnyashchy, "The Poet, History, and the Supernatural: A Note on Pushkin's 'The Poet' and *The Bronze Horseman*," in *The Supernatural in Slavic and Baltic Literatures: Essays in Honor of Victor Terras*, ed. Amy Mandelker and Roberta Reeder (Columbus, Ohio: Slavica, 1988), 40.

25. Levkovich also cites the thirteenth stanza of "Ezerskii" in which the poet is likened to the wind in addition to the eagle and the heart of a maiden.

26. I. V. Izmailov sees the essential difference between "God Grant That I Not Lose My Mind" and two contemporaneous poems with similar imagery and thematic content ("From Pindemonte" [*Iz Pindemonti*] and "The Wanderer" [*Strannik*]) in the way the poems treat liberation ("Liricheskie tsikly poezii Pushkina 30-kh godov," in *Pushkin: Issledovaniia i materialy*, vol 2 [Leningrad: Akademiia nauk SSSR, 1982], 37). Whereas in "God Grant That I Not Lose My Mind," Izmailov argues, liberation becomes invalid by its association with madness—it leads eventually to re-enslavement, in the latter two poems liberation is validated by its association with reason.

27. This coincidence of imagery undoubtedly reflects common cultural, literary, and social milieux, and not direct influence. Gogol could hardly have known Pushkin's poem in manuscript since the latest date argued for "God Grant That I Not Lose My Mind" is November 1835. Though Gogol did write Pushkin in December 1834 about his troubles getting "Notes of a Madman" through the censor (*Polnoe sobranie sochinenii*, 7 vols. [Moscow: Izdatel'stvo Akademii nauk, 1937–52], 3:699), it seems just as improbable that Pushkin could have been influenced by Gogol's work, which was written in 1834 and published in *Arabeski* in 1835.

28. Gogol', *Polnoe sobranie sochinenii*, 3:213.

29. Ibid., 3:213–14.

30. The academy edition (3:1248) states that the version that has come down to us is incomplete or uncompleted. The fair copy [*belovoi*] of the poem, like its symmetry, indicates that the poem was probably close to completion, that earlier versions existed, and that corrections were made. Indeed, some corrections on the fair copy have come down to us. The Academy edition (3:1248) describes the autograph as "fair copy, with corrections, autograph; apparently either not fully preserved or unfinished" [*belovoi, s popravkami, avtograf; povidimomu, sokhranivshiisia ne polnolst'iu ili nezakonchennyi*]. To a critic like Stanley Fish, of course, the whole argument of whether or not the poem is unfinished has little to do with the poem itself, given that a poem is primarily not an objective fact, something that is found, but a construction of its readers. Thus those who see the poem as unfinished will probably be able to argue as cogently for its being unfinished as those who see it as finished (and with a unifying purpose) will be able to argue for its being finished. See, for example, Fish's famous "How to Recognize a Poem When You See One," in *Is There a Text in This Class?* (Cambridge, Mass.: Harvard University Press, 1980), 322–37.

31. There may be nothing in all Pushkin's work that is at the same time so intensely personal, powerful, and uncharacteristic as "God Grant That I Not Lose My Mind." Neither in his private correspondence nor in his lyric poetry does Pushkin come as close to the confessional mode as in this lyric poem. In fact, it is not unreasonable to assume, although impossible to prove, that this poem in particular—in contrast to other unpublished poems—was unpublished or uncompleted or both precisely because of its personal nature. Perhaps in this poem, more than any other, the persona of the poem and the poet come closest together. There is nothing in Pushkin's letters on the subject of madness in general or on his personal fear of madness, nor would one expect there to be.

32. The extent to which form should reflect content—should a poem about madness be somewhat disjunctive—raises the issue of imitative form. Yvor Winters, who coined the term *imitative form*, or *expressive form*, in English *(In Defense of Reason* [Columbus: Ohio University Press, 1986], 41), saw it as a fallacy, employing it pejoratively to describe art, romantic poetry in particular, that, to quote Henry Adams, "had to be confused in order to express confusion" (414). The notion of imitative form can obviously be abused, but even in neoclassical poetry it is often quite appropriate that form, in some way, imitates content. Imitative form, in fact, provides the foundation for the classical theory of decorum. The idea of imitative form has been fruitfully applied to the novel as well. In Dostoevsky's *The Idiot*, the theme of chaos seems to be reflected not only in the events and characterization but also in the novel's structure and even point of view. On the other hand, incoherence is not always mad, nor is madness always incoherent.

33. Gershenzon, *Mudrost' Pushkina*, 24–27.

34. Gofman, "Problema sumasshestviia," 62. The most extreme position in this regard was expressed by Merezhkovskii who quoted the second and third stanzas of "God Grant That I Not Lose My Mind" as an example of Russia's "rebellion against culture," "its dissatisfaction with the forms of human culture ... and its attraction to chaos." See D. Merezhkovskii, "Pushkin," in *Vechnye sputniki* (Moscow: Respublika, 1995), 496–97.

35. An unfinished work need not be incomplete, as scholars of Melville's *Billy Budd* have long concluded. See Harrison Hayford and Merton M. Sealts Jr., Introduction to *Billy Budd, Sailor* by Herman Melville (Chicago: University of Chicago Press, 1962), 39.

36. Whether the expression *ne dai mne Bog* is seen as a prayer or simply a wish will be determined by one's interpretation. Certainly the use of *Bozhe* (Lord) would have made the case for a prayer stronger, as in *Ottsy pustynniki i zheny neporochny* ["Hermit Fathers and Immaculate Women"]. On the other hand, Nabokov translates *Ne dai mne Bog soiti s uma* as "The Lord Forbid My Going Mad." See also Roman Jakobson (*Selected Writings*, ed. Stephen Rudy [The Hague: Mouton, 1981], 3:74–75), who admits two different interpretations of the expression "*dai vam Bog*" [God grant you] in Pushkin's "*Ia vas liubil*" ["I Loved You"]. Responding to Jakobson, Saveli Senderovich suggests that the phrase "*dai vam Bog*" in "*Ia vas liubil*" is as much ambivalent as ambiguous, such that it may indicate

an unconscious attraction to painful experience as well as a conscious desire to escape it ("Vnutrenniaia rech´ i terapevticheskaia funktsiia v lirike: O stikhotvorenii Pushkina 'Ia vas liubil...'" *Révue des études slaves* 59, nos. 1–2 [1987]: 321).

37. R. D. Laing, *The Politics of Experience* (New York: Ballantine, 1967), 157.
38. Ibid., 133.
39. C. G. Jung, *Modern Man in Search of a Soul*, trans. W. S. Dell and Cary F. Baynes (New York: Harcourt, 1933), 111.
40. Ibid., 248–50. A light/dark antimony does not dominate the poem, but most of the poem may take place at night: stanzas 2 and 3 probably do, stanza 5 definitely does, and stanza 4 probably takes place in a dark cell.
41. Ibid., 254.
42. Ibid., 279.
43. J. E. Cirlot writes that, "in contrast with the city, the house, and cultivated land, which are all safe areas, the forest harbors all kinds of dangers and demons, enemies and diseases. This is why forests are among the first places in nature to be dedicated to the cult of the gods, and why propitiatory offerings were suspended from trees (the tree being, in this case, the equivalent of a sacrificial stake)" (*A Dictionary of Symbols*, trans. Jack Sage [New York: Philosophical Library, 1971], 112).
44. C. G. Jung, *The Spirit in Man, Art, and Literature*, trans. R. F. C. Hull (Princeton, N.J.: Princeton University Press, 1966), 13. For the wind as a creative force, see stanza 13 of Pushkin's "Ezerskii," which bears some striking resemblances to "God Grant That I Not Lose My Mind."
45. Jung, *Spirit*, 18.
46. Gofman, "Problema sumasshestviia," 62.
47. Laing, *Politics*, 133.
48. Levkovich acknowledges the presence of romantic elements in the early Pushkin, but Dmitry Čiževsky argues that these elements were part of Pushkin's "romantic vocabulary" throughout his career (*Alexander Sergeevich Pushkin, Evgenij Onegin: A Novel in Verse*, ed. Dmitry Čiževsky [Cambridge, Mass.: Harvard University Press, 1967]). For example, in *Evgenii Onegin* (1.58), the narrator speaks of "the fever of rhymes" [*goriachka rifm*] and "the holy delirium of poetry" [*poezii sviashchennyi bred*]. There are also similarities in diction to "The Demon" [*Demon*]—"the rustling murmur of the oak grove" [*shum dubrovy*] and "the singing of the nightingale" [*pen´e solov´ia*]—as well as to other poems. "Conversation of a Bookseller with a Poet" [*Razgovor knigoprodavtsa s poetom*], for example, contains "the rustling murmur of forests" [*shum lesov*], "fiery ecstasy" [*plamennyi vostorg*], and "violent whirlwind" [*vikhor´ buinyi*], which seems as destructive as the whirlwind [*vikhor´*] in "God Grant That I Not Lose My Mind."
49. Sixteen of the thirty lines of the poem have masculine rhymes in *a*: four in stanza 1; two in stanza 2, four in stanza 3, four in stanza 4, and two in stanza 5. All the rhymes are couplets except for the second set in stanza 1, which is an enclosed pair (lines 3 and 6).
50. Laing, *Politics*, 139.

51. J. Thomas Shaw, "The Problem of Unity of the Author-Narrator's Stance in Pushkin's *Evgenij Onegin*," *Russian Language Journal* 35, no. 120 (1980): 28–35.

Chapter 4. Madness and the Common Man

1. The confrontation with the statue occurs approximately one year after the flood. But few details suggest a time when Evgenii might have died, and even these are ambiguous. Pushkin may have left the time of Evgenii's actual death purposely vague. See note 34, below.

2. Pushkin might, of course, be hinting at his need to escape the tsar's "prison house" for the freedom of the country.

3. *The Queen of Spades* is one of the most formally and aesthetically self-contained works in nineteenth-century Russian literature. Dostoevsky was one of the few who tried to extend the parameters of the work, seeing in the passionate, rash, and determined Germann a rebel against the established order, the first true ideological criminal in Russian literature. The narrator of *A Raw Youth*, for example, speaks of Pushkin's Germann as "a colossal figure, an unusual, completely Petersburg type—a type from the Petersburg period." See F. M. Dostoevskii, *Polnoe sobranie sochinenii*, ed. V. G. Bazanov et al., 30 vols. (Leningrad: Nauka, 1972–90), 13:113.

4. Although this exact line has not been found in any of the Greek authors, by the late fourth century B.C., even Greek writers believed this saying to have been stated by some venerable author. It is generally considered to be the most cited Latin adage to come down to modern times. A distinction must be made between Greek myth, culture, and literature, on the one hand, and Greek science, on the other. Greek physicians tended to see madness as a mental illness with treatable physical causes. See George Rosen, *Madness in Society: Chapters in the Historical Sociology of Mental Illness* (New York: Harper, 1969), 74.

5. For examples from Greek literature of madness as punishment for disrespect of a god (usually Dionysius), as well as a discussion of the relationship between madness and punishment in Greek culture, see Rosen, *Madness in Society*, 76–78. "It is important to recall that Dionysus, the god known for his power to inflict madness on others, was himself once afflicted with madness by Hera; myths record that in this state he wandered through Egypt and Syria until he was healed by Rhea in Phrygia and initiated into her mysteries" (Lillian Feder, *Madness in Literature* [Princeton, N.J.: Princeton University Press, 1980], 39).

6. *The Bronze Horseman* does not attempt to portray the historical Peter; it is more concerned with constructing an image of Peter and exploring his legacy as embodied in his city, empire, and monument.

7. The subtitles of Pushkin's works—like Gogol's—show experimentation with genre typical of literary romanticism. In his discussion of *Eugene Onegin* Dmitry Čiževsky cites Pushkin's novel in verse as a paradigm of the "free" romantic poem, in which the very subtitle [*roman*, novel] constitutes "a deliberate challenge to

classical poetics" (Alexander Sergeevich Pushkin, *Evgenij Onegin: A Novel in Verse*, ed. Dmitry Čiževsky [Cambridge, Mass.: Harvard University Press, 1967], xv–xx, quote at xv). For a discussion of *Dead Souls* as a mixed genre form, see Frederick T. Griffiths and Stanley J. Rabinowitz, *Novel Epics: Gogol, Dostoevsky, and National Narrative* (Evanston, Ill.: Northwestern University Press, 1990), 60–95.

8. When Dostoevsky wanted his reader to link his *povest'*, *The Double*, with Pushkin's *The Bronze Horseman*, he archly called his "prose" work "A Petersburg Poem" [*Peterburgskaia poema*].

9. For a discussion of the panegyric tradition as the basis of the introduction, see Wacław Lednicki, *Pushkin's "Bronze Horseman": The Story of a Masterpiece* (Berkeley: University of California Press, 1955), 43–47.

10. Feofan Prokopovich, *Sochineniia*, ed. I. P. Eremin (Moscow: Nauka, 1961), 126.

11. Petr Krekshin, *Kratkoe opisanie*, in *Zapiski russkikh liudei*, ed. I. P. Sakharov (Petersburg: Sakharov, 1841), 4.

12. For references to the most important belles lettres in this tradition, see Xenia Gasiorowska, *The Image of Peter the Great in Russian Fiction* (Madison: University of Wisconsin Press, 1979), 119–20.

13. Lednicki has shown that Pushkin's paean of Petersburg was partly conceived as a polemical rebuttal of Mickiewicz's satirical attack against the city in his *Suburbs of the Capital, St. Petersburg* and *The Review of the Army* (*The Story of a Masterpiece*, 20–23).

14. I will give the Russian translation of the biblical passage for reference and comparison, but a full Russian translation of the Bible was unavailable in Russian during Pushkin's time. Since it is doubtful that Pushkin read the text in Church Slavic, his knowledge of the Bible was probably drawn from French editions, several versions of which are to be found in his library. Interestingly, the Russian translation of John stresses even more the Word as the beginning and origin. "In the beginning there was the Word, and the Word was with God and the Word was God. It was from the beginning with God. Everything was begun through Him (It), and without Him (It) nothing would have begun, which was begun. In Him (It) was life and life was the light of mankind. And light in the darkness [*vo t'me*] shone so the darkness [*t'ma*] did not encompass it." In the Russian the word *It* [*Ono*], which begins the second verse, stands for the Word. But in the objective case, since the same word would be used for either Him or It, the text further fuses God and the Word.

15. I shall be using the "literal" translation of *The Bronze Horseman* found in Walter Arndt, *Pushkin Threefold: Narrative, Lyric, and Ribald Verse* (New York: Dutton, 1972), 400–27. I occasionally give alternate translations to call attention to verbal echoes or to stress meanings not covered by the English. The Russian text, *Mednyi vsadnik*, is in A. S. Pushkin, *Polnoe sobranie sochinenii*, ed. V. D. Bonch-Bruevich, 17 vols. (Moscow: Akademiia Nauk SSSR, 1937–59), 5:135–49.

16. Roman emperors were officially deified. Deification of heroes, like Heracles, is not uncommon in Greek mythology. Michael Grant writes: "And so Heracles became the exemplar of Euhemerus' doctrines that all gods really once had been

men, and phenomena such as Roman emperor worship were deduced from the same idea" (*Myths of the Greeks and Romans* [New York: Mentor, 1962], 240).

17. In many respects Pushkin's deific treatment of Peter in the introduction exceeds his glorification—Lednicki says "canonization" (*The Story of a Masterpiece*, 57)—of Peter in the heroic-romantic verse tale *Poltava*, in which Peter is much more personally present. One need only compare the sections following the same line "One hundred years have passed" to see the difference. *Poltava* essentially focuses on Peter's victory in battle, which is the "monument" Peter has erected to himself. In *The Bronze Horseman* the narrator focuses on Peter's legacy.

18. Lednicki, *The Story of a Masterpiece*, 68–69

19. The Peter of *The Bronze Horseman* is, of course, Pushkin's creation as well, but Peter has a whole history beyond the poem, whereas Evgenii is fiction.

20. Perhaps the most notable exception in this regard is Richard Gregg's "The Nature of Nature and the Nature of Eugene in *The Bronze Horseman*," *Slavic and East European Journal* 21, no. 2 (1977): 167–79.

21. For a different view of Evgenii's name, see Svetlana Evdokimova, "'Mednyi vsadnik': Istoriia kak mif," *Russian, Croatian and Serbian, Czech and Slovak, Polish Literature* 28, no. 4 (1990): 450. Evdokimova notes that Pushkin probably uses Evgenii's name ironically as "a semantic oxymoron." Lednicki presents the exact opposite point of view by arguing that Pushkin transforms the defects of the parodistically portrayed Evgenii in a satire by Kantemir to virtues in his own Evgenii (*The Story of a Masterpiece*, 70–71). Evdokimova further argues that eighteenth-century Russian writers often use *blagorodnyi* [noble] ironically, applying it to characters that do not live up to their names. But it is doubtful that Pushkin was much influenced by the irony of eighteenth-century Russian literature.

22. Pushkin may have empathized with his hero's situation because he saw it as a metaphor of his own in Russian society. On the other hand, though Evgenii may belong to the hereditary nobility, he seems far less concerned with the fate of his family line and class than was Pushkin. Pushkin, however, did not place family line or class over personal merit. For Pushkin's views on this matter, see Carl R. Proffer, ed., *The Critical Prose of Alexander Pushkin* (Bloomington: Indiana University Press, 1969), 118–20.

23. Lednicki, *The Story of a Masterpiece*, 33.

24. A. N. Radishchev, *Polnoe sobranie sochinenii*, 2 vols. (Moscow: Izdatel'stvo Akademiia nauk SSSR, 1938), 1:150. After the great flood, God promises that he will never again unleash such a scourge on mankind, creating a rainbow as a sign of this contract (covenant).

25. In P. A. Viazemsky's encomium to Peter, the great tsar Peter still rules over his city, protecting it with his mighty hand [*derzhavnaia ruka*] (*Sochineniia v dvukh tomakh* (Moscow: Khudozhestvennaia literatura, 1982), 1:85.

26. "And the Lord brought us forth out of Egypt with a mighty hand and with an outstretched arm [*rukoiu sil'noiu i myshtseiu prostertoiu*], and with great terribleness, and with signs, and with wonders" (Deut. 26:8). The outstretched arm is the sign of divine power, the power that governs peoples and controls the elements,

such as the waters. It is the power that permits the Jews to cross the Red Sea and consigns the Egyptians to the waves. Russia, it appears, owes her liberation from bondage and her salvation to Peter. Terribleness and wonders are concepts that are later directly applied to Peter as well.

27. According to Rosen, in Greek culture proneness to violence and wandering were considered the most characteristic aspects of madness. The violent mad, in the cultural stereotype, were particularly prone to throw stones (*Madness in Society*, 98).

28. Wandering is a common form of punishment in many traditions. God curses Cain by making him a wanderer. The Wandering Jew is a common stereotype of the Jew as a rejected and alienated people, condemned to eternal wandering. The gods' terrible wrath toward Odysseus is shown in their postponement of his return home.

29. See "The Great Confinement," in Michel Foucault, *Madness and Civilization: A History of Insanity in the Age of Reason*, trans. Richard Howard (New York: Vintage, 1988), 38–64.

30.
> And I am the cause of all this. It is terrible
> To lose one's mind. It is better to die.
> We look at a corpse with respect,
> We say prayers for the deceased. Death
> Is the great equalizer. But a man deprived
> Of mind, becomes something other than a man.
> In vain is he given speech; he cannot cope with
> Words; the beast recognizes in him
> One of its own; he is ridiculed by everyone;
> He is subject to everyone's will; he is not even judged by God. (7:207–8)

31. "What is repeated, in fact, is always something that occurs ... *as if by chance*" (Jacques Lacan, *The Four Fundamental Concepts of Psychoanalysis*, trans. Jacques-Alain Miller [New York: Norton, 1977], 54). Dostoevsky would adopt this device in *Crime and Punishment* when Raskolnikov aimlessly wanders and "happens" to wind up at the scene of the crime.

32. Here the narrative probably means "rises suddenly from sleep," gets up, and begins to move around.

33. It took many months of wandering, madness, a chance occurrence, a concatenation of circumstances, and profound despair for Evgenii to make this threat, not so much a personal threat (Evgenii knows that Peter has nothing to fear from him personally) but a threat from history, the arena that matters most for Peter. Evgenii has one tremendous moment—perhaps the greatest in all Russian literature—but he must, as he knows, pay the price. He has incorporated all that into his consciousness.

34. The narrator mentions that the previous spring (*proshedsheiu vesnoiu*) a barge came to the island on which Parasha's little house has washed up and hauled

it away. Evgenii's cold corpse was found in the house. He was buried on the very spot. If the previous spring means the spring before the hypothetical time of writing, then Evgenii wandered Petersburg a rather long time: seven or eight years (from 1825 to either 1832 or 1833). Another detail also indicates that the hypothetical time of writing is somewhat distant from the events: In reporting the response of Alexander I to the flood, the narrator underlines the distance between the writing and the narrative by stating that at the time of the events (1824) ("during that terrible year," *v tot groznyi god*) Alexander (who died in 1825) was still ruling with glory. Further, the narrator mentions that the memory of the flood is still fresh (*Ob nei svezho vospominan'e*, 1.93). He would hardly call a memory being fresh for an event that happened recently, only a year ago. The point is that it made a lasting impression.

The hypothetical time of narration, however, does not necessarily have to coincide with the actual composition of the text. First of all, stating that Evgenii's body was cold when found probably indicates that he had not just died; but it also implies that he had died relatively recently, otherwise there would not have been a corpse. It is also improbable that not a blade of grass had grown (*Ne vzroslo tam ni bylinki*) on the island in the last seven years. Given the contradictions in the text, we have two choices. We can concede that we cannot establish how long Evgenii wandered Petersburg and therefore eschew any conclusions having to do with the length of his madness and his wanderings, or we can argue that Pushkin opens up the interpretative possibilities for each option. Perhaps the most reasonable conclusion is that Evgenii was fated to wander Petersburg, unquestionably becoming increasingly mad, for several years after his confrontation with Peter. The narrator's statement that it was *only* this last spring that his body was found may simply be a literary device for explaining why his sad tale can now be told.

35. Evgenii has accepted the Petrine ideology of meritocracy. Peter is often depicted as the first worker of, and for, the state, someone who does not spare himself for the cause, who expects others to follow his example, and who can become enraged when others do not show comparable diligence and commitment.

36. One is reminded of what Pushkin wrote about Radishchev's rebellion against Catherine the Great: "When we realize what harsh people surrounded the throne of Catherine, the crime of Radishchev appears to be the act of a madman. A petty official, a man without any authority, without any backing, dares to rise up against the general order, against the autocracy, against Catherine!" ("Aleksandr Radishchev," 12:32).

37. The exigencies of genre tend to keep Peter and Evgenii apart, maintaining and even emphasizing the distance between them. In the confrontation scene, however, both in and outside Evgenii's imagination, the two texts—and protagonists—come together thematically, metaphorically, and linguistically. The confrontation marks the place where the story of Evgenii threatens not only the monument but also the story of Peter, that is, history. As ode and *povest'* merge, so do their protagonists. Each becomes infected by the narrative mode of the

other. Madness in its various manifestations raises Evgenii to Peter's level, but the fusion Pushkin suggests, through a romantic use of madness, is also achieved through the manipulation of narrative and genre.

38. Noting the solemnity of tone and the Slavonicisms used to describe Evgenii's most dramatic encounter with Peter, Briusov sees that some equation between the two heroes has been temporarily achieved: "This is no longer 'our hero,' who 'lives in Kolomna and serves in some institution'; this is a rival of 'the terrible tsar,' about whom one must speak in the same language as about Peter himself" [*Eto uzhe ne "nash geroi," kotoryi "zhivet v Kolomne, gde-to sluzhit"; eto sopernik "groznogo tsaria," o kotorom dolzhno govorit' tem zhe iazykom, kak o Petre*] (Briusov, *Moi Pushkin*, 80).

39. That, of course, does not exclude the possibilities that both the narrator's and Evgenii's points of view are being represented at the same time.

40. E. R. Dodds, *The Greeks and the Irrational* (Berkeley: University of California Press, 1964), 64–101; Ruth Padel, *Whom Gods Destroy: Elements of Greek and Tragic Madness* (Princeton, N.J.: Princeton University Press, 1995), 94–95.

41. "Phaedrus," *The Works of Plato*, trans. Benjamin Jowett (New York: Random House, 1928), 284. For a discussion of the relationship of madness and prophecy in the Old Testament and in Near Eastern religions in general, see Rosen, *Madness in Society*, 21–70. In Greek literature, Plato's *Phaedrus* contains perhaps the most interesting view of madness, especially its relationship to prophecy. Plato describes three kinds of madness: a madness almost all agree is a great evil or misfortune (clinical insanity) and two beneficent kinds of madness that are great gifts to mankind—the madness of prophecy and the madness of those possessed by the Muses. Though Plato associates the source of great truths with the madness of prophecy, in *Timaeus* he makes an important distinction between the source, form, and interpretation of prophecy. Identifying the source of divination in human beings with the organ of the liver, Plato comments on the nature of divination:

> And herein is a proof that God has given the art of divination not to the wisdom, but to the foolishness of man. No man, when in his wits, attains prophetic truth and inspiration; but when he receives the inspired word, either his intelligence is enthralled in sleep, or he is demented by some distemper or possession. And he who would understand what he remembers to have been said, whether in a dream or when he was awake, by the prophetic and inspired nature, or would determine by reason the meaning of the apparitions which he has seen, and what indications they afford to this man or that, of past, present or future good and evil, must first recover his wits. But, while he continues demented, he cannot judge of the visions which he sees or the words which he utters; the ancient saying is very true, that "only a man who has his wits can act or judge about himself and his own affairs." And for this reason it is customary to appoint interpreters to be judges of the true inspiration. Some persons call them prophets; they are

quite unaware that they are only the expositors of dark sayings and visions, and are not to be called prophets at all, but only interpreters of prophecy. (*The Dialogues of Plato*, trans. B. Jowett, 4 vols. [New York: Scribners, 1901], 563)

In other words, the madman or diviner or oracle or prophet receives, perceives, and conveys the highest truths, truths that come from the gods, but he himself does not understand what he says, reports, or writes. It is the task of those more rational, intelligent, and sane to interpret the meaning of the oracle's, or prophet's, message. The message is intricately encoded, and, as such, it is incomprehensible; it must be decoded for mortals to understand what it entails.

42. "Folly for the sake of Christ is a form of sanctity found in Byzantium, but particularly prominent in medieval Russia: the 'Fool' carries the ideal of self-stripping and humiliation to its furthest extent, by renouncing all intellectual gifts, all forms of earthly wisdom, and by voluntarily taking upon himself the Cross of madness" (Timothy Ware, *The Orthodox Church* [London: Penguin, 1963], 118).

43. Even in the Old Testament, some of the prophets behaved in bizarre manners. Yehezkel Kaufmann, for one, has argued that the prophets were "for the most part, psychically abnormal" (*The Religion of Israel: From Its Beginnings to the Babylonian Exile*, trans. Moshe Greenberg [Chicago: University of Chicago Press, 1960], 276). There were also false holy fools, those the church considered to be impostors. In Shakespeare, the king's fool is neither holy nor mad; yet he has a certain license to tell the king truths that no one else would dare utter. In *King Lear*, the fool is a pretend fool. He is wiser than the king when the king is sane. The king becomes wiser than his fool not when the king grows foolish but when he goes mad.

44. For a detailed study of holy fools in literature, but especially in Dostoevsky, see Harriet Murav, *Holy Foolishness: Dostoevsky's Novels and the Poetics of Cultural Critique* (Stanford: Stanford University Press, 1992); Konrad Onasch, "Der Typus des 'Jurodivy' im Werks Dostoevskijs," *Dostoevsky Studies* 1 (1980): 111–21; and Frances Hernandez, "Dostoevskij's Prince Myshkin as a Jurodivyj," *Rocky Mountain MLA Bulletin* (March 1972): 16–21. For an attempt to understand the holy fool more in terms of a universal pagan (shamanism) rather than Christian religion, see Ewa Thompson's provocative study *Understanding Russia: The Holy Fool in Russian Culture* (Lanham, Md.: University Press of America, 1987). As Harriet Murav points out, some nineteenth-century scientists came to view involuntary foolishness as a serious mental disease; others saw some cases of voluntary foolishness as a fraudulent attempt to deceive the gullible public for personal gain (*Holy Foolishness*, 6–8). The phenomenon of false prophecy, of course, has often been the object of frequent condemnation. See Isaiah 28:7–8; Jeremiah 23:14, 29:23.

45. The hagiographer constructs sanctity out of the wanderings of the holy fools, the model for which is Jesus' "homelessness" (Murat, *Holy Foolishness*, 27).

46. "It might be noted that here children are especially fitting representatives of the foolish world, unable to recognize the saint in the seeming madman" (Murat, *Holy Foolishness*, 26).

47. Karamzin reports a similar story about the holy fool Nikola and Ivan the Terrible. Ivan had just savagely dealt with Novgorod and was preparing the same for Pskov. The humility of the people of Pskov impressed Ivan greatly, and he was already relenting when he visited Nikola, who offered Ivan a piece of raw meat as a gift. When Ivan refused, saying that he was a Christian and did not eat meat on Lent, the fool replied, "You do worse; you feed on human flesh and blood, forgetting not only the fast, but God himself." Nikola also threatened Ivan, predicting misfortune. Nikola, in fact, "so frightened Ivan that he left the city immediately." Pskov did not completely escape Ivan's bloodlust, but it fared well in comparison to what happened in Novgorod and what would happen soon thereafter in Moscow. See N. M. Karamzin, *Predaniia vekov* (Moscow: Pravda, 1987), 593–94.

48. For a complete dismissal of the role of God in *The Bronze Horseman*, see A. D. Briggs, *A Comparative Study of Pushkin's* The Bronze Horseman, *Nekrasov's* Red-Nosed Frost, *and Blok's* The Twelve (Lewiston, N.Y.: Mellen, 1990), 153.

49. Mazeppa says something "bold" [*slovo smeloe*] that angers Peter, who grabs Mazeppa by his moustaches and threatens him. Mazeppa misspoke, but for a nobleman to be grabbed by the mustache or by the beard is the most unforgivable of insults. Reagen's pulling of Gloucester's beard in *King Lear* is perhaps the earliest sign that she has taken leave of her senses. We can assume that Pushkin was familiar with this famous scene in Shakespeare's play. As in *The Bronze Horseman*, Pushkin pits the personal against the political. Mazeppa could hardly be blamed for viewing Peter's behavior as an unforgivable insult. On the other hand, Russia's destiny, tied to Peter, must supersede personal scores.

50. Dostoevsky may have used Mariia as a source for Mar´ia Lebiadkina, the holy fool in *The Possessed*. Whereas Mariia is not presented as especially religious—if anything she goes against family and religious practice in marrying Mazeppa—Mar´ia Lebiadkina is a figure of considerable religious significance. Half-mad and half–holy fool, she accuses Stavrogin of being an imposter, just as Mariia accuses Mazeppa. But Dostoevsky takes the prophetic and visionary aspect of his character much further. Mariia does not see the relationship between Peter and Mazeppa; it is encoded in the text, unbeknownst to her, as part of her mad accusation against Mazeppa. The narrator reveals the significance of her comparison by setting up the semantic resonances with Peter several pages before she visits Mazeppa. In Dostoevsky, Mar´ia Lebiadkina can knowingly speak the truth to Stavrogin because she is presented as a holy fool, and her insight and clairvoyance in the Dostoevskian text are confirmed by her religious status.

51. Ernest J. Simmons states that he preferred "strange or monstrous creatures" (*Pushkin* [Cambridge, Mass.: Harvard University Press, 1937], 12).

52. Xenia Gasiorowska, *The Image of Peter the Great in Russian Fiction* (Madison: University of Wisconsin Press, 1979), 107.

53. Rosen writes: "Clearly, the acts of the prophet were no trifling matter. Unless counter-measures were taken, the hostile forces which he released could lead to catastrophe" (*Madness in Society*, 47).

54. In Pushkin, monuments are not just stone; they listen, and, when angered or challenged, they come to life and respond.

55. In the ancient world, the mad were not always seers, though seers were often mad. Though Ajax, Agave, Hercules, and Orestes go mad, they do not possess divine powers. On the other hand, the powers of divination or special understanding are invariably associated with madness.

56. Padel discusses the relationship between melancholia (black bile) and dark seeing (insight in madness) (*Whom Gods Destroy*, 47–77).

57. "Clearly, by the fifth century B.C., a medical view that madness was caused by black bile had become sufficiently current among the people for the words derived from this idea to be used in daily speech and to serve as synonyms for other terms denoting mental derangement" (Rosen, *Madness in Society*, 93).

58. Padel, *Whom Gods Destroy*, 50.

59. Ibid.

60. Ibid., 53.

61. Ibid., 56. According to Padel, "*Problem 30* put madness at the center of ideas about genius for the modern world" (57). But the Renaissance probably associated melancholia and black powers with black magic and the devil.

62. Ibid., 71.

63. Donald Richardson, *Hercules and Other Legends of Gods and Heroes* (New York: Gramercy, 1996), 183.

64. Padel, *Whom Gods Destroy*, 65. "As the opposite of consciousness, madness sees wrongly. Darkly, as Ajax sees. But as the intensification of consciousness, madness sometimes sees more clearly than the sane. Both thoughts turn up in tragedy. Both left their mark on us.... Madness is the blackest, wrongest possibility of consciousness, a blackness without light. *And* it is a way of seeing in through the dark, seeing truths unavailable to normal minds: a dark through which someone (not always the mad person) may see more clearly. Two possibilities. Greek tragedy set going the long echoes of both" (66).

65. Rosen, *Madness in Society*, 49.

66. Gregg, "The Nature of Nature," 174–75.

67. Mistaken perception related to madness is an important theme in Greek drama and culture. Ajax and Agave are the most obvious examples.

68. Joseph de Maistre wrote: "His terrible arm is still extended over their posterity, who press around his august effigy. Looking at him, one does not know whether this bronze hand protects or threatens" (*St. Petersburg Dialogues*, trans. Richard A. Lebrun [Montreal: McGill-Queens University Press, 1993], 5). Pushkin had both volumes of this work in his library. The pages of both volumes are cut.

69. Evgenii's mad gaze and filmed-over eyes resemble the image of the tsar as recorded by contemporaries and later rendered by artists and writers. "Pilnyak,

Merezhkovsky, and even Alexey Tolstoy agree that Peter's gaze is burning with insanity and this is not just poetic license. One diplomat reported that it was 'painful to bear'" (Gasiorowska, *The Image*, 74). George Gutsche argues that Peter's descent from the pedestal indicates not so much a diminution of power as a diminution of moral stature (*Moral Apostasy in Russian Literature* [DeKalb: Northern Illinois University Press, 1986], 31–35).

70. This is not insignificant elevation. Rivers in the ancient world were considered to be gods.

71. *Julius Caesar* 1.2.133–34.

72. Scholars have often identified Evgenii with the river, in terms of revolt. See, for example, Iurii Borev, *Iskusstvo interpretatsii i otsenki: Opyt prochteniia "Mednogo vsadnika"* (Moscow: Sovetskii pisatel', 1981), 382.

73. One could certainly argue, as some scholars have, that Evgenii's ascription of responsibility to Peter for his fate is nothing more than a crazed idea with no basis in the text—inner or outer. But to so argue is to turn *The Bronze Horseman* into a sentimental, even bathetic text, rather than one that treats its middling hero with existential seriousness and treats both Peter and Evgenii on an equally serious level.

74. To Merezhkovsky, it was Evgenii's threat to Peter that unleashed the floodgates that would eventually bring an end to the Petersburg period of Russian history. Some critics have seen the threat as serious enough to force Peter to descend from his pedestal to quash it, even if Evgenii only imagines Peter descending from his pedestal—or even if Pushkin only imagines Evgenii imagining it. See, for example, David Bethea, "The Role of *Eques* in Pushkin's *The Bronze Horseman*," in David M. Bethea, ed., *Puškin Today* (Bloomington: Indiana University Press, 1993), 117.

Chapter 5. Madness and the River

1. Ruth Padel, *Whom Gods Destroy: Elements of Greek and Tragic Madness* (Princeton, N.J.: Princeton University Press, 1995), 50.

2. Ibid.

3. Heracles performed his twelve labors in expiation for murders he committed against his own family after he had been made mad by his enemy Hera.

4. A. D. Briggs, *A Comparative Study of Pushkin's* The Bronze Horseman, *Nekrasov's* Red-Nosed Frost, *and Blok's* The Twelve (Lewiston, N.Y.: Mellen, 1990).

5. The Finnish seas are also a metonymic substitution for Russia's northern enemies, especially Sweden.

6. Michael André Bernstein, *Foregone Conclusions: Against Apocalyptical History* (Berkeley: University of California Press, 1994).

7. See also the variations of *vozmushchennyi* ("indignant," lines 1.142, 1.161, 2.4). In line 2.4, the Neva is described as reveling in its rebellious rage.

8. Apep's hatred for and rivalry with Re probably derives from the fact that Apep was once a sun god, who was displaced by Re. In his daily struggle with Re, Apep thus comes to embody the principle of permanent rebellion. See R. T. Rundle Clark, *Myth and Symbol in Ancient Egypt* (London: Thames, 1959), 208–12; Hans Bonnet, *Reallexikon der Ägyptischen Religionsgeschichte* (Berlin: de Gruyter, 1952), 51–53; and Erik Hornung, *Conceptions of God in Ancient Egypt*, trans. John Baines (Ithaca, N.Y.: Cornell University Press, 1971), 158–60.

9. The identification of Peter with the river is less common than the other identifications. But for the identification of the two in terms of birth, see Daniel Rancour-Laferriere, "The Couvade of Peter the Great: A Psychoanalytical Aspect of *The Bronze Horseman*," in *Puškin Today*, ed. David M. Bethea (Bloomington: Indiana University Press, 1993), 76–81.

10. On a number of occasions Pushkin explicitly identifies Peter with revolution, even the Revolution incarnate [*La Révolution incarnée*]. See "O dvoriantsve," 12:205. The issue of Peter as the personification of revolutionary madness is treated in detail in chapter 7.

11. Stanley Fish, "How to Recognize a Poem When You See One," in Stanley Fish, *Is There a Text in This Class: The Authority of Interpretive Communities* (Cambridge, Mass.: Harvard University Press, 1980), 322–37.

12. Abrams, for example, writes of Blake's interpretation of Satan, in which Blake stated that Milton was "of the Devil's party without knowing it." "Blake formulated what is, I believe, the earliest instance of that radical mode of romantic polysemism in which the latent personal significance of a narrative poem is found not merely to underlie, but to contradict and cancel the surface intention" (Fish, "How to Recognize," 251). Abrams also cites Shelley, Keble, and Coleridge in this regard (252–53).

13. Georg Lukács, *Studies in European Realism* (New York: Grosset, 1964), 11.

14. Ibid., 21.

15. Tolstoy says that "the god of poetry forbade him" to carry out his intention and "ordered him to bless" rather than curse his character (A. P. Chekhov, *Sobranie sochinenii*, 12 vols. [Moscow: Gosudarstvennoe izdatel'stvo khudozhestvennoi literatury, 1960–64], 8:546). But Tolstoy was not the only one who expressed this idea. See, for example, the statement by A. B. Fokht, a professor of medicine at Moscow University, in A. P. Chekhov, *Polnoe sobranie sochinenii*, ed. N. F. Bel'chikov, 18 vols. (Moscow: Nauka, 1977), 10:409.

16. For a survey of the reactions of contemporary readers, see Chekhov, *Polnoe sobranie sochinenii*, 10:408–14.

17. As Bakhtin argues, a classic writer is one who creates works that look forward to ideas and types of which he may be unaware.

18. "The river is not just whatever water you see in the channel, but the banks, the floodplain, in fact, the valley itself, from bluff to bluff. It is anywhere the water has been and could potentially go" (Isabel Wilkerson, "The Mississippi Reclaims Its True Domain," *New York Times*, 18 July 1993, sec. 4:3).

Chapter 6. Madness and the Tsar

1. Wacław Lednicki argues that Mickiewicz played a decisive role in the changing attitude toward Peter the Great because of the Polish poet's influence on Pushkin (*Pushkin's "Bronze Horseman": The Story of a Masterpiece* [Berkeley: University of California Press, 1955], 55–56). "Mickiewicz's vision of Petersburg as an ingredient in the poetic content of *The Bronze Horseman* became in the final analysis a factor destroying the integrity of the 'Northern Palmyra' in Russian poetry and literature" (56). Lednicki admits, however, that Pushkin was probably not conscious of how Mickiewicz had invaded *The Bronze Horseman*.

2. Even the fiction writers who portray Peter as a "madman" (Pilniak, for example, in *His Majesty Kneeb Piter Komondor*, 1919) probably intend the word in a more metaphoric sense, that is, not technically insane but eccentric and excessive in many of his habits and ideas. But Gasiorowska writes: "Pilnyak, Merezhkovsky, and even Alexey Tolstoy agree that Peter's gaze is burning with insanity" (Xenia Gasiorowska, *The Image of Peter the Great in Russian Fiction* [Madison: University of Wisconsin Press, 1979], 74). In Greece also, as in most cultures, the word *mad* could be used loosely to describe eccentric behavior (George Rosen, *Madness in Society: Chapters in the Historical Sociology of Mental Illness* [New York: Harper, 1969], 91).

3. In Pushkin's day, the city, as a physical reality, had long been more the creation of Catherine the Great, Peter's heir, than it was the creation of Peter himself. Catherine, of course, commissioned the sculpting of the monument.

4. For the Egyptians, to be dead is not the same as not to exist. Just because Apep is continually killed does not mean he cannot be continually rejuvenated. See Erik Hornung, *Conceptions of God in Ancient Egypt*, trans. John Baines (Ithaca, N.Y.: Cornell University Press, 1971), 160.

5. Veronica Ions, *Egyptian Mythology* (New York: Bedrick, 1962), 39.

6. Many of the depreciatory words and phrases in *Poltava* that Pushkin uses to describe Mazeppa he also uses with the river, Evgenii, and Peter in *The Bronze Horseman*. Thus *Mazepa mrachen* ("Mazeppa is somber," 5:34); *B ego dushe prokhodiat dumy, / Odna drugoi mrachnei, mrachnei* ("In his soul pass thoughts, / Each more somber that the last," 5:43); *Ho mrachnye strannye mechty / V dushe Mazepy* ("But somber, strange dreams pass / Through Mazeppa's soul," 5:44).

7. It is a hidden or black sun. The black sun has frequently been associated with melancholia, the traditional source of madness in Western culture. Hence Julia Kristeva's *Black Sun: Depression and Melancholia*, trans. Leon S. Roudiez (New York: Columbia University Press, 1989). The black star or planet has traditionally been Saturn, the astral source of melancholy, and its concomitant, madness. The black sun also plays an important role in Mandelstam's poetry about Petersburg. Victor Terras traces the image of the black sun in Mandelstam to the work of Viacheslav Ivanov ("The Black Sun: Orphic Imagery in the Poetry of Osip Mandelstam," *The Slavic and East European Journal* 45 [2001]: 52). See Ruth Padel's

discussion of the image of the black sun (*Whom Gods Destroy: Elements of Greek and Tragic Madness* [Princeton, N.J.: Princeton University Press, 1995], 58–59). In a videotaped interview, a survivor of Auschwitz recalls: "I saw the sun in Auschwitz, and the sun was black—the sun was destruction."

8. The night the Bronze Horseman chases Evgenii is not pitch dark. It is twilit (*ozaren*) by the moon (*luna*), but a pale moon (*blednaia luna*). Evgenii can hear the pounding hooves in the dark, but some light is necessary so that he can see Peter's outstretched arm. Moreover, the moon is not an unbefitting light for madness.

9. Peter's inability to protect the people from the river seems both curious and significant from a historical perspective, since it was well known that Peter's greatest fear as a child was of water and that he worked hard to overcome it. (Gasiorowska cites Voltaire's work in this connection [*The Image*, 114].) Some of Peter's later activities and projects might reasonably be seen as a form of overcompensation, the desire to master his fear by controlling and conquering its source: Peter's early naval exercises, his passion for sailing, the founding of a new capital on the Neva near the Gulf of Finland, his interest in ship building, the construction of embankments, the obsession with northern and southern ports, and, most important, the creation of a Russian navy.

10.

> Thus saith the Lord, In this thou shalt know that I am the Lord: behold, I will smite with the rod that is in mine hand upon the waters which are in the river, and they shall be turned to blood. (Ex. 7:17)

> And the Lord spake unto Moses, Say unto Aaron, Take thy rod, and stretch out thine hand upon the waters of Egypt, upon their streams, upon their rivers, and upon their ponds, and upon all their pools of water, that they may become blood; and that there may be blood throughout all the land of Egypt, both in vessels of wood, and in vessels of stone. (Ex. 7:19)

> And the Lord spake unto Moses, Say unto Aaron, Stretch forth thine hand with thy rod over the streams, over the rivers, and over the ponds, and cause frogs to come up upon the land of Egypt. (Ex. 8:5)

> And I will stretch out my hand, and smite Egypt with all my wonders which I will do in the midst thereof: and after that he will let you go. (Ex. 3:20)

> Wherefore say unto the children of Israel, I am the Lord, and I will bring you out from under the burdens of the Egyptians, and I will rid you out of their bondage, and I will redeem you with a stretched out arm, and with great judgments. (Ex. 6:6)

11. J. Thomas Shaw, ed., *The Letters of Alexander Pushkin* (Madison: University of Wisconsin Press, 1967), 780.

12. A. D. Briggs, *A Comparative Study of Pushkin's* The Bronze Horseman, *Nekrasov's* Red-Nosed Frost, *and Blok's* The Twelve (Lewiston, N.Y.: Mellen, 1990).

13. *Poetical Works of Shelley*, ed. Newell F. Ford (Boston: Houghton, 1975), 366.

14. Peter has changed from *Poltava* and "*Stansy*" ("Stanzas," 1828), where he is presented as forgiving even those who fought or revolted against him.

15. An anecdote about the Bronze Horseman underlines the grave danger facing Petersburg if the horse and rider descend from the pedestal and leave the square. Alexander I evidently planned to evacuate the monument because of his fear that Napoleon would invade the city. But a certain Major Baturin reported to the authorities that he had dreamed that the Bronze Horseman had descended from his pedestal and galloped up to the palace where Alexander was residing, informing him that as long as the statue stayed in place Petersburg would never be in danger. See Aleksandr Feinberg, *Zametki o "Mednom Vsadnike"* (Moscow: Grit, 1993), 38.

16. Gasiorowska, *The Image*, 87–88.

17. Quoted in ibid., 90; my emphasis—G.R.

18. For a more detailed discussion of Peter's propensity to terrifying episodes of rage, see ibid., 85–89, 112–13.

19. The effigy, the death mask, of Peter the Great has influenced some writers to present Peter as a stiff, frozen figure with a mask-like face: Tynianov, for example, in the *Wax Effigy*. But, in reality, Peter was the embodiment of ceaseless activity and endless schemes and plans, a man constantly in motion. Pushkin is not attempting to create the historical Peter at all. In fact, he needs to create the godlike Peter before he can return him to the world and thus highlight the discrepancy between the two.

20. Peter was often seen as a modern-day Hercules overcoming tremendous obstacles in order to realize his idea. The horse's attempt to crush the snake, according to Wacław Kubacki, "is an old stoic Herculean symbol of surmounted obstacles, crushed enemies and superstitions" (*Palmira i Babilon* [Wrocław: Wydawn. Zakladu Narodowego im. Ossolinskich, 1951], 38).

Chapter 7. Madness, Narrator, and Author

1. On observing Ajax's madness, Odysseus comments: "For I see we are but phantoms, all we who live, or fleeting shadows" (*The Complete Plays of Sophocles*, trans. Sir Richard Claverhouse Jebb [New York: Bantam, 1967], 6).

2. For a list of the many novelists and poets who showed, right up to the revolution, obvious antipathy toward Petersburg, see Wacław Lednicki, *Pushkin's "Bronze Horseman": The Story of a Masterpiece* (Berkeley: University of California Press, 1955), 53–54.

3. George Rosen, *Madness in Society: Chapters in the Historical Sociology of Mental Illness* (New York: Harper, 1969), 33.

4. Vladimir Toporov maintains that the polar tensions between life and death,

salvation and despair, light and darkness (like the dozens of antinomies discovered by generations of scholars) define the Petersburg myth in Russian literature ("Peterburg i peterburgskii tekst v russkoi literature," in Liubava Moreva, ed., *Metafizika Peterburga*, 205–35 [Petersburg: Eidos, 1993]). One can count the following among the many antimonies found by scholars:

> immortality/ephemerality, large/small, movement/stasis, will/fatalism, freedom/necessity, rebellion/acquiescence, state/individual, social/private, order/chaos, cosmos/chaos, order/nature, man/nature, natural/artificial, natural/unnatural, creation/destruction, birth/death, pagan/Christian, Petersburg/Moscow, nobility/people, tyrant/victim, center/periphery, land/water, future/past, reason/madness, East/West, Russia/Europe, Russian/Finn, light/dark, dry/wet, empty/full, water/stone, land/water, wind/stone, past/future.

5. Although we must keep in mind, among other things, the addressee of Pushkin's letters, the following comments in a rough draft of a letter to Chaadaev (19 October 1836) give us an interesting perspective regarding Pushkin's thoughts about the state of the clergy and religion in Russia:

> As for the clergy, it is outside society, it is still bearded. One does not see it anywhere, not in our salons, not in literature; it does not belong to good society. It is not above the people, it does not wish to be of the people. Our sovereigns have found it convenient to leave it where they found it. Like eunuchs, it has no passion but for power. Consequently, it is dreaded. And, I know, a certain one, in spite of all his energy, yielded to it on one grave occasion. I was outraged by this at the time. Religion is, fortunately, foreign to our thoughts and to our habits, but there is no need to say so. (J. Thomas Shaw, ed., *The Letters of Alexander Pushkin* [Madison: University of Wisconsin Press, 1967], 798)

6. "Russian poets have grown up in a world of Orthodox customs, and their work is unwittingly saturated with the symbolism of the Eastern Church. Precisely the Orthodox tradition, which severely condemned the art of sculpture, which did not admit it into churches, and which understood it as a pagan or diabolical vice (the two concepts were equivalent for the Church), suggested to Pushkin the close association of statues with idolatry, with devilry, with sorcery. It is enough to read Gogol's deliberations on sculpture for us to understand how inseparably plastic art was linked to the concept of paganism in the Russian view: '[Sculpture] was born along with a definitely formed pagan world, it expressed [this world] and died along with it.... It was as remote from Christianity as the pagan faith itself' ("Sculpture, Painting, and Music," 1831). On Russian soil, sculpture was closely associated with whatever was un-Christian, even anti-Christian, in the spirit of the Petersburg tsardom" (Roman Jakobson, "The Statue in Puškin's Poetic Mythology," in *Language in Literature* [Cambridge, Mass.: Harvard University Press, 1987], 362–63).

7. David M. Bethea, *The Shape of Apocalypse in Russian Fiction* (Princeton, N.J.: Princeton University Press, 1989), 51. Also see Bethea for a discussion of the debate about the horse's independence of its rider or the inability of the rider to control the horse (51–52).

8. In his literary epic, *Taras Bulba*, Nikolai Gogol does not focus on the Cossacks as horsemen. By contrast, Isaac Babel (*The Red Calvary*) focuses on the Cossacks as equestrian warriors and lovers of horses. Both the author and narrator reveal a profound ambivalence toward the Cossacks and their horses.

9. Jean Marquès-Rivière, *Amulettes, talismans et pantacles* (Paris: Payot, 1949). Quoted in J. E. Cirlot, *A Dictionary of Symbols* (New York: Philosophical Library, 1962), 152.

10. Jorge Luis Borges, "Stories of Horsemen," *New Republic*, 19 May 1982, 8.

11. This is given substantial support when the final version of the poem is compared to earlier variants and to an earlier genealogical poem, *Ezerskii*.

12. For a rather frank expression of Pushkin's views, see his diary entry of 22 December 1834, which recounts his conversation about the nobility with Grand Duke Michael (12:334–35). Also see his notes for a work on the nobility (12:205).

13. In a rough draft to his letter to Chaadaev, Pushkin writes. "Have you read Tocqueville? I am still all hot and bothered and quite frightened by the book" (Shaw, *Letters*, 798).

14. "Peter the Great, who in himself is universal history" (ibid., 780).

15. Ibid., 37–38.

16. Ibid., 379

17. Ibid., 793

18. According to Peter's *Table of Ranks*, which was promulgated in 1722 and lasted, with modifications, until 1917, hereditary nobility (the right to pass noble status onto one's children and the right to own serfs) was conferred on all army officers (those who reached the twelfth rank in the military) and on commoners in the civil and court services who reached the eighth rank. Under Catherine, those occupying lower ranks (*lichnye dvoriane*) were granted only personal nobility. In 1845, army, court and civil ranks entitling their holders to hereditary nobility were raised.

19. Pushkin told the Grand Duke Michael in 1834: "All the Romanovs are revolutionaries and levellers" (Diary, under 22 December 1834 [12:335]). Grand Duke Michael thanked Pushkin for admitting him into the Society of Jacobins (*Spasibo, tak ty menia zhaluesh' v iakobintsy!*).

20. B. H. Summer, *Survey of Russian History* (New York: Reynal, 1943), 133.

21. Of course, Pushkin's social origins were in both the hereditary (the Pushkins) and service nobility (the Hannibals). Some critics have argued that the poem is, in part, a thinly disguised commentary on the Decembrist uprising. See, for example, D. D. Blagoi, *Sotsiologiia tvorchestva Pushkina: Etiudy* (Moscow: Federatsiia, 1929), 308–28; George Gutsche, *Moral Apostasy in Russian Literature* (DeKalb: Northern Illinois University Press, 1986), 37–42, 158–60.

Conclusion

1. Joseph Frank, *Dostoevsky: The Seeds of Revolt: 1821–1849* (Princeton, N.J.: Princeton University Press, 1976), 310. Although Pushkin called his narrative poem [*poema*] a *povest'*, for the great Russian critic Belinskii, the *poema*, which still retained some of the seriousness of the epic, addresses itself to the most profound ideas and moral questions. In calling his *povest'*, *The Double*, a *poema*, Dostoevsky emphasizes that his work, though in prose, is *generically* the same as Pushkin's and of the same high seriousness of purpose. For Belinskii's definitions of the *poema* and its distinction from other genres, see V. G. Belinskii, *Polnoe sobranie sochinenii*, 13 vols. (Moscow: Akademiia Nauk SSSR, 1953–59), 6:414–15.

2. A few words need to be said about the version of Pushkin's text that Dostoevsky knew, since crucial passages of *The Bronze Horseman* were not restored until 1857. Although *The Double* was published in 1846, the revised version of 1866 is considered the standard version and the one almost invariably translated. Because of problems with the censorship, exacerbated by the personal notations on the manuscript made by Tsar Nicholas I himself, Pushkin did not publish *The Bronze Horseman* in his lifetime. The version that Zhukovskii published in *Sovremennik* in 1837 had significant changes and deletions in the crucial lines 430–38—where Evgenii challenges and threatens the monument. Pushkin's original lines (434–38) were restored in the 1857 Annenkov edition of Pushkin's works, with the exception of ellipses for "You'll get yours" [*Uzho tebe*]. For the journal version of *The Double*, Dostoevsky had at his disposal the 1841 edition of *The Bronze Horseman* (which was based on the version published by Zhukovskii in *Sovremennik* in 1837). For the revised version of *The Double* (1866), he had at his disposal the Annenkov and later editions of *The Bronze Horseman*, in which lines 434–38 were restored with the exception of *"Uzho tebe."*

3. For the generally positive image of the city before Pushkin, see N. P. Antsiferov, *Dusha Peterburga* (Peterburg: Brokgauz-Efron, 1922), 45–62; Wacław Lednicki, *Pushkin's "Bronze Horseman": The Story of a Masterpiece* (Berkeley: University of California Press, 1955), 43–51.

4. Antsiferov, *Dusha Peterburga*, 73.

5. The main idea of the *pochvenniki*, or "men of the soil," was that Russia could be saved by a reconciliation of its educated classes with the common people, the *narod*. The *pochvenniki* argued that only the Russian people had preserved the purity of Christianity (Russian Orthodoxy) in their hearts, and thus the salvation not only of Russia but all European civilization could come about only through the acceptance of their faith—or at least the principles of their faith. The *pochvenniki* took a middle position regarding Peter the Great, arguing that much in Peter's ideas was beneficial and should be retained but that Russia had already assimilated all it possibly could from the West and now had to pursue a path peculiar to its own nationalistic spirit. In the 1870s Dostoevsky retained his idealistic notions about the potential of the Russian people, but he began to approach the Slavophiles in his attitude toward Peter the Great, rejecting almost the entire

Petrine project, which he increasingly came to believe was alien to the Russian people and detrimental to their spiritual development—and therefore an impediment to the salvation of Russia itself.

6. There is much myth about the myth of Petersburg. The idea of Petersburg as the most abstract city in the world has gained currency as almost the dominant topos of the Dostoevskian version of the myth. Although the Underground Man states that Petersburg is "the most abstract and intentional city in the whole world" [*samyi otvlechennyi i umyshlennyi gorod na vsem zemnom share*] (F. M. Dostoevskii, *Polnoe sobranie sochinenii*, ed. V. G. Bazanov et al., 30 vols. (Leningrad: Nauka, 1972–90), 5:101 [hereafter *PSS*]), few descriptions of Petersburg in Dostoevsky substantiate this claim. It is Bely who picks up on the Underground Man's idea (with a little help from Tolstoy's Karenin) and integrates it into his novel about the city. Dostoevsky is far more apt to focus on the city's slums and phantasmagoric qualities. But even the phantasmagoric qualities of Petersburg, as Lotman shows ("Simvolika Peterburga i problemy semiotiki goroda," *Trudy po znakovym sistemam* 8 [1984]: 35–40), were not the creation of Gogol or Dostoevsky (the canonizers of this idea) but the reworking of longstanding popular stories and literary writings of the 1820s and 1830s—many by a group of writers (such as Odoevsky) who were close to Pushkin.

7. Dostoevsky refers to line 16 as "the little window hacked through to Europe" [*prorublennoe v Evropu okoshko, PSS*, 23:358].

8. Dostoevsky unquestionably viewed Svidrigailov (the details of whose suicide recall *The Bronze Horseman*, see note 15, below) as a Petersburg figure emblematic of the worst aspects of Peter's legacy: "the most frightful moral dissoluteness" [*strashneishaia raspushchennost' nravov, PSS*, 20:14].

9. *PSS*, 27:62. There are several depreciative descriptions in Dostoevsky's later works having to do with the Bronze Horseman. In *A Raw Youth*, the narrator describes the city as a mirage that will disappear into thin air with the lifting fog. After the city disappears only two things will remain: the Finnish swamp and, in the middle of it, "as a decoration, the bronze horseman on a heavily panting, overdriven steed" [*dlia krasy, bronzovyi vsadnik na zharko dyshashchem, zagnannom kone," PSS*, 13:113). This, of course, is Dostoevsky's reduction of the last lines of the first part of *The Bronze Horseman*. In the note to *A Diary of a Writer* mentioned above, Dostoevsky describes a Petersburg abandoned except for Germans, dilapidated buildings, and, in the middle of it all, Peter's monument [*pamiatnik Petra*]. Dostoevsky always fantasized that Petersburg was only a mirage that would disappear one day with the fog. For other derogatory references to the *prorublennoe v Evropu okoshko* in the *Diary*, see especially the second chapter of the June 1876 issue, entitled *"Moi paradoks"* (*PSS*, 23:38–42).

10. Evgenii's troubles also begin after returning home from visiting: "*V to vremia iz gostei domoi / Prishel Evgenii molodoi*" (1:10–11).

11. As Antsiferov shows, water has always symbolized the principle of primordial darkness and chaos, often in the form of a sea monster. Water, then, becomes an appropriate symbol in both Pushkin's and Dostoevsky's texts, not only for

nature's revolt against Peter's order but also for the mental dissolution of the heroes (N. P. Antsiferov, *Byl' i mif Peterburga* [Petrograd: Brokgauz-Efron, 1924], 57–60).

12. Fedor Dostoevsky, *The Short Novels of Dostoevsky*, trans. Constance Garnett (New York: Dial, 1945), 509. The passage continues for another eight lines to describe the weather: in particular, the howling of the wind and the rushing of the water. The English translations of *The Double* from the Garnett translation have been checked—and amended when necessary—with the Academy edition. The pagination from the English, followed by the Russian from the Academy edition, will appear in the text.

13. This is a clear literary echo. As we saw in the previous chapter, the narrator frequently uses *uzhasnyi* [horrible] to describe Evgenii's experience. See lines 1:92 [*uzhasnaia pora*, a terrible time], 1.71 [*uzhasnyi den'*, a terrible day], 2.40 [*vid uzhasnyi*, a terrible sight], 2.91 [*uzhasnye potriaseniia*, terrible shocks], 2.94 [*uzhasnye dumy*, terrible thoughts], 2.132 [*proshlyi uzhas*, the former horror], and 2.155 [*uzhasen on*, how terrible he is].

14. "The weather was awful: there was a thaw; snow was coming down and it was raining—just as at that unforgettable time when at that terrible midnight hour all the misfortunes of Mr. Goliadkin had begun" (596; 1:213).

15. The most important indirect reference in Dostoevsky's later works to *The Bronze Horseman* is probably Svidrigailov's suicide in *Crime and Punishment*, which Dostoevsky was still working on when he revised *The Double*. Before his suicide, Svidrigailov wanders around town on a night very much like the one described in *The Double*. It is July but, nevertheless, the night is pitch black, rainy, cold, and damp, with a chilling and howling wind. The following description alluding to a possible flood precedes Svidrigailov's second nightmare. "Through the nocturnal gloom and darkness there resounded a cannon shot, then another. 'Ah, the signal. The water is rising,' he thought; 'toward morning, it will pour out into the lower areas and streets, it will flood the basements and cellars, the sewer rats will come up, and in the rain and the wind people will start, soaked and cursing, moving their rubbish to the upper floors'" (*PSS*, 6:392).

16. Hegel's famous "slaughter-bench at which the happiness of peoples, the wisdom of states, and the virtue of individuals have been victimized" (G. W. F. Hegel, *Reason in History: A General Introduction to the Philosophy of History*, trans. Robert S. Hartman [New York: Liberal Arts Press, 1953], 27).

17. Pushkin writes in a letter to Chaadaev (19 October 1836): "And Peter the Great, who in himself alone is universal history!" (J. Thomas Shaw, ed., *The Letters of Alexander Pushkin* [Madison: University of Wisconsin Press, 1967], 780).

18. The only "Peter" in *The Double* is Goliadkin's drunken, untrustworthy, and mocking servant Petrushka. He is usually not around when Goliadkin wants him: "Petrushka is not here" [*Petrushki net*]. But "*Petrushki net*" might also mean "there is no Peter." Goliadkin is parodically cast as the true child (son) of Peter: Iakov Petrovich. It is, as Terras might say, another role in which Dostoevsky has cast Goliadkin, but a role that he is completely incapable of playing.

19. The Table of Ranks is, in fact, the only one of Peter's reforms that survived essentially intact to 1917.
20. Hegel, *Reason in History*, 43.
21. Lednicki, *Pushkin's "Bronze Horseman,"* 50.
22. Freud argues that the double in primitive thought is a guarantee of immortality, but in the course of civilization it came increasingly to represent death (Sigmund Freud, "The 'Uncanny,'" in *Collected Papers*, 5 vols. [New York: Basic, 1959], 4:386–91).
23. Although several Soviet critics have argued that Goliadkin is basically a good man who is a victim of an oppressive social and political system, most critics have found little worth in Dostoevsky's hero and almost no convincing social causes for his condition. For Soviet critics who emphasize the disfiguring effects of the social environment on Goliadkin, see V. V. Ermilov, *F. M. Dostoevskii* (Moscow: Gosudarstvennoe izdatel'stvo khudozhestvennoi literatury, 1956), 62–65; L. Grossman, *Dostoevskii* (Moscow: Molodaia gvardiia, 1962), 70–72; G. M. Fridlender, *Realizm Dostoevskogo* (Moscow: Nauka, 1964), 68–81; F. Evnin, "Ob odnoi istoriko-literaturnoi legende: Povest' Dostoevskogo 'Dvoinik,'" *Russkaia literatura* 3 (1965): 3–26; V. E. Vetlovskaia, "Sotsial'naia tema v pervykh proizvedeniiakh Dostoevskogo," *Russkaia literatura* 3 (1984): 91–94. Many Western critics, commenting on Goliadkin's situation, also place a great deal of blame on the social and political order in Russia under Nicholas I. See, for example, René Girard, *Dostoievski: Du double à l'unité* (Paris: Plon, 1963), 52–53; Rudolf Neuhäuser, *Das Frühwerk Dostojewskis, Literarische Tradition und gesellschaftliche Anspruch* (Heidelberg: Winter, 1979), 163–75; Dominique Arban, "Le statut de la folie dans les oeuvres de jeunesse de Dostoievski," *Zapiski russkoi akademicheskoi gruppy v Ssha* 14 (1981): 30; and Frank, *The Seeds of Revolt*, 306–9. Grigor'ev gives perhaps the most negative assessment of *The Double*. In an unpublished letter to Gogol of 17 November 1848 he describes the depressing effect that *The Double* had on his spirit: "As you read this monstrous work, you feel yourself devastated and thrilled as you merge with its absolutely insignificant hero. You come to feel sad that you are a human being and you become convinced that man could not be other than he is described here" (quoted in V. Ia. Kirpotin, *Molodoi Dostoevskii* [Moscow: Gosudarstvennoe izdatel'stvo khudozhestvennoi literatury, 1947], 248). Goliadkin has repelled many Soviet critics as well. See, for example, Kirpotin, *Molodoi Dostoevskii*, 242–46; and Ermilov, *Dostoevskii*, 70–71. Victor Terras—who describes everything about Goliadkin as petty, shabby, and trite—argues that Goliadkin is Devushkin without any of Devushkin's positive attributes: "The evil in Goliadkin Junior is as petty and wretched as the good in Goliadkin Senior is shabby and indifferent. Consequently, where the struggle between truly 'romantic' *Doppelgängers* would reflect a struggle between heaven and hell, the struggle between the two Goliadkins is only a wretched intrigue, carried on by two underlings for nothing more than a snug little job. What difference does it make, which of the two— or if either—occupies a desk at the 'department,' a flat on Shestilavochnaia?... One wonders if Goliadkin is really entitled to a *Doppelgänger*, for in order to have

a "dual personality," one must have a personality in the first place" ("Problems of Human Existence in the Works of the Young Dostoevsky," *Slavic Review* 23 [1964]: 85–85).

24. Dostoevsky's approach to Goliadkin has seemed to many even harsher in light of his sympathetic treatment of Devushkin, the hero of *Poor Folk*, his first novel. See, for example, Terras, "Problems of Human Existence," 85; and Kirpotin, *Molodoi Dostoevskii*, 243–45. On the other hand, *The Double*, like *Poor Folk*, also parodies the works of Gogol—in this case "The Nose," itself a parody of the theme of the double. Dostoevsky reintroduces the seriousness of the double theme that Gogol had made ridiculous.

25. Critics have viewed Dostoevsky's consistent maintenance of both a sympathetic and deprecating stance toward Goliadkin as highly problematic. Frank notes that "Dostoevsky's work of this period often contains a puzzling ambiguity of tone because a character is often shown simultaneously both as socially oppressed and yet as reprehensible and morally unsavory because he has surrendered too abjectly to the pressure of his environment" (*Dostoevsky: The Seeds of Revolt*, 307). The grotesque effect of this point of view is also discussed by N. S. Trubetzkoy, *Dostoevskij als Künstler* (The Hague: Mouton, 1964), 49.

26. V. V. Vinogradov, "K morfologii natural'nogo stilia: Opyt lingvisticheskogo analiza poemy *Dvoinik*," *Izbrannye trudy* (Moscow: Nauka, 1976), 111–13; Trubetzkoy, *Dostoevskij als Künstler*, 48–49; Victor Terras, *The Young Dostoevsky: 1846–1849* (The Hague: Mouton, 1969), 128–33.

27. Vinogradov, "K morfologii," 113–40; Mikhail Bakhtin, *Problems of Dostoevsky's Poetics*, trans. Caryl Emerson (Minneapolis: University of Minnesota Press, 1989), 211–27.

28. Terras, *Young Dostoevsky*, 206–31; M. F. Lomagina, "K voprosu o pozitsii avtora v *Dvoinike* Dostoevskogo," *Filologicheskie nauki* 14, no. 5 (1971): 4–9. Space does not allow a detailed analysis of Dostoevsky's technique of transcribing consciousness. Basically the narrative appears to be told by still another double of Goliadkin who has the feelings of Goliadkin Senior, but who, in contrast to Goliadkin Senior, can see through Goliadkin Junior's "treachery." In order to preserve his "innocence," Goliadkin Senior must pretend that he has no knowledge of Goliadkin Junior's designs until they are exposed. Alternatively, one might posit that the narration is a brilliant and unique example of *erlebte Rede* in which the narrator transcribes two different levels of Goliadkin's consciousness (and subconscious) simultaneously.

29. The subtitle for chapter 1 reads as follows: "How Titular Councilor Mr. Goliadkin woke up. How he fitted himself out and set off for where he was going. How Mr. Goliadkin justified himself in his own eyes and how later he came to the conclusion that it was better to act boldly, with an openness not devoid of nobility. How Goliadkin finally got to where he was going" (1:334).

30. Terras, *Young Dostoevsky*, 124.

31. Ibid., 168–69.

32. Konrad Onasch, *Dostojewski als Verführer* (Zürich: EVZ, 1961), 28–29.

33. Evgenii's threat to the monument was missing in the versions that Dostoevsky had at his disposal in 1846. Dostoevsky knew, however, that a serious threat uttered by Evgenii had been censored. In his 1846 review of *The Bronze Horseman*, Belinskii emphasizes that the words Evgenii addressed to the monument had obviously been left out [*nedostaet slov, obrashchennykh Evgeniem k monumentu*] and that those words obviously contained the idea of the poem. Izmailov argues that Belinskii's words indicate that he knew the original lines, either through friends at *Sovremennik* or through those who prepared the first posthumous edition of Pushkin's works in 1841. Although Dostoevsky and other literary figures close to Belinskii may also have known the original lines, it is clear even in Zhukovskii's edition that Evgenii threatened the statue. Dostoevsky could hardly have been less perceptive than Belinskii about the omitted lines (*The Double* appeared in print before Belinskii's analysis of *The Bronze Horseman*), assuming that Belinskii did not know what had been omitted. For the most complete discussion of the publishing history of *The Bronze Horseman*, see Izmailov's excellent treatment in A. S. Pushkin, *Mednyi Vsadnik*, ed. N. V. Izmailov (Leningrad: Nauka, 1978), 227–42.

34. For Briusov, this is not so much a return to sanity as *prozrenie* [insight] (Valerii Briusov, *Moi Pushkin: Stat'i, issledovaniia, nabliudeniia*, ed. N. K. Piksanov [Moscow: Gosudarstvennoe izdatel'stvo khudozhestvennoi literatury, 1929], 79).

35. Richard Gregg, "The Nature of Nature and the Nature of Eugene in *The Bronze Horseman*," *Slavic and East European Journal* 21(1977): 174–75.

36. Psychologists have often studied autoscopy, the hallucination that a mirror image of oneself exists outside the self. See Robert A. Rogers, *Psychoanalytical Study of the Double in Literature* (Detroit: Wayne State University Press, 1970), 14–15.

37. Catherine Nepomnyashchy has argued—perhaps a bit too enthusiastically—that madness gives insight not only to Pushkin's Evgenii but also to "all the downtrodden clerks and social nonentities in Russian literature" (Catherine Theimer Nepomnyashchy, "The Poet, History, and the Supernatural: A Note on Pushkin's 'The Poet' and *The Bronze Horseman*," in A. Mandelker, ed., *The Supernatural in Slavic and Baltic Literatures: Essays in Honor of Victor Terras*, (Columbus, Ohio: Slavica, 1988), 43.

38. Terras, *Young Dostoevsky*, 256.

39. Ibid., 183.

40. Donald Fanger, *Dostoevsky and Romantic Realism: A Study of Dostoevsky in Relation to Balzac, Dickens, and Gogol* (Chicago: University of Chicago Press, 1962), 162.

41. D. S. Merezhkovskii, "*Vechnye sputniki: Pushkin*, *PSS* 13:344.

42. In the analysis of madness and rebellion, I shall be relying on the last chapters of the 1846 journal version of *The Double*, since Dostoevsky considerably toned down the theme of rebellion in the revised version of 1866. For the most complete description and analysis of the differences between the 1846 and 1866 versions of *The Double*, see R. I. Avanesov, "Dostoevskii v rabote nad *Dvoinikom*,"

in N. K. Piksanov, ed., *Tvorcheskaia istoriia: Issledovaniia po russkoi literature* (Moscow: Nikitinskie subbotniki, 1927), 154–91; and Evelyn Harden, "Translator's Introduction," in Fyodor Dostoevsky, *"The Double": Two Versions* (Ann Arbor: Ardis, 1985), xxvi–xxi. After the critical failure of *The Double* became apparent to him, Dostoevsky contemplated a radical revision of the novel. In the early 1860s he made some notes for revision (see *PSS*, 1:432–36), but they did not enter the 1866 version. In fact, Dostoevsky, for various reasons—financial as well as artistic—actually abandoned his ambitious plans to transform the old novel (which he always believed contained one of his most original ideas) and, instead, merely made cuts in the original—first by eliminating repetitions (Belinskii criticized the novel as exasperatingly repetitious) and then by deleting as much as possible those ideas of rebellion, "freethinking," and imposture [*samozvanstvo*] for which he already had envisioned other more appropriate novelistic forms. Most critics, like Avanesov, hold that the cuts Dostoevsky made in the 1866 version harm the novel and that the complete overhaul Dostoevsky contemplated could never have been successfully achieved using the basic structure and characterization of the 1846 text. See, for example, A. L. Bem, "'Nos' i 'Dvoinik,'" in A. L. Bem, ed., *U istokov tvorchestva Dostoevskogo*, (Prague: Petropolis, 1936), 159–61; W. J. Leatherbarrow, "The Rag with Ambition: The Problem of Self-Will in Dostoevsky's 'Bednyye lyudi' and 'Dvoinik,'" *Modern Language Review* 68 (1973): 616; and Gyula Kiraly, "Kompozitsiia siuzheta romana *Dvoinik: Prikliucheniia Gospodina Goliadkina*," in *Acta Litteraria Academiae Scientiarum Hungaricae* (Budapest: Magyar Tudomanyos Akademia, 1969): 11:239–56.

43. When Dostoevsky revised *The Double* in 1866, he had already become committed to the creation of more active, romantically conceived rebels. Germann in *The Queen of Spades* had become a more important figure for the Dostoevskian hero and the depiction of Petersburg. In fact, Dostoevsky's notes for his revision of *The Double* reveal that he is no longer thinking of the meek Goliadkin but rather of the proud Raskol'nikov. To transform Goliadkin into an active revolutionary, a radical of the 1860s, as Dostoevsky had planned, involved more than revising the old story; it meant writing an entirely new novel.

44. For a negative evaluation of Evgenii's love for Parasha, see Svetlana Evdokimova, "'Mednyi vsadnik': Istoriia kak mif," *Russian, Croatian and Serbian, Czech and Slovak, Polish Literature* 28, no. 4 (1990): 452.

45. In his plans for revision *(PSS*, 1:435), Dostoevsky describes the German woman as a lame, exceedingly poor woman who had once helped Goliadkin. V. N. Zakharov notes that the novel never really shows Goliadkin in love. See his "Zagadka 'Dvoinika,'" *Problemy izucheniia Dostoevskogo* (Petrozavodsk: Petrozavodskii gosudarstvennyi universitet, 1978), 35.

46. In his notes for the revision of *The Double* (*PSS*, 1:432–36), Dostoevsky focuses on the relationship that should obtain between employees and their superiors [*nachal'stvo*]. But as with many of these notes, they shed much more light on Dostoevsky's projects of the 1860s than on the text of *The Double*. For an interpretation of these fragments, see Bem, "'Nos' i 'Dvoinik,'" 152–53. Imposture

as rebellion is the subject of *Boris Godunov*, not *The Bronze Horseman*. For a discussion of *samozvanstvo* in Dostoevsky in terms of the demonic, see Harriet Murav, "Representations of the Demonic: Seventeenth Century Pretenders and *The Devils*," *Slavic and East European Journal* 35, no. 1 (1991): 56–70. For an especially insightful examination of the question of *samozvanstvo* in Pushkin, see Caryl Emerson, *Boris Godunov: Transpositions of a Russian Theme* (Bloomington: Indiana University Press, 1986), 88–141.

47. From an ancient biblical point of view, God alone is king in Israel. This view makes suspect the claims of even "legitimate" kings. In the eighth century B.C., killing one's predecessor was the most common path of succession to the throne. See Robert M. Seltzer, *Jewish People: Jewish Thought* (New York: Macmillan, 1980), 19–27.

48. Goliadkin's first name, Jacob [*Iakov*], further underscores the theme of imposture in *The Double*. In the Bible, Jacob, the younger brother, succeeds in usurping the position of his elder twin brother, Esau, by deceit, just as Goliadkin Junior usurps the position of Goliadkin Senior—at least in Goliadkin Senior's imagination. Esau calls attention to the importance of Jacob's name when he speaks to his father of Jacob's deception: "Was he, then, *named Jacob* that he might *supplant* me these two times? First he took away my birthright and now he has taken away my blessing" (Genesis 27:36). The Hebrew root *aqab* [supplant] is associated with the name Jacob. Whereas the Bible treats the succession to the leadership of all Israel with requisite seriousness, *The Double* presents as travesty Goliadkin's being passed over for a petty position in the tsarist bureaucracy. Moreover, Goliadkin Senior and Junior, in contrast to Esau and Jacob, are not reconciled in the end. Dostoevsky was also undoubtedly aware of the idea of the meek, Christlike Jacob as the progenitor of the Russian race, propounded, for example, in the well-known sixteenth-century *Tale of the Kingdom of Kazan*. If Dostoevsky had this Jacob in mind in *The Double*, he again was using it parodically.

49. See B. A. Uspenskii, "Tsar and Pretender: *Samozvanstvo* or Royal Imposture in Russia as a Cultural-Historical Phenomenon," trans. David Budgen, in Iu. Lotman and B. A. Uspenskii, *The Semiotics of Russian Culture*, ed. Ann Shukman (Ann Arbor: University of Michigan, 1984), 263, 272.

50. Caryl Emerson's characterization of Dimitrii as a risk taker and adventurer, as a person who chooses to create himself—and thus a character rather dear in some ways to Pushkin's heart—highlights again the reductive and parodic nature of Dostoevsky's project with Goliadkin, whose greatest fear in life is imposture [*samozvanstvo*] (Emerson, *Boris Godunov*, 123–26).

Index

absence: displacement in *The Bronze Horseman*, 154; and loss in "God Grant . . . ," 71; madness as negation or absence, 75; religion as, 168–69
ace as symbol in *The Queen of Spades*, 28, 48
Aeschylus, 12, 15
Alekseev, M. P., 74
Alexander I, tsar, 96, 177
ambiguity: in *The Bronze Horseman*, 102, 129–30, 142–43; in "God Grant . . . ," 78; in Pushkin's works compared to Dostoevsky's, 195–96; time, duration of madness and ambiguity, 102; in *The Queen of Spades*, 22, 23, 34–35
anger: in Biblical tradition, 158; in Greek tradition, 156–57; Neva as source of Evgenii's mad anger, 124–26, 138; of Peter the Great, 157; punishment linked to, 122–23; as source of madness in *The Bronze Horseman*, 104–5, 118–23
Antsiferov, N. P., 4
asylums, eighteenth-century images of, 10, 72–75, 80
author. *See* author/narrators
author/narrators: alienation of, 163–64; author as distinct from narrator, 169; in *The Bronze Horseman*, 94, 97–100, 131–34, 162, 164–65, 197–98; during confrontation scene in *The Bronze Horseman*, 164–65; in Dostoevsky's *The Double*, 189–91; Evgenii conflated with, 109–11, 124, 128, 159, 165–67; fear of social changes, 171–72; frightened by madness, 130; Germann in *The Queen of Spades* and, 59, 103; as mad "Other," 167; Neva river in *The Bronze Horseman* and, 131–34, 142; as participant rather than objective observer, 142; persona in "God Grant . . . ," 67, 84; Peters-burg and, 163; punishment by, 103; in *The Queen of Spades*, 65, 198–99; reader as resistant to perspective of, 139; role in *The Bronze Horseman*, 162; subject/object switch in "God Grant . . . ," 70; as subject of *The Bronze Horseman*, 197–98; sympathy for Evgenii in *The Bronze Horseman*, 94, 97–100, 99–100, 105–6, 124; three-stage process of development and, 84; truth, access to, 163–64
avarice, 27–28

backshadowing, 132
Bakhtin, Mikhail, 189
Balzac, Honoré de, 140
Batiushkov, Konstantin, 7, 24, 73–74
Belinsky, V. G., *viii*
Bernstein, Michael André, 132
Bethea, David M., 173
Bible, the, and Judeo-Christian literary tradition: anger as divine, 158; outstretched hand, as Biblical allusion, 153–54; Peter the Great's characterization and, 91–94, 96, 117, 127; possession and madness in, 14, 168; prophecy in, 15; punishment and, 90–91
"Blessing of Madness, The," (Dodd), 111
Borges, Jorge Luis, 173
Boris Gudunov, 112–13, 175
Bronze Horseman, The: anger as source of madness in, 104–5, 118–23; author/narrator's role in, 164–65, 197–98; chase scene in, 123, 151; chronology in, 102, 148, 155–56; confrontation scene in, 101, 106–11, 114, 116–17, 120–22, 124–25, 127, 128, 154, 157, 159, 161; critical strategies described, 7–8; darkness in, 128–29, 146–56, 160; Dostoevsky's *The Double* and, 4–5, 181–96; as hybrid text, 197; irony in, 96, 98; laudatory ode as element of, 91–92; as lyric, 198; poetics of, 100–101, 109–10, 136, 146, 147–50, 154, 159–60, 167–68; psychoanalytic criticism and, 8; punishment of Evgenii, 12, 102–4; repetition used in, 100–101; story vs. plot in, 155–56; synopsis, 89, 95. *See also* Evgenii *(The Bronze Horseman)*
Brothers Karamazov, The (Dostoevsky), 6, 35–36
bureaucracy and bureaucrats, 183, 186–87
Byronic hero, 3–4, 71

Captain's Daughter, The, 174–76, 197
cards: card playing as social context, 3–4; as signifiers, 51, 60–61; as symbols in *The Queen of Spades*, 48; transformation of in *The Queen of Spades*, 28
Catherine II, tsarina, 177
Cervantes, Miguel de, 16–18, 130, 196, *viii*
Chaadaev, Petr, 176
chaos and the irrational: in "God Grant . . . ," 69; in Pushkin's works, *vii–ix*
Chekov, Anton, Tolstoy on, 140–41
choice: of Achilles, 50; Evgenii's confrontation as a choice, 122; in *The Queen of Spades*, 33–34, 35, 56–57; as refusal of symbolic order, 56–57; unconscious choice and truth, 55
chronology, *viii–ix*; ambiguities in *The Bronze Horseman*, 102, 148, 155–56; chronological context of works, 3, 65
citations, conventions used, *x*
coincidence: in *The Bronze Horseman*, 100; as compulsion in Freudian analysis, 54; in *The Queen of Spades*, 53–54
countess *(The Queen of Spades)*: as mother figure, 55, 57; as the Other and object of desire, 51–52; as witchlike or demonic, 54–55
Creativity: as enhanced by madness, 68–70, 77. *See also* poetic madness
Crime and Punishment (Dostoevsky), 35, 182–83

darkness: in Greek tradition, 118; outstretched hand linked to, 151–53; Peter equated with, 128–29, 146–56, 160, 171; as possession and madness, 159
Decembrist revolution, 175, 178, 179

Deleuze, Gilles, 48, 56
democracy, Jacksonian democracy as madness, 176
demonic, the. *See* devils and the demonic
Derzhavin, Gavrila, 92
desire: Germann in *The Queen of Spades* and, 32; the Other as object of desire, 50–58; in *The Queen of Spades*, 50–58; truth and, 51
devalorization of madness: as context, 24–26; Dostoevsky and, 26, 191–92; Gogol and, 25–26; in *The Queen of Spades*, 23–24, 26–31
devils and the demonic: in *The Bronze Horseman*, 168–69, 172; in *The Brothers Karamazov*, 35–36; Countess in *The Queen of Spades* as witchlike or demonic, 54–55; in Dostoevsky's works, 112, 171–72, 174; madness as demonic possession, 14–15; in Pushkin's works, 171–72; *samozvanstvo* as, 194–95
Devils, The (Dostoevsky), 112, 171–72, 174
"Devils" (Pushkin), 171–72
Dodd, E. R., 111
Don Quixote (Cervantes), 16–18
doppelgängers. *See* doubles (doppelgängers)
Dostoevsky, Fyodor: ambiguity in works of, 195–96; *Crime and Punishment*, 48, 182–83; devalorization of madness, 26, 191–92; *The Devils*, 112, 171–72, 174; *The Double*, 8, 26, 174, 181–96; on Evgenii in *The Bronze Horseman*, 128; on Germann in *The Queen of Spades*, 39, 59–60; *The Idiot*, 17–18, 21, 112; madness as theme in works of, 4–5, 6; Petersburg and, 144, 181–82; Pushkin's influences on, 5, 35, 155, 174, *viii*, *x*; *The Queen of Spades*, 22, 37, 39, 59–60; on the supernatural, 123

Double, The (Dostoevsky), 8, 26, 174; Peter the Great demythologized in, 182; as reworking of *The Bronze Horseman*, 181–96
doubles (doppelgängers): Goliadkin's confrontation with his double, 185; in "The Nose" (Gogol), 25–26; *samozvanstvo*, 194–95; statue as Peter's double, 172
dreams: in *The Bronze Horseman*, 94, 95, 98, 164; in *The Brothers Karamazov*, 35–36; Evgenii's aspirations, 94, 95; as Evgenii's torment, 98; in *Poltava*, 113–14; in *The Queen of Spades*, 27, 32–33, 45–46, 51; as wish fulfillment, 45–46

ego: devalorization of, 38–39; as obstacle to truth, 44, 47
ego psychology. *See* Freud, Sigmund, and Freudian psychology
Egyptian mythology, 135–36, 147
Elisha (Biblical prophet), 15
Emerson, Caryl, 22
Euripides, 11
Evgenii *(The Bronze Horseman)*: anger as source of madness, 104–5, 118–23; as antithesis of Peter the Great, 95; author/narrator conflated with, 109–11, 124, 128, 159, 165–67; author/narrator's sympathy for, 94, 97–100, 105–6, 124; characterization of, 4, 8, 18; confrontation scene, 101, 106–11, 114, 116–17, 120–22, 124–25, 127, 128; contrasted with Germann in *The Queen of Spades*, 94–95; as cursed, 12, 117–18; death of, 101; destruction of as impersonal, 129; dreams of, 94, 95, 98, 164; as Everyman, 94–95, 127–28; Goliadkin in *The Double* compared to, 183–86; heroic stature of, 94, 106; as holy fool, 112–13, 116; insight and mad clarity, 110–11, 121, 128, 139, 191;

Evgenii *(continued)*
　madness as inevitable, 162; madness of, 96–97, 99; Neva as co-victim, 124–25, 142; Neva as source of anger, 124–26, 138; as paranoid, 119–20; Peter the Great and, 89, 90, 95, 101, 120, 129 (*See also* confrontation scene *under this heading*); as possessed, 139; punishment of, 12, 102–4, 120–23, 121; as rebellious, 12, 104, 119–20, 124, 127, 137–38, 178, 179; as representative of social class, 175–76, 178; romantic analysis of, 121–22; three progressive stages of madness, 184–85; transgression of, 103–4; as victim, 124–26, 179; as "waking," 100; as wanderer, 101

Falconet statue, 121; outstretched hand in pose of, 151–54; as an Ozymandias, 155; Peter as idol, 165–66, 170, 172–73; as Peter's doppelgänger, 172; Peter the Great as the bronze horseman, 145
Fanger, Donald, 192
fire, 69, 120–21
Fish, Stanley, 139
floods: aftereffects of flood, 127; and madness in Greek tradition, 131; as punishment, 153–54; as rebellion, 142, 176, 177; as social change, 142–43
forests, 69, 76, 79
Forster, E. M., 40–41
Foucault, Michel: on madness, 9; on separation and imprisonment, 73; wandering and madness, 99
Frank, Joseph, 181
Freud, Sigmund, and Freudian psychology: on coincidence as compulsion, 54; the ego, 38; gambling analysis, 41–43; the id, 41; Lacan and, 39; madness as metaphor, 61; personality, model of, 38, 39–40; punishment and, 43

"Gambler, The" (Dostoevsky), 35
gambling: card playing as social context, 3–4; Dostoevsky's "The Gambler," 35; as prophetic, 31–32; in *The Queen of Spades*, 31–32, 33–34; as symbol of life, 49, 58
genius. *See* poetic madness
genre, 4, 91, 196–99; *The Bronze Horseman* as hybrid text, 197
Germann (*The Queen of Spades*): author/narrator's attitude toward, 59, 103; as challenge to social order, 124; characterization of, 6–7, 31–32; choices of, 33–34, 35, 56–57, 122; Countess as mother, 55, 57; Dostoevsky on, 39, 59–60; ego deterioration of, 40–41; as Everyman, 198–99; Evgenii in *The Bronze Horseman* contrasted with, 94–95; as gambler, 41–43, 49, 53; as heroic, 49–50, 59; imagination of, 26–30, 30–32, 35; madness as breakthrough, 199; obsession and, 46; paternal relationships, 45, 48, 51–53, 57, 58; as prophetic or revolutionary, 59–60; punishment of, 34, 43, 49, 55–56, 59, 103, 121; reductiveness of imagination, 30–31; refusal of symbolic order, 56–57; Saint-Germain and, 51–53, 57; social order challenged by, 59; as symbolic of social transformations, 59
Gershenzon, Mikhail, 78, *vii*
"God Grant That I Not Lose My Mind": absence and loss, 71; ambiguities in, 78; as anti-romantic, 68, 70–72, 76–77, 78–79; chronological information, *viii–ix*; creative freedom and madness in, 68–70; critical strategies described, 7; eighteenth-century images of

madness in, 72–75, 80; as lyric, 89; madness as plague, 24; persona in, 70; poetics of, 68–69, 70–71, 83–84; as romantic, 68, 69–70, 76–77, 78–79; romanticism vs. realism in, 75; social consequences of madness, 70– 71; subject/object shifts in, 70; text and translation, 65–67; as unfinished work, 68, 77–78; violence in, 69, 79, 129

Gofman, M. L., on Pushkin, 35, 82

Gogol, Nikolay, 4, 6; irony in works of, 25–26; "Notes of a Madman," 5, 25–26, 75–76, 189; parodies, 10; "Portrait," 29

"Golden Pot, The" (Hoffmann), 6, 10, 25, 69

Goliadkin (*The Double*, Dostoevsky): confrontation with double, 185; as Everyman, 190–91; Evgenii in *The Bronze Horseman* compared with, 183–86; humiliation as fear, 193–94; as puppetlike, 189; three progressive stages of madness, 184–85; as without redeeming features, 188–89

Greek literary tradition: anger and violence linked to madness in, 156–57; choice of Achilles, 50; darkness in, 118; duration of madness, 102; Evgenii's madness and, 129; madness as curse, 13–15; madness associated with black flood in, 131; melancholia, 118; paradigms of madness, 8; prophetic madness in, 12–14; punishment and madness, 11–12, 14, 90, 99, 102; tragedy in, 161; violence linked to madness, 11–12, 13, 15, 156–57, 196; wandering and madness in, 98–99

Gregg, Richard, 119–20, 191

Grigor'ev, Apollon, vii

Guattari, Félix, 48, 56

heroes: Byronic hero, 3–4, 71; Evgenii in *The Bronze Horseman* as heroic, 94, 106; Germann in *The Queen of Spades* as heroic, 49–50, 59; Goliadkin in Dostoevsky's *The Double*, 188–89; as mad holy fools, 8

History of Pugachev, The, 197; chronological information, ix

Hoffmann, E. T. A., 5, 25, 67, 69; madness as prophetic in works of, 10; romanticism and madness in works of, 6

holy fools, 8, 15, 99; decline of social and religious acceptance of, 116; Nikolka in *Boris Gudunov*, 112–13; Peter the Great and, 116; prophecy and, 112–13; in Russian tradition, 112; as speakers of truth, 112–13; Tsar and fool, 112–13, 115

homelessness, 163

horses and horsemen, 173–77; Neva as horse, 135

humiliation, 70–71, 83; madness and, 102–3; Peter the Great as humiliated in Dostoevsky's works, 188; as source of madness, 193–94

hypersanity (madness as breakthrough), 81, 82–83

Iakobson, Roman, 170

id, the, 41

ideas as crimes, 103

Idiot, The (Dostoevsky), 17–18, 21, 112

imagination: as inferior to objective reality, 122; Lacan, 60; madness as failure of imagination, 26–30; reductiveness of Germann's imagination, 30–31; romantic madness and, 23. *See also* mirror stage of Lacan

imprisonment, 83; Foucault on, 73; insane asylums, 10, 72–75, 80; madness and, 70–71

insight: Evgenii in *The Bronze Horseman* and mad clarity, 110–11, 121, 128, 139; genius and, 65; madness and, 121

intertextuality, 3–4
irony: in *The Bronze Horseman*, 96, 98, 135, 166; Dostoevsky's use of, 189; in Gogol's works, 25–26

Jeremiah (Biblical prophet), 15
Jung, Karl, 81–83

Keats, John, 71
Khvostov, Dmitri, 147
King Lear (Shakespeare), 5, 16
Krekshin, Petr, 92

Lacan, Jacques, and Lacanian psychology: autonomy and linguistic imagination, 60; devaluation of the ego, 38; Freud and, 39; Germann in *The Queen of Spades*, analysis of, 61; language and the Other, 56; mediation rejected in, 43–44; mirror stage, 38, 43–47; the Other as object of desire, 50–58; psychotic *vs.* neurotic personalities, 56; subjectivity and, 56; symbolic order, 56–57, 58–61; truth and the symbolic, 44, 47
Laing, R. D., 48, 50, 56; hypersanity (madness as breakthrough), 81, 82–83
language: Germann's use of language, 27–29; Lacan and access to truth, 60; linguistic reduction and madness, 50–51; loss of as punishment, 59; madness as loss of, 58; the Other and, 56; truth and the symbolic in Lacanian psychology, 44; the Word in *The Bronze Horseman*, 117, 145, 158
Lednicki, Wacław, 4, 95
Levkovich, Ia. L., 75
Liza (*The Queen of Spades*), 27, 32, 58
Lomonosov, Mikhail, 92
love, in *The Bronze Horseman* and *The Double*, 183–84
Lukács, Georg, 140

madness: as creative freedom, 68–70; creativity and, 77; as death-in-life, 40, 59, 83, 100; as demonic possession, 14–15; devalorization of, 23–31, 191–92; eighteenth-century images of, 10, 72–75, 80; as failure of imagination, 26–30; as freedom or liberation, 122; Freudian psychology and, 40; genius, 79; as humiliation, 70–71, 83, 102; hypersanity and madness as breakthrough, 81, 82–83, 198–99; insight and, 65, 110–12, 118–19; Jacksonian democracy as madness, 176; as journey of discovery, 198–99; literary traditions of, 5, 7, 11 (*See also* the Bible and Judeo-Christian literary tradition; Greek literary tradition); medical paradigms and treatments, 7, 9–10, 74; as negation or absence, 75; as plague or contagion, 17–18, 24, 73, 80, 126, 144, 157, 162, 178–79; poetic madness or genius, 24–25, 69–70, 75, 79, 80–81, 112, 118; as possession, 14–15, 99, 168; as price for truth, 47; as punishment or curse, 11–12, 13–14, 90, 99, 117–18, 199; rebellion as, 118, 124–29, 175, 178–79; as reward, 199; as sacred and prophetic, 9–10 (*See also* holy fools); as self-destruction, 79–80; social consequences of, 70–71, 72–73, 117–18; as spiritually transformative, 80–83, 198–99; truth linked to, 7, 11, 12–14, 34, 47, 50, 112–15, 129–30; valorized in "God Grant . . . ," 80–85; violence linked to, 11–12, 13, 15, 129–30, 196
Mariia (*Poltava*), 113–14
materialism, 27–28, 59; romantic psychoanalysis and, 61
Mazeppa (*Poltava*), 113–15, 124
melancholia, 118, 151
Merezhkovsky, D. S., 128, 192

Index

Mermaid, The, 100, *ix, vii*
mirror stage of Lacan, 43–47; defined and described, 44
Moscow, as vanquished old order, 169–70
Myshkin (*The Idiot*, Dostoevsky), 17–18, 21, 112

Nabokov, Vladimir, 29
Name-of-the-Father, 56–59
narrators. *See* author/narrators
nature: romanticized vision of, 141; as ultimate reality, 131. *See also* Neva river
Neva river, 89, 92–93; after effects of flood, 127; as anthropomorphized character, 8–9, 131–34, 137, 141–42; conflated in madness with Evgenii and Peter, 159; deconstructivist readings, 132, 139–42; Evgenii linked with, 137–39, 142–43, 159; flood as punishment, 153–54; as horse, 135; linked with Peter the Great, 134–37; as pagan force, 171; as subject to Peter, 145; as victim, 124–25, 142; as villain or destructive beast, 133–34
Nicholas I, tsar, 176–77
"Nose, The" (Gogol), 25–26
"Notes of a Madman" (Gogol), 5, 25–26, 75–76, 189
numerology, 39

odes and odic tradition, 91–92, 109, 197
Odoevsky, Vladimir, 4, 5, 6, 10, 25
Onash, Konrad, 190
Other, the: author/narrator as Other, 167; language and, 56; as object of desire, 50–58; truth accessible only through interaction with, 60
outstretched hand, 127; Biblical allusions, 153–54; as oppression and darkness, 151–53; as protection, 152–53

panegyrics, 153
Paracelsus, Theophrastus, 82
paranoia, 119–20, 191
Petersburg, 7; as aberration, 155–56; author/narrator's relationship with, 163; in *The Bronze Horseman*, 147; construction as violent act, 136–37; Dostoevsky and, 144, 181–82; in Dostoevsky's *The Double*, 186–87; as monument of Peter's mad power, 160; as pagan world, 169–71; in Russian literary tradition, 144, 181–82
Peter the Great, 7; Alexander I, tsar, contrasted with, 96; Biblical literary tradition and characterization of, 91–94, 96, 117, 127; as the Bronze Horseman, 145; bureaucrats as successors, 186–87; as darkness, 128–29, 146–56, 160, 171; demythologized by Dostoevsky, 182–83, 186–88; Evgenii and, 116–17; Evgenii as antithesis of, 95; Evgenii's challenge to (*See* confrontation scene *under The Bronze Horseman*); Germann and, 60–61; as godlike figure, 90–94, 101, 113, 135–36, 146–47, 166, 171; historical tsar, violent rages of, 157–58; holy fools and, 116; as idol, 165–66, 170, 172–73; linked with Neva river, 134–37; as mad, 128, 136–37, 144, 146, 156–61; Neva river as subject to, 132; odic tradition and, 91–92; in *Poltava*, 113, 115; as protector, 95–96; as revolution incarnate, 178, 179; in Russian literary tradition, 7–8, 163; sculpture of, 95–96; as source of madness, 162–63; as sun god, 135–36, 146–47, 171; as threat to Russia, 128, 142, 160–61; undermined by the Neva, 127; Word as power, 117, 145, 158. *See also* Falconet statue
plague, madness as plague or contagion, 17–18, 24, 73, 84, 126, 144, 157, 162

Plato, 12–13, 15, 112
Poema, 91
poetic madness, 24–25, 75, 79–81; demonic possession and, 14; in Hoffmann's works, 69; hypersanity and, 82–83; *vs.* insanity, 70; insight and, 65; melancholia and, 118; poetry as measure of sanity, 67; as prophetic, 12–13; Shakespeare and, 112
Poltava, 8, 113–15, 124, 197
Poprishchin (Gogol, "Notes of a Madman"), 5, 75–76, 189
Poshlost', 29, 31, 35
The Possessed (Dostoevsky). See *The Devils* (Dostoevsky)
possession: in Biblical tradition, 168; as darkness and madness, 159; of Evgenii in *The Bronze Horseman*, 119; madness as, 99; madness as demonic possession, 14–15
Povest, 91–92
power, use of word, 159
Prokopovich, Feofan, 92
prophecy, 9–10; in *The Bronze Horseman*, 112; as a curse, 13–14, 118; as divine or demonic, 14–15; gambling and imagination as prophetic, 31–32; Germann as prophetic or revolutionary, 59–60; Greek tradition and, 112; holy fools and, 112–13; in Judeo-Christian tradition, 15; madness linked to truth, 12–14
psychoanalytic criticism: "fragmentary code" in *The Queen of Spades*, 23; Freud and ego psychology, 37; "God Grant . . . " and, 7; historical context for, 38; Lacan and anti-ego psychology, 37; *The Queen of Spades* and, 6–7. See also Freud, Sigmund, and Freudian psychology; Lacan, Jacques, and Lacanian psychology; romantic psychology

Pugachev rebellion, 124, 174–76, 197, *ix*
punishment: anger linked to, 122–23; in the Bible and Judeo-Christian literary tradition, 90–91; of Evgenii in *The Bronze Horseman*, 12, 102–4, 120–23, 121; flood as punishment, 153–54; Freudian analysis, 43; of Germann in *The Queen of Spades*, 34, 43, 49, 55–56, 59, 103, 124; in Greek literary tradition, 11–12, 14, 90, 99, 123; of idea "crimes," 103; loss of language, 59; loss of sexuality, 59; repetition as punishment, 55–56
Pushkin, Aleksandr: and Batiushkov, 7, 24, 73–74; as "father of madness" in Russian literature, 4–5; fear of future as represented by Germann, 59; fear of social change, 59, 60, 95, 124, 176; French romanticism as context of, 9; genre choices of, 196–97; Gofman on, 82; Greek literary tradition and, 8; on Petrine revolution, 176–77; on poetry, 24; as realist rather than romantic, 75; reputation of, 69, 91, *vii*; romanticism and, 24, 75; in Western literary tradition, 5. See also *specific works by title*.

Queen of Spades, The: ambiguity in, 22, 34–35; author/narrator in, 198–99; chronological information, *viii–ix*; the countess as the Other and object of desire, 51–52; critical strategies described, 5–7; deception in, 22; Dostoevsky on, 22, 37, 39; as intertextual or hypercontextualized, 3–4; "lyrical" reading of, 61; as parody, 26; supernatural interpretations of, 22–23; synopsis of, 22–23, 26–29

Radel, Ruth, 111
Radishchev, A. N., 152–53, 166

Index

readers and reading: deconstruction of Neva river in *The Bronze Horseman*, 132, 139–43; reader as resistant to perspective of author/narrator, 139; retrospective reading, 21, 132, 156, 167; subjective theories of reading, 139–40

reason: as acceptable loss, 68; French romanticism and, 9; madness as absence of, 75

rebellion: in *The Captain's Daughter*, 174–76; as contagious, 126; Decembrist revolution, 175, 178, 179; Evgenii's rebellion against Peter, 104, 119–20, 124, 127, 137–38, 178, 179; flood as similar to periodic rebellion, 176; Goliadkin as petty rebel, 192–94; as madness, 12, 118, 124–29, 175, 178–79, ix; Neva flood as rebellious, 142; Peter and the Neva as rebellious, 136; Petrine revolution as rebellion against social order, 176; the Pugachev rebellion, 124, 174–76, 197, ix; three forms of rebellion, 175–76; as tragic, 161

reduction, 32, 34

Reeder, Roberta, 26

religion: as absence, 168–69; Pushkin and, 170. *See also* the Bible and Judeo-Christian literary tradition

repetition: in *The Bronze Horseman*, 100–101; as compulsion, 54; Germann and, 30–31; Lacanian psychology and, 54; poetic use of, 100–101, 114–15, 148–50, 159–60; as punishment, 55–56

romanticism: Byronic hero, 3–4, 71; epiphany and madness, 34, 35; French romanticism, 9; genius conflated with madness, 24; Germann in *The Queen of Spades* as romantic hero, 23, 59; madness as sacred and prophetic, 10; valorization of madness, 6, 23, 25, ix–x. *See also* poetic madness

romantic psychology: analysis of Germann in *The Queen of Spades*, 47–50; devalorization of the ego, 38–39; Germann's mad choices valorized, 61; madness as spiritually transformative, 80–83; madness linked to truth, 7; valorization of madness in, 56, 111–12

romantics: madness as insight and, 111–12; valorization of madness, 111–12

Rusalka (The Mermaid), 100, ix, viii

Russian literary tradition: Petersburg in, 144, 181–82; Peter the Great in, 7–8, 163

Saint-Germain, in *The Queen of Spades*, 51–53, 57

Samozvanstvo, 194–95

Saul (Biblical prophet), 15

sculpture, 117

seven as symbol in *The Queen of Spades*, 28, 48

sex and sexual imagery: punishment and loss of sexuality, 59; in *The Queen of Spades*, 48

Shakespeare, 5, 16, 119, *viii*; imagination as inferior to objective reality, 122; madness in, 122; poetic madness, 112

Shelley, Percy Bysshe, 70, 155

skies, 69, 76, 79

sleep, 164. *See also* dreams

snakes, 136

social changes: in *The Bronze Horseman*, 95; flood as, 142–43; Peter as sponsor of, 128; in *The Queen of Spades*, 59, 60; Russia in peril, 128

Sophocles, 102–3

Stählin, Jacob von, 157–58

subjectivity/objectivity, subject/object switch in "God Grant . . . ," 70

supernatural, 32–33; in *The Bronze Horseman*, 117, 122, 123–24; in *The Brothers Karamazov*, 35–36; in *Poltava*, 113–14; in *The Queen of Spades*, 22. *See also* devils and the demonic
"Sylph, The" (Odoevsky), 25
symbolic order in Lacanian psychology, 58–61

Terras, Victor, 190
three: as symbol in *The Queen of Spades*, 28, 48–49; three forms of rebellion, 175–76; three progressive stages of madness, 184–85; three-stage process of development and author/narrators, 84
Tolstoy, on Chekov, 140–41
translations, source of, x
truth: author/narrator's access to, 163–64; derangement and, 14–18; desire and, 51; holy fools as speakers of truth, 112–13; Lacanian psychology and, 44, 47; madness as price for truth, 47, 50; madness linked to, 7, 11, 12–14, 34, 47, 50, 112–15; order and, *viii*; prophecy and madness, 12–14; romanticism and, 7; unconscious choice and, 55; in the Western tradition, 11

Viazemsky, Petr Andreevich, 95–96, 176
Vinogradov, Viktor, 189
violence: in "God Grant . . . ," 69, 79, 129; in Greek tradition, 11–12, 13, 15, 156–57, 196; of the historical Peter the Great, 157–58; madness linked to, 11–13, 196; Neva river as violent or chaotic, 131; Petersburg's construction as violent act, 136–37

wandering, 163–64; in *The Bronze Horseman*, 101; holy fools, 99; madness and, 98–99; Saint-Germain as Wandering Jew, 52–53
whirlwinds, 69, 76, 82
Word, 158

Zachariah, 173–74

PUBLICATIONS OF THE WISCONSIN CENTER
FOR PUSHKIN STUDIES

David Bethea, Alexander Dolinin, Thomas Shaw
Series Editors

Realizing Metaphors: Alexander Pushkin and the Life of the Poet
David M. Bethea

The Poetics of Brevity: Alexander Pushkin's Little Tragedies
edited by Svetlana Evdokimova

Pushkin's Tatiana
Olga Hasty

The Imperial Sublime: A Russian Poetics of Empire
Harsha Ram

Pushkin and the Genres of Madness: The Masterpieces of 1833
Gary Rosenshield

www.ingramcontent.com/pod-product-compliance
Lightning Source LLC
Chambersburg PA
CBHW070939230426
43666CB00011B/2495